MY
PASHTUN
RABBI

MY
PASHTUN
RABBI

A JEW'S SEARCH *for* TRUTH, MEANING,
And HOPE *in the* MUSLIM WORLD

A
MEMOIR
of the EMIRATES

DAVID EDEN

ISBN (Print) 978-1-54393-155-6
ISBN (eBook) 978-1-54393-156-3

Printed in the United States of America

First Printing

10 9 8 7 6 5 4 3 2 1

Dedicated to the memories of:

Hilal Al Falahi

Mark Leimsieder

Harvey Horwitz

Sid Rosner

&

Stephen D. Isaacs

CONTENTS

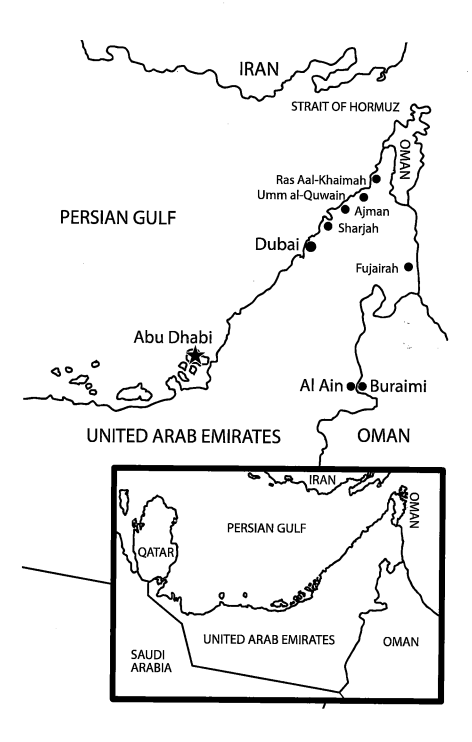

MY
PASHTUN
RABBI

CHAPTER 1

Into the Land of
"Insha'Allah, no problem"

THE MORNING OF THE FIRST FULL DAY OF RAMADAN AT 8:10 a.m., I stood for the second time in front of a door marked "Women's Toilet." *This* was a classroom? And *my* classroom?

Excited to get to my first hour teaching at United Arab Emirates University, I'd given myself ample time to find my schoolroom. Now I was ten minutes late. I'd lost another ten trudging in from the gate where my ride had been obliged to drop me—taxis, their drivers being uniformly men and non-Emiratis, were barred from the "girls'" campus. The only males allowed to enter were professors, some of us Western expats, and South Asian laborers, neither of these classes deemed men in the UAE.

Other than what I'd determined from a Xeroxed map, the layout was unfamiliar. New-faculty orientation had omitted visits to any of UAEU's facilities, including its famed Islamic Center. When several in my cohort pointed this out to the dean, an affable white-haired Canadian, he had commandeered a van and escorted us on a personal tour. We'd done no more than cruise by the female campus here at Maqam. At the sight of its high perimeter masonry wall topped with barbed wire, I had asked whom the high security was meant to keep out. The answer I anticipated was "terrorists." But the dean let out a peculiar laugh. "It's not to keep anyone *out*! It's to keep the girls *in*!"

Now that I was behind the wire, I looked around for signs of the activities that would motivate young women to flee. There seemed to be no activity at all. The morning sun was already brutal, the temperature nudging 100°F. My search for Building 66 took me past a few structures in generic cement-block architecture, access roads and concrete sidewalks. I identified the highest thing around, a flagpole from which the UAE's green-black-white-red banner waved. This would logically be the center. From there, I could spot one of the major buildings identifiable on my map and orient. A big bluish one.

I confirmed what was typed on the other paper I clutched: *Building 66. Room 04*. Standing at the base of the pole, I turned a slow circle, scanning the buildings. No quads. No lawns. A few stunted trees. I can't recall now what I had pictured as the women's campus of the United Arab Emirates national university. But I'm sure it wasn't this. The place looked less like a place to study than an old, nondescript corporate office park. This was my refuge from the wreckage of the life I'd fled back in Cleveland?

Doors on distant buildings opened and young women streamed out, clad head to toe in black. I checked my watch. Seven fifty-three. So, those buildings were the dorms the map identified. Building 71 was in front of me. That put Building 66 to my right, a distance of maybe a hundred yards.

As I turned to hurry off in that direction, something in my peripheral vision pulled me up short. Stepping through a door in the wooden construction fence behind Building 66, amid the rolling waves of girls in black, a flash of color. I turned back and squinted against the glare—I was facing east and the sun was still low. Yes, one of the dozens of women streaming out of the dormitories like flocks of starlings stood out in dramatic chromatic relief. She wore the traditional *sheyla*, but not in black -- in flaming, flamboyant, flamingo pink.

The mystery was arresting and kindled a sense that the uniformity of my new work environment might not be so uniform after all. But that would have to be filed for later contemplation. I was due at Building 66. Room 04, which turned out to be—or at least so identified by its sign—a women's toilet.

First reaction: panic. Was I, a freshman member of the faculty, about to make a fool of myself and reveal that I was so stupid I couldn't find my classroom? I scampered, sweat pouring from my head, my shirt soaked, around all three floors of Building 66, scrutinizing the number above every door. Which brought me back, even more anxious, to Room 04, Women's Toilet.

I noticed that three young women stood nearby, uniformly attired and looking bemused. They confirmed this was indeed the room assigned to the class for which they were registered. I learned their names—Fatima, Mariam and Sheikha—and asked them to meet me right there for the next scheduled session. Thus ended Day 1 of *Computer-Assisted Reporting*. Class dismissed. The students seemed unfazed. I can't say the same for myself. An enrollment of three? And a restroom to teach in?

I braced myself for another trudge in the heat and set off back across the sand and a sidewalk to Building 71, home to the Mass Communication department's administration. Fulminating silently, I fought the loop I was sliding into. This just couldn't be true. This was absurd. This was a farce. But of course it was—all three! Not yet two full weeks in the UAE, I was already feeling like an old hand.

Thirteen days earlier, amid the throng pushing and shoving outside Dubai Airport's old Terminal 1, whether by some act of divine providence or mere serendipity, I had found the driver sent by my new employer. I was soon sprawled on the back seat of a white Camry and despite full-blast a/c, dripping sweat. Not just pouring perspiration but pasted to the seat, my black t-shirt as limp as a dishrag.

As the man at the wheel, a quiet South Asian, negotiated thick traffic we passed a long series of banners lining the airport road. They featured a boy of maybe ten, smiling, in a wheelchair, wearing a form-fitting Superman leotard-shirt. The banners with the boy, his smile, and wheelchair drove home what I'd just done: Flown a third of the way around the world to spend three years in a country whose language, customs, even its alphabet, were indecipherable to me. Add to that an alien take on Superman.

I was working over those strange, jet-lagged epiphanies as we traversed a floating bridge and merged onto a congested concrete highway. I counted twelve lanes. From the ground, Dubai was hardly the vision I'd peered out at in the bright morning light, nose pressed to the acrylic shield of an economy-class window: a string of glittering skyscrapers, sharp-cut rhinestones strung along a sapphire sea. B-roll used on gushing American TV stories about the Miracle City of the Middle East. From my backseat vantage point, that skyline was somewhat less inspiring, though very much a work in progress. Even from this distance, the progress looked frantic.

Most cities, I reassured myself, lose their magic and appeal as one closes the distance. Just like people. The longer shot is more forgiving. Manhattan from the last rise going west on the Long Island Expressway, especially when the old towers were there. San Francisco from the Golden Gate. Cities like Paris, more breathtaking the closer you get, are the exception that proves the rule. That generally applied to cities of the past. Then, of course, there were cities of the past such as Cleveland, the one I'd just left, its unending rust-belt downturn eased only moderately by the national real estate bubble.

Dubai, a committed city of the future, was riding a magic carpet, delirious with *nouveau*-riches and content with the dreams that money *can* buy. Toast of the financial media, the sheikdom gushed wealth: the world's tallest building going up and biggest shopping malls, one alleged to have an indoor ski slope. A secular Mecca. We passed a building that looked like the conning tower of the world's largest nuclear submarine, home to Zayed University, a billboard extolling Dubailand, another the Dubai Outlet Mall. I was curious to see the place, feel it around me. My immediate destination, however, lay elsewhere, deep in the desert. Al Ain, in the sister emirate of Abu Dhabi, sounded quite different from Dubai. It lay an hour or so south, my driver said—so far, the only words he'd spoken.

Unemployed for more than a year, the divorce to cap a dead-end marriage stalled short of finalization, I'd applied in a seat-of-the-pants way for a teaching job. Financial desperation wasn't my motivator. I had a decent nest egg tucked away in investments, and the Dow was lounging in the 14,000 range. I needed something to do. I needed to *get out* of my life.

My search for jobs at American journalism schools kicked up nothing. Then I was struck by a new idea: the farther flung the better.

One item in the United Arab Emirates University's online application had almost turned me off for good, the box marked "Religion." I stared at the space a good thirty seconds, debating leaving it blank. But, really, how could I be surprised? I wanted to teach at a university in the heartland of the Islamic world. Their place, their rules. I filled in the answer. No way was I going covert with this element of my identity. I had a hunch my reply on that question alone would put an end to the matter.

But the prospective employer emailed almost immediately to set up an interview—a teleconference. One member of the panel of three, a female professor from Egypt, pointed out that I had neither a PhD nor non-Stateside teaching experience. Further—now I could practically hear her looking over the rims of her glasses at the rest of the committee—I had never taught full time. Valid objections, it seemed to me, all overruled by her two colleagues, both Americans.

The interview had been followed by a nearly summer-long silence. I'd pretty much forgotten the idea when an email turned up with two attachments, a contract and an e-ticket on Emirates to Dubai. Departure date two weeks away, start date only four. The salary, the equivalent in local currency of about US$80,000 a year, would put me just under the IRS's limit for exemption on foreign-earned income, but would be tax-free in the UAE. Perks: rent-free luxury housing, a fat furniture allowance, high-end healthcare, annual round-trip airfare from the US to the UAE for myself and my son, and an end-of-contract bonus. The escape hatch I'd been trolling Google for, in the form of an exotic working vacation, with eighty thousand in pocket money? I didn't negotiate any terms. Since the contract wasn't binding until I got to Al Ain and signed it in person, what did I have to lose but some time? Time being the thing I had too much of, I signed the attachment, scanned to a digital copy, attached it to an email and hit SEND.

In reply UAEU's Mass Com department chair, one of my two advocates in the interview, emailed her congratulations. I'd been selected over more than seventy-five other applicants, she said, and was earmarked to be "our expert in journalism." The second paragraph departed from the official-sounding, cheerleading stuff. Dr. Beverly got surprisingly personal and noted what had inspired her to push hard for me: the discovery, via Google, of the lawsuit I'd brought against my previous employer, a Cleveland TV station. Never thought I'd hear that cited as a factor in my favor. "You have courage," said my prospective boss. "David versus Goliath. We could use you here." Her email closed with one more observation, carefully worded. "Our journalism technician scarcely knows English, yet she is advising the newspaper in both languages."

A warning? An odd flash of color in a landscape of shimmering, raven black? Either way, it was what intrigued me most.

Cruising out of Dubai, I told myself again that the abrupt, utter change would be good for me. Life had laid me low. The UAE was on a high. Maybe the perfect moment for our lives to intersect. For a whole host of reasons, at any rate, here I was on the sleek, six-lane E-66, headed into the interior. The landscape outside had turned to something less urban. Dunes, a few scrub trees. A backdrop to *Beau Geste*, the world of the Foreign Legion. The a/c had dried the sweat, and my T-shirt felt almost crisp. My blue Cleveland Indians cap wasn't a Panama hat, but I fancied myself a character from Graham Greene.

Those romantic reflections were pierced by a steady, very annoying two-beat beep. A ping. Ping-ping. Ping-ping. The noise came from the dashboard, but the driver looked oblivious.

"Is it possible to turn that off?"

He nodded and let up on the accelerator. I watched the needle. When it dropped below 120 kmph, the irritating sound ceased. "Thank you."

He acknowledged that with a nod and a glance in the rear-view mirror. How must his latest passenger look to him, a burly, bearded, sleep-deprived middle-aged *schlump* in sunglasses and a blue cap? Whatever his thoughts, the driver directed none of them my way. We drove on in restful silence, packed in a tight caravan of luxury sedans, SUVs, Toyota pickups, laborer-crammed Tata buses—an Indian make, I remembered from somewhere—and open-sided six-wheelers hauling camels and goats. High-tension lines followed the ribbon of smooth concrete, framing sand dunes that rolled into the distance like massive breakers on Oahu's North Shore. I had seen plenty of deserts, from the Sonora and Mojave to the Negev, but nothing as arid as this. Nor had my previous experience included a yellow road sign bearing the image of a camel, a *Ghostbusters*-like slash bisecting its midsection.

I was working out what that could mean—dromedaries banned not to cross the highway? Or banned from it to get to Al Ain?—when the ping-ping came back.

I caught the driver's eye in the rearview mirror, my look imploring. That got him to speak. "If I go slower, under one-twenty, it turns off. Over that, it makes the noise. It's the radar."

"Are we in a hurry?"

He shrugged. "It will take us longer to get to the hotel." Maybe his usual passengers had limited knowledge of the relationship governing speed, time and distance. With something approximating a smile, he added, "*Inshullah*, no problem. We will get there later, *inshulluh*."

In-SHULL-*uh*? The phrase, stress on the middle syllable "*SHULL*," befuddled me.

The highway narrowed to four lanes, fronded palms filing down the median. Off and on the car pinged, and my nerves resigned themselves to being worked.

I noted a sign telling us we'd passed into what was to be my home emirate. The dunes turned red and swelled taller. Shortly, we exited the highway into that landscape onto a road skirted by a high security fence. This terrain was familiar from my reconnaissance via Google Earth: the border with Oman and the "twin city" of Buraimi, contiguous with Al Ain.

"We'll be at the hotel in maybe, *inshulluh,* ten minutes," the driver said.

The Intercontinental sat at the city's edge in a walled compound. It was precisely noon—for me, three a.m.—when I staggered out at the drive-up. The desk informed me as I checked in that there was a meeting set by UAEU for nine the next morning. I was confident I could easily sleep most of the intervening twenty-one hours. Even through the exhaustion, I felt an eagerness to make my first foray out. Looking from the shade of the lobby onto the surrounding landscape, I noted that the dominant life forms were the date palm and the automobile. The land was wide and flat around the resort compound, but featured no pedestrians. Sidewalks did flank the roads—and could have fried eggs, literally and fast. Even the short stretch to the bottom of the Intercon's drive up looked like heat stroke waiting to happen. Google Maps had shown me that the Al Ain Oasis lay just two miles west, beyond the Hilton we'd passed. I'd pictured myself walking there from the resort compound. So much for that idea. Walking the other way was a non-starter; the Oman border and its fence formed the northern boundary of the Intercontinental's spread.

A bellman, South Asian, took my bags and me to the fourth floor. Deposited in my room, I opened the sliding door and stepped onto the balcony. It was the first I'd been truly outside and not under the shade of a passenger pickup or drop off. Blast-furnace-hot wind held me in a bear hug. The cool interior beckoned. I slipped back inside, drew the blackout curtains, and fell into bed.

And, of course, was suddenly wide-awake. Back home, my career had blown up. Well, I'd dynamited whatever bridges might have been behind me. Fired from the CBS affiliate where I had spent two years as managing editor and executive producer of news shows, I'd sued, won a pyrrhic victory, and walked away with a settlement decent enough it came with a non-disclosure clause and headlines. Only fair, as I'd surely never work in TV or mainstream media again.

The marriage, too, was behind me. It had been played out for years; only paperwork remained. There'd been no ill will, just no will at all. My wife and I had agreed we'd wait for Max to finish high school, but my mother-in-law's death, followed by my court case, kept delaying the inevitable. Now Max was starting his sophomore year of college.

So, surfing the net, I'd spotted an escape hatch and dived for it. Down a rabbit hole that had deposited me in this air-conditioned room with its balcony overlooking a swim-up bar. The room was cool, the mattress firm, and I was starting to feel drowsy.

Did I have regrets? Neither I nor the ceiling staring back at me knew the answer. More pressing to me was the question of whether I had a future. It involved an unsigned contract and a promise of physical comfort, but I had no idea what I was getting myself into *this* time.

The next morning gave me a few ideas on that front. The event gearing up in the Intercontinental's Jebel Hafeet Room seemed less like an informational meeting for incoming international faculty at an institution of higher learning than a UN family retreat, for refugees.

For a moment, I thought the doorway in which I stood was a wormhole or some such cosmological portal, taking me back to my first day of college and the first run to the dining hall. The room before me, curiously circular, felt suffused with the same put-a-good-face-on-it anxiety. The intervening years, in the trenches of journalism and civil court, had taught me a few things about reading casts of strangers. This room was more strained than the freshman dining commons at Miami of Ohio, thirty-eight Septembers earlier. With pause in the time warp, the read I got was quiet bedlam ready to erupt into pandemonium. I stepped through.

The Jebel Hafeet crowd had come from everywhere in the world, some trailing spouses and screaming children, but some like me beyond that age, and many apparently there solo. I sensed I might not be the crowd's only forlorn foreigner who'd come to the end of whatever road he'd been on. I scanned the throng for another one-man tribe marooned on this arid shore. Naturally, I gravitated toward voices speaking English. A diminutive white-haired guy took a seat in an arc of chairs. I blatantly stared. Finally, it hit me: Ray Walston. The fellow, who looked like Bill Bixby's Uncle Martin in the 1960s sitcom "My Favorite Martian," started chatting with a middle-aged, American-sounding couple. A blonde in a floral-print dress teetering on spike heels and an athletic man, they took seats close to his.

I felt sheepish about gravitating toward my own demographic. Cave in to lazy cowardice on the first day? Diverse faces, multi-national and multi-hued, gave me the same message—we've got at least this in common, we're here to make our last stand. Possibly our only stand. And, as if evoked by that locution, here was General Custer now. But not a fellow Yankee. The guy striding in, about my age, could have been cast as a Pommie officer in *Bridge Over the River Kwai*. His ruddy complexion, wavy brown-grey mop, prominent nose, angular chin, blustery, jovial air, along with the mischievous glint in his eye, screamed "Limey." The newest arrival, a bloke if I'd ever seen one, moved to a semi-circle of chairs and selected a seat near the trio I'd been studying. We each caught the other's eye and nodded a greeting. Maybe an acknowledgment. Could he, I wondered, be a foxhole buddy here?

"Tony," he said, extending his hand. "Brisbane.

"David," I responded, accepting it. "Cleveland."

That was the extent of our initial meeting.

Soon the meeting got underway and the undercurrent of tension rose to the surface. We'd all signed on with the understanding that we'd be billeted a week at the Intercon, then move to university-provided luxury housing. The interim HR director promptly corroborated a rumor that had apparently been swirling, though of course I'd been oblivious—no such housing. All hell broke loose. The Jebel Hafeet Room turned into the cantina bar in *Star Wars*. The interim HR director, a hapless American, said he'd found out only days earlier that our prospective landlord, having found someone who would pay higher rents than the university, was reneging. He had decided against informing us so as to avoid "concern." Given the mutiny he had on his hands, I suspect he regretted that call.

Calls of "liar!" rained down on him as the arrows must have at the Little Big Horn. There was even louder, polysyllabic howling in Arabic.

His story sounded doubtful and many around me voiced their suspicions. He had just found out? Does he take us to be fools? Weren't we talking about dozens of apartments? And had the university not had a contract? Of course! was the answer. But that didn't matter, observed the Ray Walston lookalike. The upshot, in his encapsulation: UAEU was giving up without a fight; the landlord no doubt had *wasta*.

Whatever that was, it trumped a written agreement. I thought of the unsigned one in my black canvas bag, and added *wasta* to my mental list of things to find out about, right below *in-SHULL-uh*. For the moment I focused on making the acquaintance of Uncle Martin, who seemed to be in the know. Brian, he said as we shook, from Toronto, but an old Mideast hand, having just relocated from Oman.

Although agitated voices filled the air the people in my little group seemed oddly relaxed. Tony gave a summation that was concise if not entirely sensitive to the concerns of many of our colleagues. "Two months stuck in the Intercon with free food, a pool, a bar, and a gym? By me that's soft duty."

The athletic guy, Dan, concurred. He was unemployed—looking at selling real estate—and had tagged along with Carol, the blonde, his wife. She'd be teaching just three days a week, and happy to hang other days by the pool. Dan said something about the hotel's Horse & Jockey Club being the finest bar in Al Ain. Tony footnoted that there were only three competitors. Brian affirmed this, and endorsed the Intercon overall. He was a new hire like us, but had spent eight years in Oman teaching English as a second language. UAEU had hired him to teach something called "UGRU." That, too, went on my list.

In the life ended two days before, I would have watched, listened, maybe nodded, and said nothing. When the meeting adjourned, I would have walked away and resumed whatever I'd been doing. Here I was about to begin a new teaching job at a major Arab national university as the "journalism expert," with no idea what I was supposed to teach, and now apparently no place to live, just an interim place to stay at a nice hotel. I wasn't yet doing anything I could walk away and resume.

I began paying attention to people and groups around us, carrying on in languages I didn't understand, but carrying on vociferously. For those who'd come here with families in tow, the open-ended prospect of life in a hotel room had to be daunting. I looked to the groups speaking in Arabic. They wouldn't be genuine Emiratis, as this meeting was for us expats. So what countries did they hail from? I'd come here determined to meet people from all over. But for the moment, I was getting attached to the North American-plus-an-Aussie tribe.

Brian and I got to chatting and I started in on my questions. "My driver from Dubai kept saying '*in-SHULL-uh* this' and '*in-SHULL-uh* that.' I'm hearing it this morning, too. What does it mean?"

The UGRUist let out an odd chuckle, like the chirp of baby birds. "The '*SHULL-uh*' you heard is actually a slurred form on Allah. A literal translation is 'God willing.' The phrase is commonly pronounced '*inshallah*' although purists will say, *insha'Allah*. Everyone says, '*Inshallah*, no problem,' which means 'God willing, things will go the way you want.' But *inshallah, or insha'Allah,* means one thing to the person who says it and another to the person who hears it. So, '*inshallah,* no problem,' which you heard as '*in-SHULL-uh,* no problem,' may mean the person wants things to go your way, or may mean the person just wants *you* to go away."

Tony guffawed. "What '*in-SHULL-uh'* or '*inshallah'* or '*insha'Allah'* means, I believe is the person's not going to lift a finger to influence the outcome or take any responsibility. Pure resignation to all-powerful fate. That way, when something inevitably gets bollixed up, it's *God's will* that it did. It's not the person's fault. Hence, no problem... unless it is for you!"

The absurdist analysis was ominous, but I liked it. Having just lived through what felt like an era of blame and recrimination, I felt a certain appeal in such an approach to life.

Brian resumed. "Take us. We were just told our housing doesn't exist. To the university, '*insha'Allah,* no problem.' They'll simply have everyone stay here until they find alternatives. They've got the funds. For people who have kids, it's a different story. *Insha'Allah,* big problem, if you're a family of five and just found out you're sharing one hotel room indefinitely."

Tony capped the discussion with a smirk. "And while we're sympathetic with their plight, *insha'Allah,* no problem for us." Tony, like Brian, was a language purist.

After the meeting—which apparently had no business to conduct other than to convey a hearty welcome and a dose of bad news—new faculty was directed to tables outside the Jebel Hafeet room. There we were to sign our contracts. I hung back with Tony and Brian, watching people who moments later had been deeply upset now scrambling to be first to make the commitment. Behind each table sat a pair of young men in crisp white robes and headcloths, some tied and others held down by black crowns. Assisting them were young women draped in black. These were "official Emiratis" like the ones I had seen at Passport Control at the airport.

"What do you call that here?" Tony asked Brian, pointing not so discreetly at the Emirati's attire.

Brian explained that in the UAE the male's white robe is called a *kandura* and the head covering a *ghutrah*. He mentioned that some Emiratis tie it with a little tail and others use the black crown, a *tagiyyah*, and wear a prayer cap under it. The women's gown, he went on, is an *abaya* and the head covering is a *sheyla*. "You won't find many here who wear the veil." None in the room did, at least at the moment. Brian added that the UAE, unlike Saudi Arabia, allowed women to drive and to go out in public unescorted by male relatives. I had yet to meet an Emirati socially, but at least had made the acquaintance of someone who seemed to know the lay of the land.

After the rush subsided I went to the proper table, received my "official" contract and was politely handed a pen. I asked for time to read the document. I assumed it was the same one that had been sent to me, and that I'd printed and brought with me now. But given that I was about to make a three-year commitment, I figured it was worth five or ten minutes to be sure.

"*Insha'Allah*, no problem," said the young man in white.

But there was a problem. I compared the two versions. The new copy included a clause the old one hadn't, and it deemed a part of my salary a bonus that could be cancelled at any time.

"I have a problem with this contract," I told the university representative.

"Other people do, too," he replied, with a smile. "Sign it like the others. *Insha'Allah*, no problem. Everything, *insha'Allah,* will be fine. We also need your passport. It will be returned to you with your three-year visa after you pass your health test, *insha'Allah*. Maybe two weeks, *insha'Allah*."

The medical "screening" had been part of the fine print I'd read back in Ohio. But nothing about it indicated my passport would be held hostage until I'd passed. I felt duped. Lured in and ensnared. Four uses of "*insha'Allah*" in a single statement did nothing to put me at ease, either. But what could I do? Not sign, make a big public snit, and go back to my terminated life? Quit before I'd begun? I signed the contract and forked it over, folded into my passport. That didn't sit well, either. I didn't even have a photocopy of the picture and basic-info page. I was trapped.

The unease stuck with me, despite being handed, at the next table, a check for thirty thousand dirhams—at 3.67 to the USD, nearly eighty-two hundred bucks. My furniture allowance. As I had no apartment for the foreseeable future, I had no reason to spend any of it on furniture. Next, I was directed to the Union National Bank table. There, Tony stood in front of Brian and me, arguing with an official.

"If you deposit it with us," I heard the Emirati man tell him, "you can use your money right away. We will give you this." He dangled an ATM card. "But if you want to use another bank, *insha'Allah*, no problem. HSBC also has a table here. Your paycheck, however, will be deposited in this account and you can transfer it to another bank later. *Insha'Allah*, no problem."

Loud enough for Tony to hear, Brian said, "The university chancellor owns the bank the university uses. They've already set up accounts. The chancellor is Sheikh Nahyan, if you didn't know."

"A son of Zayed," Tony offered. "One of twenty-some. They run Abu Dhabi and the UAE."

I'd read a few things about Zayed on the internet.

"Sheikh Zayed bin Sultan Al Nahyan," Brian said. "Founder of the UAE. The man who made it a country. Deceased. He's a god here. His picture, by decree, is everywhere. He'd be a saint if this were a Catholic nation. Abu Dhabi's got a billion-dirham mosque named for him. It's breathtaking."

Tony grumbled something about "being locked into the company store." He harrumphed, "I already have an HSBC account in Brisbane. They are not going to control my money and me like that." He stomped off to the other bank's table, which so far had no customers.

"Trust me," Brian said to me quietly. "You want to do it this way. Tony will find out. His check will take a while to clear. We don't get paid until the end of September."

Following his lead and handing over my check, I was immediately rewarded with a UNB Visa debit card, packed with thirty-thousand dirhams and ready to hit the town.

But before I could get my first taste of Al Ain beyond the Intercon's gates, we were herded to lunch at the hotel's main restaurant, Arabesque. The quality of the buffet was encouraging. But we ate in a hurry, as buses were waiting for us at the hotel's entrance.

Our first outing was not, as I had imagined, to see the campuses— segregated by sex—where we'd be teaching. We were taken to the nearby Al Ain Mall. A mobile phone was, evidently, a necessity. In the UAE, Brian explained, your mobile phone number is your primary connection to everything, including utilities, since street addresses aren't used. (Mail may be received at the workplace, if one's employer receives mail; otherwise, rent a post office box, if you can find one.) We were encouraged to sign up for a prepaid service called *Wasel*. The phonetic similarity between *Wasel* and *wasta* fed my hunch that the telephone monopoly, Etisalat, also belonged to someone connected.

Three things stand out from my first venture. Scores of yellow Smiley Faces hung everywhere in the shopping center, another flashback to the mid-sixties. A flock of grade-school boys, Emirati by their *kanduras*, bumper skated on an ice rink. Outside, where I'd just been, it was 115°F. Worse, the whole place reeked. I had never smelled anything quite like it, except as a child stuck at holiday gatherings with the overlaid cheap scents of aunts and grandmothers. Each Emirati woman seemed to have a signature fragrance. Mixed with the score of perfume boutiques misting their wares, the air was cloying.

Scariest of all, there was only one refuge from that perfumed atmosphere, the food court. There the dense musk of American fast food cancelled out all else. KFC, Pizza Hut, Hardees and Burger King dominated the trays of Emirati families, many trailing overweight children. America's exports doing their grim work. I couldn't even escape it here, but there was a Lebanese Grill and *gelato*.

I acquired nothing but a Nokia, the same model as Brian's, an Etisalat SIM card with my new "050" phone number, and *Wasel* cards worth 500 minutes. At 500 dirhams, twenty-seven and a quarter cents per minute, all on my new university-arranged debit card.

The ride back to the neutral air of the Intercon took just a quarter of an hour on smooth city streets lined with green lawns and fragile flowers. We passed the Hilton and I took note; some new faculty was billeted there.

Only a few pedestrians braved the late afternoon heat, and there seemed to be nothing out there worth the risk of sunstroke. Still, I returned from that first field trip determined to avoid being confined. I was locked into the University's bank, had surrendered my passport, and was bound by a contract that guaranteed me nothing until I passed a health exam.

Yearning to get out on my own, or at least not as part of a herd, I stepped onto my balcony, clutching my phone. I had only one phone number other than Brian's. I called Dr. Beverly and she picked me up that evening in her second-hand Chevy Blazer. She'd heard about the housing fiasco.

"I bet you can do with a few hours away from the hotel," she said, pulling out onto the highway.

What I recall from that night tour were a lot of high-beams, several near accidents in roundabouts, South Asian families curiously lining the sides of the roads to picnic on the lawns, a humongous pearled jewel-box sculpture marking one of the main downtown circular intersections, a big Pizza Hut sign presiding over another, mobile phone stores everywhere, and lots of signs for "saloons."

"Saloons?" I asked. "Isn't this a dry country? I mean in the other sense?"

Beverly laughed. "They're beauty parlors. Barber shops. They just don't know how to spell."

We ended up at Paco's Mexican cantina in the Hilton. The sixty-something feminist from Nebraska via Ohio U. broke the bad news. She had been removed from the department's chairmanship. I'd suspected there was more to her alacrity in offering me a tour than a desire to welcome the new guy. I might not have known *wasta* from UGRU or the ins and outs of *insha'Allah*, but reading blunt omens wasn't foreign to me. It's bad news when the boss who hired you is booted downstairs.

Beverly's follow-up question stunned me. "Are you the new chair?"

My look of astonishment answered her question. It was clear that she had no clue what was going on and was looking to me, a colleague who'd been on board only a matter of hours, for answers.

I joked that the situation was Kafkaesque.

"That's UAEU in a nutshell," Beverly said, ruefully. "But at least I can still teach. If the new chair's not you," she theorized, "it's got to be Dr.

Ali from Penn State. The one in Erie, Pee-Ay," she added with some disdain. "He's originally from Djibouti." She sipped her Heineken. "I guess I tried to change things too quickly and angered people with *wasta*. Watch out for that! But I need this job. It's two more years before I'm eligible for Social Security. Who's going to hire me back home? I like it here."

That soliloquy gave me pause. "Well, not that it means much but no one has said a word to me. Hell, classes start in less than two weeks and I don't even know what I'm teaching."

"I don't know either!" She laughed, but now I clearly heard the edge of hysteria in it. "I wonder who's going to tell us. And now I've got no office. Maybe we can share one."

"By the way," she added. "I don't know whether *they* know you're Jewish. I haven't told *them*."

They? *Them*? I'd been kidding about the Kafka thing.

Whoever were the *they* or *them* who might or might not know, was *their* knowing or not knowing a bad thing? Did the faculty/staff know? Had Beverly brought me here to hint that I'd better lay low?

Was religion going to be an issue?

The contradiction hit me. My being a Jew couldn't be a secret—the fact was on the application I filed! Yet, Beverly was intimating I'd be wise to do just what I had decided against, go covert with it. She was giving me more insight on department politics, but I was distracted through the rest of our beer and fajitas. The repeated keyword—*they*—was soon to take on meanings it hadn't carried in my prior lives. I'd been in the UAE a few days. No passport. No housing. No boss. And now a secret religious identity?

The next morning saw us moving on to the big time, Dubai's Festival City. Set on a man-made canal, this was not a mere mall but a vast shopping and lifestyle center anchored by IKEA, Panda Hypermarket and the UAE's only ACE Hardware. Attached were two hotels—an Intercontinental and Crowne Plaza. Most of the shoppers were South Asian and Western, but there was a smattering of visible Emiratis, resplendent in their black and white. I was heartened to find a conveyor-belt sushi eatery.

The most interesting parts of the excursion were the rides up and back. Moraig, a New Zealander with a few years in Al Ain, engaged by the HR department to accompany us, held court on our luxury motorcoach. Tony, Carol, Dan, Brian and I had boarded Moraig's bus because it was free of screaming children. It was one of a fleet UAEU keeps to transport female students on Thursday to their homes, scattered all across the country and back to their hostels in Al Ain on Saturday night. Angling north on E-66 to Dubai, Moraig regaled us with advice, a mini crash course in survival for Western expats.

Two things she said particularly struck me. Tony lit on a third.

When Carol told Moraig that she was the new director of interdisciplinary studies and knew the acting provost, Moraig nodded sagely and said, "Ah. *Wasta*." When Dan told about his plans to get a job selling high-end real estate in Dubai, Moraig offered him her local savvy, too. "They keep saying the economy is good. You shouldn't have any trouble." She revealed the reason we lost our housing. Prices for Al Ain's residential real estate had doubled in six months. The builder was promised more money so he just broke his contract with the university. "Nothing will happen to him because he has *wasta*," she concluded. "He's related to Zayed."

"*Wasta*?" I asked. I'd given up on figuring out by context what it meant. Time to ask.

Brian piped up from across the aisle. "Connections. Who you know."

"If you have *wasta*, you're golden," Moraig offered. "Nobody can touch you. Especially if you are related to Zayed and his family, the al Nahyan. They run Abu Dhabi and the UAE. You'll see."

Carol nodded. She'd apparently seen already. And now she was one of my college's higher-ups. That struck me as good news, given what I'd heard from Beverly. I needed an ally.

On the way back to Al Ain, the talk turned to food and spirits. Moraig said something about "a place to buy pork," which surprised me. Tony's ears pricked up when she mentioned two places that sell alcohol. The rub, Moraig added, was that expats were supposed to go to the central police station and register to get a special permit entitling them to buy two bottles a month. "But don't worry about it!" she gushed. "You'll see!" The better liquor store was called Spinney's on the other side of town, where she went, and there was another somewhere near the Hilton.

I looked at Tony, who was absorbing this crucial intelligence and jotting it into a pad.

"Isn't this against all the rules here?" I asked Moraig.

Tony had a quick response. "You must have missed Rule Number One."

"Namely?"

Finishing up whatever he was scribbling, he gave us a broad grin. "There are no rules."

It may have been the very day after that trip that Carol—as she, Dan, Brian, Tony and I lunched at Arabesque—posed the Jewish question. I had cracked a sardonic joke about something or other and Carol called me out. "You're Jewish!?" she said, supremely confident of her Jewdar.

I nodded.

"I thought so!" she said, proudly "I knew there was *something* about you."

"It took you this long?" Dan asked. "I figured that out the first time we met David."

Tony and Brian hummed their respective confirmations.

"I have a lot of Jewish friends," Carol added.

Naturally. She was from Florida and knew New York and Jersey Jews. Curiously, Carol added, "You could be a borscht-belt comedian."

Finally came the morning for the medical screening, the hoop I needed to jump through for the return of my passport and finalization of my contract. Carted off from the Intercon once again, we were dropped at the regional health center. The air conditioning was broken. The few women, including Carol, were separated from the men and led away. A crowd of male South Asians, mostly Pakistanis and Bangladeshis, queued up. Tony, Brian, and I gamely joined them—but to wait for what we weren't sure.

"They've thrown us in with the chattel," Tony chortled, sweat wetting his brow.

I histrionically wiped my forehead. "I can't believe they don't have a special line for us rather than throw us in with common laborers?" Brian gave a soft laugh and confirmed the thought that had just struck me. "We *are* laborers. Like them. You've signed your contract and *they* hold your passport. What can you do? *They* know that." Tony let out a guffaw. "Golden handcuffs, David," he laughed.

At dusk that day I paid my first visit to the Horse & Jockey Club, eager to blow off steam. Inside the pub-themed bar Carol and Dan were cradling wine glasses. Dan took one look at me. "What happened to you?!"

I deflected to Carol, sipping a white wine. "What happened to you?"

She related how the women were taken to an air-conditioned room and were given the standard tests—BP, urine, blood, chest X-rays. "That part was quick and easy. Then I had to wait on the bus for hours for the men. You were one of the last." She giggled. "You didn't look too happy."

"*Insha'Allah*, no problem," Dan laughed. "Looks like you need a drink."

"*Insha'Allah*, big problem!" I was still steamed. "I'll take a beer."

I peeled off the bandages and revealed my black-and-blue inner arms where technicians took my blood. Dan plunked a Heineken in front of me. "*They* took my blood pressure. Highest ever in my life. I waited in line for more than an hour for a chest X-ray. Finally, I played the white-man card."

Dan nodded sympathetically. "Had to do that a lot when I was on the tennis tour."

"I hate doing it," I whined.

"*Insha'Allah*, no problem," Dan laughed. "You *will* play that card again." He added another wink and shifted to Moraig's Kiwi accent. "You'll see!"

Three days into my new-life adventure and my sense of adventure was wearing thin.

CHAPTER 2

Rule Number One

AFTER OUR FIFTH OR SIXTH CONSECUTIVE WADE THROUGH the buffet at Arabesque, enjoyable but increasingly monotonous, Tony and I decided to make a run for it. Brian lent us his Mitsubishi Lancer and we ventured out in search of booze. With Ramadan and the school year fast approaching, and with the prices at the Horse & Jockey Club burning holes in our wallets, we needed relief.

Tony took the wheel. Moraig had mentioned two options: Spinney's, across town, and an anonymous store behind the Hilton. Further intel revealed the second was near the dormitories for the hotel's foreign staff. A gaggle of South Asians hanging out near what looked like dormitories suggested we'd navigated unerringly. The Mitsubishi deftly slotted into a space between a Land Cruiser and Range Rover, both with opaque tinted windows; we peered out at the single-story cinderblock building. It was, indeed, anonymous. No sign betrayed the establishment's name or purpose. The two metal doors were marked simply "Entrance" and "Exit" in English. Another promising indication—anyone selling alcohol here would engage customers in the expats' *lingua franca*.

"Exit" swung open. Caught in the fluorescent light flooding through, we probably looked like a couple perps sizing up a prospect for armed robbery. Or cops on stakeout. I preferred the outlaw feeling. It fit Tony, too.

Over our first week in the country, I'd learned this much about my accomplice. Originally a "Bugle boy" from Bugle, Cornwall, he immigrated to Australia after a stint in the Merchant Marine. At 17, he left Cornwall and had circumnavigated the world several times, with a stopover in Vietnam in the 1960s, ending up in Brisbane. He was a professional rally driver and enjoyed a profitable career in energy, chiefly oil, but chucked it all to get a PhD and teach, at half his former pay. "I'm glad I did it. Starting a doctorate in your forties is insane, but I don't miss the rest."

Tony was a professor of something called "management information technology," who at 60 had been "made redundant." After seven years at Queensland U. of Technology, winning several teaching awards, he was one of the casualties when QUT gutted its faculty. With Australia's university system in a state of general upheaval, Tony saw his best option in signing on at UAEU's Business School. It was, he said with a determined tone of neutrality, a job.

Though my son's exploits were a favorite topic, Tony never mentioned children. He'd been married, too, less than a year, and following the divorce he and his ex-wife had lived together for two decades.

For years I'd told myself, and more recently found myself telling Max, struggling to find his niche at college: "All you need in life is one other person to share your foxhole. Sometimes you share it for life, other times for a year, a day, an hour—however long it takes to get through a moment of truth." Tony was living up to the sense of him I'd gotten the moment he strode into the Jebel Hafeet Room. Here's a guy who'd make a good foxhole buddy. He'd had practice at what I needed to get started on—seeing a future where none was apparent.

Clambering out of the Mitsubishi, we stood aside to allow two shop workers, South Asian, to lug four cases of liquor down the concrete steps. They proceeded to the Land Cruiser, raised the liftback and stowed the goods. The SUV's window dropped a few inches and I caught a glimpse of a white *guthra* as a hand reached out to hand the worker a wad of dirhams.

"I'd say we've found the place," Tony said.

"*Insha'allah*," I offered. Invoking God's will might still be in order, as we'd yet to step inside. There was the issue of a police permit. I eyed the uninviting building. "So, what if we get carded?"

"Carded?" Tony asked.

Right—he'd be thinking I was talking about a soccer match. "Asked to present our documents. The permit Moraig told us about with her chipper 'You'll see!'"

"Ah! Right. No time to visit the police now! So, follow Rule Number One."

We stepped through "Enter" to find ourselves in an establishment that could hardly exist elsewhere in the Arab world. A floor-to-ceiling room filled full of alcohol. One wall was a display of vodka, the bottom shelf warehousing 12-dirham liters of Cyrillic-labeled Russian and Indian jet fuel, the top tiers stocked with Grey Goose, Belvedere, Chopin, Absolut, Stolichnaya, Russian Standard, Finlandia, Smirnoff, and more, for 80 to 140 dirhams a liter. Absolut was on special: 90 dirhams for two one-liter bottles. I divided these prices by 3.67, the exchange rate having already been imprinted on my cerebral cortex. Yep, much better deals than at the state store back home.

A few boxes of Johnny Walker Blue, selling for a bit more than 500, dominated the top of the whiskey wall. Shelves below were stocked with JW's green, black and red labels, Dewar's, Glenlivet, Glenfiddich, Ballantine's, Jack Daniels, Wild Turkey, Four Roses, Canadian Club, Bushmills, and 12-year-old Chivas Regal on special for 72 dirhams. Indian scotches—Bagpiper Gold, McDowell's Green Label, MaQintosh—starting at 9 dirhams a bottle—filled the lower depths.

"Tony," I said. "Isn't Indian Scotch an oxymoron?"

"Nasty stuff, David. One of the more heinous crimes of the British Empire."

"The Blue's half the price it goes for in Cleveland," I observed.

"No taxes here. After all, what self-respecting government would tax a product that is officially not sold inside its domain? They needn't keep the prices low for us. We'd pay anything!"

"And, as you have noted, Muslims don't drink," I said, smirking, "like Jews don't eat bacon."

Tony rolled his eyes. "You saw the parking lot. Muslims don't drink except the ones that do. I hear that Saudi's consume more Scotch per capita than any people on earth." He turned away. "I'm going to check out the gin."

I placed two bottles of Chivas and one of Martel V.S. on the counter and coolly laid a 200-dirham note beside them. Tony stepped up behind me with a Gordon's gin and an Australian Chardonnay. At the register, a pudgy Indian with thick salt-and-pepper hair and matching moustache rang up my purchase, picked up the money, looked at me, and asked, "Do you have a permit?"

"Rule Number One," Tony murmured, closed-mouthed, the ventriloquist to my dummy.

I enunciated slowly. "I don't. Is that a problem?"

The vendor looked me up and down. "No problem." He pushed a button, opening the cash drawer. "I am supposed to ask, however. So I do." A believer in Rule Number One himself.

Back at the car Tony plopped his two black-bagged bottles in the back. I lowered my three to the floor between my feet and said, "When we walk into the Intercon, everyone will know what's inside."

"Indeed," Tony answered. "And our colleagues among the freshman faculty will be jealous because they're too timid to venture out to find this place. We, however, will have a fine run of it."

As he backed out, a white BMW 750i, its windows opaque, pulled in. From a tiny spot of shade in front of their dormitory, the cluster of Hilton workers watched the parade of sin buyers in their overbearing vehicles. Did they know the people inside paid more for a bottle of sin than they earned in a week, maybe even a month? Were they even allowed inside the store?

At the Intercon, once we'd delivered the keys and the Martell to Brian, Tony joined me in my room. He set up his bar on the balcony's low bamboo table, while I filled the ice bucket. A hot breeze wafted over us as we settled into the two wicker chairs. In the pool a lone couple sat at the swim-up bar.

Over Tony's shoulder, through the sliding door, BBC World, though on mute, shouted ominous, flashing-red graphics of the nose-diving financial markets. Had I known what was looming, I would have pulled everything out of the markets, chiefly that life-altering settlement from the TV station. I naively thought I'd always have that, and the illusion made my situation feel different from Tony's and my other UAEU colleagues. I had a cushion, an escape hatch. The job here was, for many, a one-and-only option. Within weeks the collapse of Lehman Brothers would be followed by cascading dominoes and havoc in the world's financial system, what would become known as The Great Recession, and my sense of invulnerability would be shaken.

"Gin or scotch?" Tony asked, Chivas in one hand, Gordon's in the other.

I pointed to the first. "Can't stand gin." I chuckled. "Back home I rarely drink."

"So you've said. Each time you've ordered a beer, if memory serves." He produced a scowl, and a grave look. "There's no *back home* for the moment, young David. *This* is your home now."

He had a point. But what was this "young David" crap he was laying on me since we'd gone on our booze run? I'd take the epithet as a token of camaraderie, along with his speaking as my senior.

"Hate gin? Just as well," Tony added. "Less chance of conflict. But I'll be sure to save the tidbit, re: your preference in liquor—which you scarcely touch—for the Al Ain *Gazette*, when it profiles you."

I half-smiled, gazing out across the Intercon's lush garden, its tropical colors muted in the sparse lighting. Drinking habits *back home* were back there—where I drank scotch only with Mark, a high school teacher and a true foxhole buddy. But here I was drinking it with Tony. Who, even if he drank gin, had foxhole potential. I idly wondered whether I did myself. Whether the whole notion was not just palaver you tell your emerging adult son.

"Right now," I told him, "I'd drink straight out of the bottle."

"Thankfully, we at last have alcohol. None too soon with Ramadan and classes quickly approaching." Cracking the Chivas, Tony poured me two fingers. "Rocks?"

I nodded.

Pouring the other glass a good two-thirds full with Gordon's, Tony plunked a few cubes into each. "Cheers." He passed me my drink and held up his own.

"To Rule Number One," he added with a twinkle in his eye, and took a long drink.

"And to Dan. His advice worked."

That advice had been to act cool and calm, like you know the drill, not like just one more Western asshole who blew into town last week. So far, a Western asshole was what I was stuck with being. Another idle thought. I drained my first scotch, plunked the glass on the table, and got up to lean on the railing. The hot breeze was blowing harder. The palms around the pool swayed, and the moon's reflection was scattered on the water. The couple laughed and clinked glasses at the swim-up bar. I sensed an interrogation coming, and wondered how much I wanted to reveal.

I'd felt subdued since those first days in the UAE. Not that I'm ever a social butterfly, but I'd been holding back. Watching. Keeping my eyes and ears open. Trying to get a fix on people, and—to the extent I could—the place. If I felt like unburdening to anyone, it would be to Tony. But I wasn't sure what I had to unload. Looking out at the pool, I tried to get a sounding on how, so far, Al Ain hit me. All I could come up with was a decided ambivalence. I didn't dislike the place; I simply hadn't had any contact with it. Or didn't want to believe I had since what I'd taken in so far was all university rules and retail. I had a nagging hunch that getting beyond the malls were going to be hard. My eye tracing the perimeter wall around me here, Oman on the other side, I recalled the barbed wire around the women's campus.

"Were you surprised buying booze was that easy?" I asked, turning back to Tony.

"I suspect the good people behind the Hilton will sell to anyone."

"And at these prices," I chortled, "I might have to become an alcoholic."

"Drinking is about all there is to do," Tony said. "Unless you love to shop." He refilled my glass. Once I'd raised my hand to signal he might stop, he set the bottle beside the table, on the balcony's floor. He cocked his head and studied his gin. "We know each other a bit now," he said, pausing for effect and leaning back in his chair. "I know why I'm here. I needed the job. But what's a Jew doing taking a job teaching at UAEU? Or for that matter, in the Arab world at all?"

I brought the glass to my mouth and sipped, to buy a moment. The wind kicked up the blackout curtains inside the room. "Because I could," I said, with a big laugh. It was an easy default reply.

"That's an *arsehole* answer," Tony responded. "They're used to Christians here, especially Pommie types—we've exploited the place forever. And while they may hate us, they tolerate us because they need us and we need their money. But a Jew? Here? If you wanted to get out of Ohio you could have gone anywhere. So I ask again, young David, why here? And what kind of Jew are you anyway?"

OK, no more *arsehole* answers. I had two questions now. I'd hit the second first.

"It depends. I've been a lot of kinds of Jew." I'd been asked versions of that question before, but I doubted Tony intended it in the same way. Orthodox, Conservative, Reform—did that stuff mean anything to him? I eased back into the wicker chair.

Should I say I pay dues to a small Orthodox synagogue? That Yiddish was spoken in the kosher home in which I was reared? That I'd married not just a *shiksa* but also a blonde from Minnesota, of Scots-German stock? (She had converted, had "official Jew papers," something nobody else in our family possessed.) That I didn't-really-kinda-believe in God, but hedged my bets, not willing to discount the possibility of *Something*? Basically, a non-observant Jew with baggage.

What kind of Jew indeed. A lot of Jews, as well as gentiles, have asked me that, and not always in the friendly way Tony had. Not "What kind of *Jew* are you?" but "What kind of Jew *are* you?"

My earliest remembered inklings of myself as a Jew are anchored in a gentile world. They feature Greenville, Ohio, birthplace of gunslinger Annie Oakley, with just one Jewish family, ours. As the first Jewish students ever enrolled at East Elementary my brother and I were sent to the principal's office during mandatory classroom prayer. Prayer was addressed to God, but I caught on quick that this was the Christians' god. After school, neighborhood boys would chase us home; my brother, slower than me, was the punching bag. Things got easier when East Elementary enrolled its first black student, in '59.

We were uprooted from that world in the spring, when my father died. and transported to a Cleveland inner-city "all-Negro" neighborhood, where my mother's immigrant parents were the last whites and Jews left. Given a peculiar secular-Jewish upbringing to age seven, I suddenly *had* to go to temple every day for a year and say the *Mourner's Kaddish* in memory of my father.

Probably a bit more listener-friendly to jump into the 1960s and Cleveland Heights, a predominately Jewish neighborhood. Having to stand my ground again, with the Italian greasers who wanted to kick the ass of the reputedly tough "Jew kid." I smiled a moment remembering those street brawls. I never started one, but I never lost. That, no question, Tony would appreciate. Toss in, for color, how I came to detest beet borscht and the stench of *gefilte* fish in the making before Passover?

All those things were way in the past, and Tony's interest was present tense.

"Before I came here, my Jewish friends asked me, 'Why are you going there? They hate us.' I'd ask, 'Who's us?' They'd respond, 'Americans. Jews. Both.'"

"Your friends have a point," Tony said. "Everybody here loathes Bush and they hate Israel."

Sure, they had a point. But I didn't want to believe that "Jew" or even "American" had to circumscribe my identity.

Tony pressed on. "And you wanted to come anyway?"

"To see for myself, and I needed to get out of my life in Ohio and *do* something. This came along so I grabbed it." I put the glass on the table. "I have an old friend. I told you about him. Bob. Former U.S. Air Force colonel. Commanded nukes in Germany. UN weapons inspector in Iraq with Hans Blix."

Tony nodded, pouring what by my count would be his third gin.

I briefly recounted my send-off by Bob, Mark and a few other fox-hole buddies. "After a couple drinks, Bob grabbed my shoulders. 'Do not tell anyone you're Jewish! Tell them you're Canadian.'"

"Because nobody hates Canadians?"

"Precisely. So I countered, 'But, what if they *ask* me whether I'm Jewish?'"

"And he replied?"

"'Just tell them you're Canadian.'"

Tony laughed. "Right. Asked 'Are you American or Jewish?' you answer 'Canadian'!"

"At least according to Bob. If anybody checks my UAEU job application they'll see 'Jewish.' If any one Googles me they'll find out because of the whole lawsuit thing. I'm just not advertising it."

Tony's look was like something out of the silent-film actor's handbook, yet hard to read. It may have said, "You're naïve if you believe that's going to work." He contented himself with a neutral—if slightly slurred—question. "Does Mohamed know?"

Mohamed, my across-the-hall neighbor, was a new professor, like us, hailing originally from Yemen but most recently Oklahoma City. So far the only Arab we'd met in our ranks.

"He hasn't asked and I haven't told."

"So," Tony said. "No Jewdar. We'll see how long it takes him to figure it out."

We clanked glasses to that, and downed the last of our drinks. He poured again for us both. This being my third, I resolved to stop counting.

"You asked what kind of Jew I am." I sat back, putting one foot on the table.

"That is the topic."

I took a deep breath. "I'm the kind of Jew who knows enough to be dangerous. I do what it takes within my code. I don't seek confrontation, but I also don't back down from schmucks and assholes no matter who they are even if I work *for* them. Journalists, which I guess I'm not any more, aren't supposed to do that. For anyone, including their bosses. I guess it's still the playground in me. You stand up to bullies. That's the kind of Jew I am."

I inhaled, caught my breath, and let out a small laugh. "And I can *daven*, but I choose not to."

"So, you're an arsehole who can *daven* but doesn't?" Tony said, laughing. "Tell me a bit more."

"I can be the biggest *arsehole* in the world if that's the only way to go." I drained my glass and Tony refilled it. "Take it right to the endgame." I raised my eyebrows and grinned like Jack Nicholson. *"If I am not for myself, who will be for me?* I told you about suing the TV station."

"Somewhat."

Maybe it was the alcohol or the fact that I was halfway around the world from *back home* and felt safe laying out the whole *megillah*. For the next thirty minutes, with a refill or two or three, I recounted how I knew the *arseholes* were concocting to fire me after a management change. Over the course of months I had gritted my teeth. TV news is like that. I knew *they* wanted to get rid of me. The beginning of the end started after I'd reported an incident in the control room with a young sports producer, the GM's son's best friend, who had overstepped his authority. Just days earlier, he had started telling anti-Semitic jokes in my presence, and I let them slide. But I thought that was odd and knew something was up. He had grown up on Long Island, and knew his way around Jews. I had mentored him, and we'd gotten along, but his attitude started to change after the new boss arrived.

Soon after I turned in my written report about the control-room incident, which included a section about the anti-Semitic jokes preceding it, the shit started hitting the fan. Memos questioning my poor job performance suddenly started flowing to my inbox. *They* were building a case to get rid of me. *They* thought I was playing "the Jew card." I knew how both ends of that game were played. I knew how *they* thought. Hell, I'd once been one of *them*. I'd been a *they*! Tony's eyes nearly exploded from their sockets when I told him that I began wearing a *yarmulke* to work—every day. Another foxhole buddy told me it would drive them crazy, and it did.

"So you sued for religious discrimination?

"No, for wrongful termination and retaliation."

"And you wore the little black skullcap?"

"No."

I described the large Rasta-like skullcap I wore. Because of where I sat in our newsroom, my colorful *kippah* popped up regularly during live broadcasts. Three months later I was fired for violating a station policy that hadn't previously existed. A year later after a five-day trial in Cuyahoga County Common Pleas Court the TV station offered a settlement that my lawyer told me I couldn't refuse. Dr. Beverly read an article about that lawsuit that moved her to hire me.

"It was never about religion, but that's what *they* thought. The *yarmulke* worked its wonders, like a red herring should."

"So it was about the jokes?"

"No, it was about assholes, or *arseholes*, or whatever *they're* called, and standing up to them if you can. At least not going down without a fight."

My former employers had, without even realizing they were doing it, or foreseeing the consequences, made my Jewishness the central part of my newsroom identity. I'd fought fire with fire. It was absurd—worthy of Kafka, in a low-rent kind of way. Tony's interrogation got me thinking—I'd followed that battle by going to a place where "Jew" would be the sum of most people's perception of me. And making that the first thing they knew about me would virtually guarantee their doing so. I'd have to let the detail filter out, find its way into context.

Maybe this getting drunk and mawkish had its benefits. Whether it was Chivas or Tony's Q&A or just that fact I was calmly reflecting on the whole firing and lawsuit episode for the first time, my life was revealing narrative cause-and-effect links I'd missed. Tony took a long sip of his gin. He lifted the bottle of Scotch, I nodded, and he refilled my glass.

I took a sip. "By the way, the young guy got a raise and a promotion. He had written an apology but they'd told him not to send it to me." I cupped the glass between my hands. "I think that worked against them. That and the fact they'd kept a secret file on me."

"Like the Gestapo!" Tony just shook his head. There was a silence. "And now you're a professor, a teacher. But you could've gone *any*where! Why here?"

Yes, the $64,000 question. What prompts a Jew to go live in an Arab and Islamic country? Not ready to address that, I deflected. "It usually takes me a year to drink a bottle of Scotch."

"I'm confident you'll be picking up the pace," Tony said.

"Enough about me and my *yarmulke*. What are you?"

"I'm not. Don't like any of it. My mum was Welsh Methodist. My dad's a Brit, a religion all its own. I'm not big on 'faith' or countries run by it. It's mucked up the world for too long."

"Well, then," I chortled. "I ought to ask you what *you're* doing here. Curious place for an atheist to spend the next four years."

"This place isn't run by religion. It's run by oil and money. Religion is just one way to control the people who live on top of the oil."

"That's an interesting angle. Sounds like the gin talking."

"It may be, but I'm not a big fan of Israel, I must tell you," Tony continued, leaning forward as if to compensate for the complete non sequitur. "It calls itself a democratic country, but religion rules it." OK, there was the transition. "You know what I mean. We can debate the historical reasons why, but I do not like what they do. Hope that's not a problem." He sat up straight and cocked his head. "Well, is it?"

I said nothing and watched his eyes grow bigger.

"*Insha'Allah*, no problem." I chuckled.

That might have been the most concise answer to his basic question: A Jew who doesn't give his own "chosen people," or Israel, a free pass. There are many of us who think Israel ought to do better, even in an insane world. No, *especially* in an insane world. Isn't that what Jews are always told about themselves? Isn't that what rips out our hearts and *kishkas*? The expectation of being "gooder." Not that I was going to get into any of that this far down in the bottle, or mention I was also a Zionist with an asterisk.

Tony cracked a big smile. "Good! Because so far I like your company."

"Go fuck yourself, my friend." We laughed even as I was saying it. "I have plenty of problems with the Israeli government. So do a lot of Jews, but it is our homeland. Period. Period. Period."

"I'm not saying I have a problem with Jews, just the Israeli government."

"Then you're a better man than me." I was feeling my oats. "I have a problem with both!"

Tony let out a roar. "What kind of crazy Jew are you? You don't get along with other Jews?"

"Sometimes I do."

"Have I told you one of my Jewish jokes yet?" Tony asked.

"No, you haven't." The breeze was refreshing, but not enough to sober me up.

"Two Jews meet on vacation," he started, "and they find out that each has lost his business and is living off an insurance claim. The first says that his business was destroyed by a fire while the second Jew says his was destroyed in a flood." He looked at me, and I nodded for him to continue. "The one who lost his business in the fire incredulously asks the other, 'How do you start a flood?'"

"Tony," I laughed. "It wasn't about the jokes."

"I have more."

"So do I."

"I know," he said. "It was about the arseholes. Now—before we call it a night, and I see whether I can find my way back to my room on all fours—one more thing." Ah, so Tony knew the first rule of the theater: leave them wanting more. His closing line was downright Seinfeldian. "What the hell's *davening*?"

CHAPTER 3

The Story of Mohamed

THE TWO WEEKS PRECEDING RAMADAN AND MY FIRST DAY of school I persisted as a trapped, stateless person. The results of the physical from hell were still finding their way through the system, and lodged in the bureaucracy somewhere along with them was my passport. OK, no big deal. The only place I would've gone was Buraimi, Al Ain's poor sister city across the border in Oman.

I used that time to learn a bit about my fellow expats, in different ways and to varying degrees stateless right along with me. Most were here because other options had dwindled or run out. Some came for first jobs, more for last jobs, a few, like Carol, for career breaks.

Much of my learning about the crew took place over meals at Arabesque, now the *de facto* faculty club. Three meals a day. It was there I learned that Carol was on sabbatical from a Florida university and that Dan, a onetime pro tennis player, had traveled the world in the '70s and lost glorious matches to some of the biggest Swedish names in the sport. Carol confirmed that she'd ended up at UAEU because she knew the acting provost. Dan planned to break into the leasing end of local real estate.

Brian was less the elfin Uncle Martin than My Morose Martian. After the first few days, he kept largely to himself. I made it a point to sit with him at meals, which meant he sometimes sat with the others, too. By ditching Oman for UAEU, he had nearly doubled his salary. Never married. No children. Sasha, a single mom of British extraction, also teaching UGRU, had joined him in coming to UAEU. A relationship I never sussed out, it extended to Brian's taking Sasha's little boy under his wing.

The freshman teacher who most intrigued me was Mohamed from Yemen via Oklahoma. He spoke not only my language, but also that spoken by the UAE's locals. Not a foxhole buddy, precisely, but friendly, a conversationalist, and eager to be an ambassador of cultural outreach, a human bridge of the Mideast-West divide. I first noticed him seated by himself at Arabesque, near a window, drinking coffee. The others had peeled off and I watched this man because I thought I'd seen him on my floor of the hotel. When he left I tailed him, discreetly. We rode in the same elevator to the same floor, where I let him exit first. He stopped directly across the hall from my door. I introduced myself and he asked whether I had a laptop and an Internet connection. I did, and was happy to put them at his disposal. Ice broken.

A naturalized U.S. citizen, he had lived in the states since he was nineteen, which I judged as about half his life, and had earned a PhD in electrical engineering at Syracuse. As he had a hearing defect, he'd made his specialty cochlear implants. Twice married, he had recently finalized divorce No. 2, and hoped to find Wife No. 3 here. He'd quit his job as an assistant professor at an Oklahoma university expressly to join UAEU's faculty. A native of Sana'a, Yemen's capital, he wanted to be closer to his children, who lived there with his first wife, and to his aging parents. He professed a commitment to his people, the Arabs. Coming back to the Mideast had a bigger purpose—"to help the Arab world learn to take care of itself." I was taken with, even moved by, his strong identification with the world from which he'd been long absent, and his inspired drive to be a part of its emergence and growth. As had Tony, in asking, "What kind of Jew are you?" Mohamed, in his zeal to serve his people, raised long dormant questions about how I fit into my own ancient tribe. Was I a Jew who wasn't a *Jew*? A hypocrite as the TV station's attorney tried to paint me in the trial?

But my being a Jew kept itself beyond the edge of our wide-ranging conversations. We talked for hours about what was wrong with America and the Middle East. My Yemeni colleague's perspective was refreshing. A practicing Muslim, although wife No. 2 had been a Polish Catholic woman, he refrained from alcohol—in itself something of a relief, as I had my work cut out for me in keeping up with Tony. We bonded first over our shared disgust with Bush, Cheney and their Orwellian War on Terror. "I hope, *insha'Allah*, Obama wins," he said. "If a black man with a Muslim father can be elected president of the United States it means anything is possible now. Maybe even in the Mideast."

He never said anything in those days about Jews, or about Israel, but he was upfront with his disappointment with the Emiratis. He decried how entitled and lazy the UAE's citizens were, and raged against the discrimination he already had experienced here. He was especially angry over a shopping trip to Carrefour, the dominant store at Al Jimi Mall. "*They* cut in front of me at the checkout line like I didn't even exist. The Filipina sales clerk just shrugged her shoulders. I came here because I wanted to help the Arab people. But already I can't stand the Emiratis. *They* look down on other Arabs." As a capper, he added, "Everyone knows they are not devout Muslims." When I learned he was being paid less than me, I was stunned. He was plainly worth much more. Was I at a higher pay grade because I was a white Westerner? I couldn't tell Mohamed about the discrepancy, so I couldn't ask.

He'd directed our conversation toward Islam, and so I asked him about the rift between Shia and Sunni. Mohamed explained the schism to me in such a way that I got it, for the first time. In a nutshell, the conflict was an ancient, never-ending, blood-and-succession feud. A religious war within Islam. A *jihad* by believers of both factions, one that would never end. Our world was endlessly trapped in it.

That covered, he moved up to the 20th century, and railed about how Islam had been hijacked by radical extremists and corrupted by oil wealth. I asked questions, as a journalist is taught, and an unfrocked journalist will do just out of habit. He didn't ask about my religion. Our topic was Islam, and it was a safe bet he wasn't in conversation with a fellow believer, Shia, Sunni or anything else. It steamed Mohamed that the oil-rich Gulf States had done little to help poorer Arab nations. He explained how all Arabs trace their roots to Yemen, including the dominant Bani Yas and the UAE's other twenty-odd tribes, forming a complex pecking order of which the Al Nahyan, a branch of the Al Falahi, resided at the to$_\textbf{r}$ made conservative Abu Dhabi, not flashy Dubai, the pre-eminent emir.

As intense as was his virtually instant resentment of his host country, where he had come expecting to feel at home, it was nothing compared to his love for Yemen and reverence for his father. He told me early on, and repeated it often, that I'd have to go there with him. The invitation was sincere, and kind, but still made me laugh. No way was I going where the kidnapping of tourists and terrorist attacks were apparently everyday events. I was intrigued, but that would have to be in another lifetime. I found it hard to get a handle on things in the relatively Westernized UAE. In Yemen? I'd be lost.

His stories about his father's exploits did make the notion tempting. The man sounded like a force to be reckoned with. "My father didn't go to school. So, in addition to the Koran, he taught himself English as a boy so he could read the great books of the world. That's how he educated himself." A nationalist revolutionary, he had led labor movements, been jailed, exiled, and returned home triumphant to became chief advisor to the country's first president after helping overthrow Yemen's last imam. The story Mohamed relished telling most highlighted his father's courage. I hoped to meet him someday.

As those opening weeks dragged on my Yemeni colleague became increasingly outraged at the university. "I was promised a villa with three bedrooms. Now I may have to live in this hotel for months. I can't have my children here. *They* are crazy and liars!" He was even talking, before we started teaching, about quitting. He had a legitimate beef, along with what I sensed was a not-brand-new resentment of the wealthier populations among his people. Hearing about the runaround Mohamed was getting from the university, I had a feeling we were all in for the same. Given I had no idea where my passport was, and what impact my health exam results had on my contract, I might already be in the midst of mine.

My fellow Western faculty was my main source of diversion from this futile worry.

d most others were hot to buy cars, "when in Rome" being
. The UAE is an automotive culture to such an extent that
mparison, might as well be Amish from coast to coast. Full-
ship here seemed to depend on an arcane combination of
tribal affiliation, *wasta*, proximity to government (itself *wasta*-linked),
and, by no means least, what one drove. Even vanity plates convey great
status in the UAE, and can easily cost as much, and often more, than a
Maserati or Rolls. Single and double digits command millions of dirhams.
What other effect would oil wealth produce in a traditionally nomadic
society? At any rate, we'd all need wheels. Dan and Brian alone elected to
rent. Mohamed was up for either, so long as he could get a deal. I wasn't so
keen on either the purchase or the rental option. It made no sense to make
any kind of commitment to a machine until my contract was certified,
which until my passport-physical situation clarified was a non-starter.
Back to the worry I was avoiding.

We'd heard tales about Sharjah, the Emirate just north of Dubai,
and its famous used-car market, the Mideast's biggest. Sharjah is an
industrial city, third largest in the UAE, predominately South Asian, and
loaded with warehouses. Because of high rents in Dubai it had become a
bedroom community for its glitzier neighbor, whose long-running boom
had been driving up rents in Sharjah, as in Al Ain. All over the gritty city,
high-rises were in various states of construction.

Mohamed was itching to check out the car bazaar. He'd found a
taxi that would take him the 200-mile round-trip for 300 dirhams, about
US$81, and asked me to go. I asked Tony to join figuring he could always
use an airing, and a three-way split was better. Since Mohamed spoke
Arabic he could facilitate the trip and any transaction Tony might wind up
getting into. This was no run-of-the-mill hunt for second-hand vehicles.
Tony was set on a Porsche, Mohamed on a Toyota SUV. I was determined
just to venture beyond Al Ain's city limits, and see what was out there.

UAEU wanted me to see what *they* thought I should see. While I was
hardly feeling rebellious, yet, I knew there had to be something else.

After piloting us through the two-hour drive up E-66, in blistering
heat, via a Corolla taxi with spotty a/c, our South Asian driver dropped us
off in downtown Sharjah. He said to call his mobile when we were ready
to leave and he'd pick us up. Mohamed told him he'd pay him when we

returned to Al Ain. I was surprised to hear that proposal accepted—a great way to keep a cab at one's disposal.

We arrived in late afternoon's scorching heat, and walked the deserted streets, nearly every square foot crammed bumper to bumper with vehicles from around the globe. The city center was a used-car lot! Signs for storefront dealers read like an atlas—"Stockholm," "Florida," "New Jersey," and "Virginia." But aside from the used cars, the streets were empty, and most shops closed until sunset.

"We came at the absolute worst time," Tony griped.

"We are idiots," I added.

Mohamed laughed and nodded like a bobble-head. And yes, Tony and I were certainly The Two Stooges, but Mohamed should have known better. After that he became the third Stooge, "Mo." Drenched with sweat, Tony and I had a pressing need to relieve our bladders. Mohamed led us to a small neighborhood mosque. "It's okay because there is no place else. No one will bother us."

And so my first visit to an Emirati mosque was made for less than noble reasons. I almost peed in the place where worshippers wash their feet before prayer. I mistook it for a trough urinal. Fortunately, Mo stopped me in time. He directed me to a small restroom with a humble hole in the floor. Then we found an air-conditioned cafeteria and guzzled fresh-squeezed fruit juices, watching the afternoon wane.

After dark, the action started, *American Graffiti* style.

Vehicles of every make, cruising slowly and being eyed by potential buyers now lined the once-empty streets. It recalled stories I'd heard of Bangkok bordellos. Everyone here, of course, was male, chiefly Arabs and South Asians, and one or another would dash over to a cruising car like a pelican diving into the sea for a fat fish. There would ensue, as in any red-light district, a brief conversation. Then buyer and seller would either drive off together, or return to the sidelines and the parade.

Mohamed explained that if a buyer and seller agreed on a price in principal, they would peel off, talk further, and if they reached an agreement, proceed to one of the scores of mechanics' shops, all South Asian, to get the vehicle "certified" as fit for sale. Cash would then exchange hands.

We enjoyed the pageant, but I saw nothing but trouble in buying a car this way. A man on the street told Mohamed to be careful because many of the cars submerged during Hurricane Katrina had ended up in Sharjah. We eventually walked into a storefront with the name of one of the States above the door—Maryland, maybe?—and were escorted into a dark back office. Served tea by several young South Asian men and greeted by the proprietor, a big Nigerian wearing a Dallas Cowboys jersey, we were grateful for the a/c. Mohamed was interested in a Land Cruiser in the Nigerian's lot. But when the seller found out I had once been the sports editor of a Dallas newspaper and, even better, had met Tom Landry, he wanted to talk football. It was all about the 'boys, not SUVs. No business was transacted that evening.

CHAPTER 4

Divine Intervention

MY COLLEAGUES' OBSESSION WITH THINGS AUTOMOTIVE, OR maybe my indifference to them, proved the decisive element of those weeks, and to a great extent, of the coming year. It all happened, it hit me later, in a circuitous, *insha'Allah*, kind of way.

The Islamic holy month began that year, 2008, on the first of September, though officially as of sundown on the last day of August, which was the day UAEU chose to start classes. I'll never understand why an Arab university would do that. Ramadan, following a lunar calendar, comes a bit earlier each year, and over the course of thirty-three years circuits all the seasons. Why not, once in a lifetime of the Christians' savior, start classes at the cusp of October? I was confident there was an Emirati logic that would explain this, but never managed to winnow it out of anyone. All we were told was that starting classes late was out of the question. Mohamed warned that by the middle of the second week, the students would be listless from fasting, and we'd accomplish nothing until the period of atonement ended.

By that final day of August, I had learned that I would be teaching two days a week, and have four-day weekends. I still didn't know where my passport was, or the status of my contract, but the schedule suited me just fine. My teaching load comprised three courses: *Computer-Assisted Reporting, Introduction to Language and Communication,* and *Writing for Media.* The reporting course excited me most. It would surely have the top journalism students. But the only textbooks for the three courses were outdated British ones, and I had—getting my assignments so late—virtually no prep time.

University regulations stated that all professors were required to file course syllabi, so I complied and submitted pure fiction. I don't know whether my colleagues did likewise. Most were more concerned with logistics, specifically ground transportation. How would we get from the Intercon to UAEU's several far-flung campuses? There were those who'd rented from EuropCar. Others thought they'd try their luck with hotel taxis and hope to flag down cabs on the street after teaching. Tony was set to go to Abu Dhabi in a few days to rendezvous with a doctor and—perhaps—buy the fellow's second-hand Peugeot, listed on a car-swap website. Mohamed was inkling more toward a rental; it seemed sensible, since he made daily reiteration of his threat to quit unless his housing situation was fixed immediately.

Sticking to my own version of the "when in Rome" approach, I told myself that something, *insha'Allah*, would fall into place, and we'd all get where we needed to be. Moreover, still a passportless, contractless and stateless person, I deemed it unwise to commit to anything.

Mohamed set out for classes early on the thirty-first by taxi and—as of teatime—had yet to report back. My first class was at eight the next morning. I remember the hour of Mo's return pretty specifically because, late that afternoon, just a couple hours before the full moon's appearance on the eastern horizon would usher in Ramadan, I was seated in the hotel lobby drinking tea. My companion, Carol, was telling me about her first day in the classroom.

Mohamed blew in, agitated. By that point in our acquaintance, I'd fairly say, more agitated than usual. "Dave," he groused, "the taxis wouldn't stop for me! I waited an hour. I cannot do this again!"

Carol, lifting a cup, pinky-extended, asked with concern, "What will you do?"

Mo had already conceived a plan. "Dave, come with me now before it gets too late."

Unceremoniously taking my leave of Carol, I hopped with him into a cab. Our mission: to investigate Emirati-owned car rental agencies clustered in a crumbling part of Al Ain's idea of downtown. We were, by the angle of the sun, on a tight timetable. At dusk the city would shut down, and until then, people would be hurrying home for the last meal before their first daylong fast. Cabs would be scarce.

Mohamed turned to me from the cab's front passenger seat, which it was his habit to occupy on our outings. "We'll go where the locals go and get a better deal. I'll negotiate in Arabic. EuropCar is a rip-off." Soon we were cruising the central streets, flanked by multitudinous mobile phone stores and "saloons," looking for the cluster of storefront auto-rental joints.

Mohamed gave it his all, but only grew angry all over again. After the second drop-in, I stayed outside. By the fifth agency, where I'd found a shady spot under an awning, Mohamed stormed out, hollering back over his shoulder in Arabic. He muttered that the manager inside was an *Egyptian*.

"He told me that because I am Yemeni, if I want to rent a car I have to leave my passport. I told him he was crazy, that I am an American citizen and a professor." Mohamed ranted that "the Egyptian"—everyone seemed to be referred to by nationality in the UAE—had told him it didn't matter what Mo claimed he was. Many Yemenis had rented cars in Al Ain and driven them across Oman's desert to their country and sold them. No Yemeni, *ergo*, could be trusted. "They are all crazy," Mohamed pronounced. "Let's go back to the hotel." He looked at me a little sheepishly. "I haven't eaten all day and I need food and drink before my fast in the morning."

On the nearly deserted street, mind-numbing heat radiating up from the pavement, Mohamed tried to hail a taxi. This had the same result you'll get in Manhattan during a rush-hour cloudburst. The same result, Mohamed ranted, he'd had trying to get back from classes. White-and-green cabs, most Corollas, many driven by men with white or henna-red beards, did drive by, all with passengers. Mohamed identified these drivers as Bahtan. By his tone, I gathered he had more sympathy with them than with Egyptians.

"They will be up all night eating," Mohamed said. "Because tomorrow they cannot eat from sunrise to sunset. Like me." That reminded him of his disgust with the UAEU administration. "They are crazy for the first month of college to be during Ramadan!"

We watched a half dozen more taxis speed past, a few without passengers. "They see me and won't stop," he grumbled. "You try, Dave."

I stepped forward and stood stoically in the street, my hand up. A taxi, a particularly old green-and-white Corolla with bald tires, quickly pulled over. Through the window, I asked the driver what it would cost to get to the Intercon.

"Fifteen dirham." The slight man, with big brown eyes, black hair, and a short, dark beard, spoke a beautifully accented English. He added a welcoming smile, a smile filled with something more than a greeting. I had a sense this man had put in his own time standing on the sides of roads.

"That's cheap, Dave," Mohamed said, and jumped into the front seat. I was more than happy for the sprawling room in the back. The a/c didn't hit me so I rolled down the window.

Nearly all of Al Ain's taxis then were independents driven by what the Emiratis call Bahtan, Pashtun from the tribal areas of Pakistan and Afghanistan. They spoke a little English—chiefly the English portion of "*insha'Allah*, no problem"—and charged whatever fare they could get away with. Their cabs had meters, more or less decorative. Those in the know agreed on the fare upfront. To see whether it might lead to conversation—Mo was busy fulminating—I complimented our driver's English.

"Thank you," he replied, pulling out into traffic. "I speak better Arabic, Pashto, and Urdu."

Maybe, I mused, I should give this man my classes at Maqam, and I should drive the cab.

"You were kind to pick us up. I think you were the last taxi on the street."

He laughed. "*Yaya*, everyone is going home for the last meal. I was, too. But I saw you and decided to stop." He caught my eye in the rearview mirror. "Maybe this will be good, *insha'Allah*."

It was *God's will* that he took pity on Mohamed and me, and stopped? Was this an act of Ramadan spirit? Not just a random event in the course of a day's traffic? Or was he saying prospectively that, *God willing*, this random pick-up of a fare might turn out to be a good thing? For whom? Small things had, all my life, led to bigger things. I decided to assume that the driver was onto something. What mattered, however, was not a theo-logical-philosophical debate raging in my head, but getting Mo back to the Intercon before the buffet closed. I wanted no part of what would happen if he didn't get fed.

"I'm David," I said to the driver.

"Noor," he replied, turning to look me in the eye. "I am Pashtun from North Waziristan."

He looked about five-and-a-half-feet tall, maybe 120 pounds soak-ing wet, and was wearing the traditional Pakistani shirt and pants, light blue, pajama-like and loose fitting. It occurred to me, somewhat irrele-vantly, that I could carry him under one arm.

"He's Bahtan, too, Dave," Mohamed said.

"*Yaya*, I am Bahtan," Noor laughed. "All taxi drivers in Al Ain are Bahtan."

I wondered what, literally, "Bahtan" meant. Eventually, I came to the conclusion it was the Emirati equivalent of Americans calling all Hispanics "Mexican."

Noor seemed personable. We chatted in English the rest of the way. My gut told me his old taxi was the answer to my transportation problem, and more. Yes, maybe this would be good, *insha'Allah*. When he dropped us off at the Intercon, I asked whether he'd like to be my regular driver.

We quickly agreed on a weekly payment, for the job of ferrying me to and from Maqam on Mondays and Wednesdays, of one hundred twenty dirhams. That worked out to sixteen dollars each round-trip, which—given the Intercon's location—was really a double round-trip. Seemed to me I was getting a great deal.

As we entered the lobby, Mohamed chided, "Dave, you could pay him less."

That first morning of Ramadan Noor's beat-up Corolla pulled up to the Intercon at 7:25. Noting a few anxious colleagues waiting for taxis that hadn't arrived, I invited them to climb in. Twenty minutes before class time, we de-cabbed at Maqam's barbed-wire main gate.

"See you at ten?" I confirmed with Noor, shutting the door on the passenger side.

"*Insha'Allah*," he replied with his ready smile, and drove off.

Twenty minutes later, I was staring at the sign that read "Women's Toilet." Room 04.

At Building 71, off the second-story promenade, I found the Mass Communications office. Inside I made the acquaintance of the secretary, Mariam, the tiniest adult I have ever met, an Emirati munchkin dressed from head to toe in black. Not a midget and certainly not a dwarf. Just teeny. Perfectly proportioned like one of those miniature ponies. By then I had had a good laugh at my plight.

Mariam listened to my problem amid the office hubbub. I wasn't sure how much English she understood but she calmly produced a document proving that indeed my class was assigned to Room 04. I told her the room was a women's lavatory, whereupon she told me I was wrong. I replied that I was not. Mariam—whom I would get to know all too well in the coming months—offered the less-than-germane information that room assignments and scheduling were the responsibility of a German company. *Ipso facto*, said company being German did not make mistakes. I wondered idly whether she'd have cited Teutonic organizational skills as proof of national infallibility had she known her interlocutor was a Jew? Of course, she may have known this—who would have perused my application if not the intimidating itty-bitty department secretary?—and maybe that's why I was assigned Room 04. It was one explanation.

I simply asked for another room. Mariam handed me a form. I paused before filling it out. With only three students, the class would surely be cancelled. This had to be a futile exercise. I asked Mariam whether she could direct me to my office. Handing me a slip of paper with yet another number, she told me to look for it on the far side of Building 71, also along the second-story promenade.

Why would I have imagined an office adjacent to my department with the others?

This number did at least belong to an office—no, make that a closet with two desks and chairs, one computer, and one working telephone. And a roommate, Dr. Beverly. I've had bad first mornings at new jobs. OK, I had no classroom, probably no class anyway, and no privacy in my so-called office on the far side. So much for a campus refuge.

"I told you we'd share an office," my colleague effused. "I know it's not much, but...."

I tried to act chipper, which isn't exactly my default setting. Could this be happening? Beverly was on the "outs" and now I was relegated to Siberia with her. The implication was obvious—on the outs before I had even started. While my irritation, and Mohamed's influence, may have been inducing a minor case of paranoia, in my bones I felt that the pint-sized Mariam had, as a matter of principle, disliked me from long before we ever met. Within weeks, a consistent pattern of my being non-informed about department meetings and everything else would remove all doubt on that score. Not that I confirmed it immediately, but this day was the start of the rich—as I no longer joked, Kafkaesque—experience that would be my tenure at UAEU. The Arabs at the institution resented its dependence on imported faculty and its turn to English as the primary language of instruction, and thus went out of their way to jack *us* at every turn.

Beverly proved sympathetic, and helpful. She was unsurprised by Mariam's reaction to the classroom scheduling. "She runs the place. Dr. Ali will find that out! I sure did."

What Beverly wanted to know right away were the names of the girls enrolled in the Women's Toilet class. She perked up at the mention of Fatima Al Falahi.

"Oh!" Beverly exclaimed. "She was my student last year. Her family has a lot of *wasta*. Her father is related to Zayed. He's well known. I've been trying to wangle an invite to see their camels for a year. They own some of the fastest racing camels in the UAE. See if you can get us both invited."

That bit of intel piqued my interest and sowed yet another seed. Maybe camels, *insha'Allah*, would lead me into the Emirati world. Well, far more likely the class would be cancelled, I'd be assigned to teach something else, and that would be that. No more Room 04, Women's Toilet.

But small things, and ridiculous screw-ups, can lead to bigger and better things.

Arrival back at the campus gate improved my mood considerably. Noor was waiting in the sand-and-asphalt parking lot. He was as chipper as I had tried to fake being for Beverly. I opened the passenger door and slid in, my head pouring sweat under the drenched blue ball cap. Desperate to feel the weak a/c on my chest, I undid the top buttons of my soaked shirt.

"How was your first class?" he asked, with his big friendly grin.

I took off my cap, wiped a hand over my forehead, thought about it, and in the end simply laughed. An easy enough question, but I didn't know how to answer.

"Noor," I said, shaking my head. "My class this morning had only three students enrolled and it was scheduled in the women's toilet."

"The women's toilet?!" He looked mortified. "They are crazy, yes?!"

"Yes, the women's toilet," I said, trying to laugh. "Naturally, I didn't go in."

On the drive back to the Intercon I told Noor the tale. When he dropped me off, I asked with a half shrug. "You'll pick me up at 12:45?"

"*Insha'Allah*, no problem," he answered.

Right. This—my passport held hostage, uncertain employment status, uncertain housing, classroom assignment that took me to the door of a women's toilet, and even Mariam—was all *God's will*. And so, no problem? I wasn't quite there yet. Problems are to be tackled, *insha'Allah* or no *insha'Allah*. Besides, it was years since I'd addressed any questions, silently or aloud, to God.

Noor's smile as he departed left me with the feeling I'd be doing that soon, and that I'd met a special man who could be my "teacher" here. I laughed to myself. Could he be my Pashtun *rabbi*?

CHAPTER 5

The Girl in Pink

INTO MY THIRD AND LAST CLASS THAT FIRST FULL DAY OF Ramadan wafted the blur of color I'd glimpsed that morning, stepping through that door in the fence. She wasn't an apparition, but did stand out like an orange atop a bushel of apples—if oranges were pink and apples were black. By the time she came in, a bit of brash individuality hit me as a great relief.

My two afternoon classes had also been scheduled to meet in Building 66, but not in Room 04. For that I gave thanks to my God. I'm sure He had never in all of eternity heard a prayer like that from a Jew standing where I was standing. It's hard to describe the relief I felt just walking into a real classroom, with real desks.

After Noor dropped me off, releasing me into the crushing mid-day heat, I diverted through a modern, hi-tech building of reflective glass, the one I'd navigated by earlier. Its a/c, as I had hoped, worked. Still, a mere fifty yards in the sun had me raining sweat from every pore. This edifice was a piece of the one-billion-dollar campus reconstruction underway throughout Maqam.

With *Intro*, my first afternoon class, due to kick off at two, I was in no hurry. In my morning reconnaissance this new building, in front of

Building 71, had caught my attention. Between the two stood that flag-pole with the Emirates' four-colored banner blowing stiffly in the breeze. Maybe that building, I'd considered, would be my shortcut, both to the Mass Com office and to the cramped lair I shared with Dr. Beverly. Maybe I'd be lucky and find an hour of privacy before afternoon classes, to decompress.

In the back of building, I discovered an oddly dark food court. Flights of four, five or more girls, all in black from head to toe, sat at tables huddling around laptops, laughing as students do everywhere. But it struck me, not a single young woman was sipping coffee or a soft drink or eating anything. Duh! It was Ramadan. The food court was closed. Still, I was pleased to see it anchored by Dunkin' Donuts. A little slice of home and a good cup of coffee when I needed one, I put a pin in that.

Building 66 did not feature such extensive catering facilities. One of the original university structures, built in the mid-seventies, it had been designed in a functional Arabic style. The white concrete-and-block three-story structure featured an open-air central courtyard to admit cross ventilation. It struck me immediately as funny that flocks of birds flitted in and out as often as flights of girls in black. A few vending machines near the front entrance sold salty snacks, fruit juices and bottled water. Or at least did the other eleven months of the year. Tucked in one corner, a stand, also dark, advertised "Magic Corn," which I later learned was a Styro cup of boiled frozen yellow kernels loaded with butter and other flavorful toppings. I noticed after the holiday that the two elderly Filipinas, who I'd watched sweep the building's floor in the morning and eyed me as I stood by Room 04, also oversaw Magic Corn.

Intro, in a second-story classroom, with broken a/c, open windows, flimsy curtains and no cross breeze, had thirty-five young women signed up, although I didn't count to see if they'd all made it. On the whiteboard I wrote my name. A chorus of voices rang out, "Welcome, Doctor David!"

After explaining I wasn't a PhD, that they should call me "Mr. Eden" or "Professor Eden," or simply "David," I handed out the syllabus. This was greeted with smiles and "Thank you, Doctor."

Not wishing to correct again regarding my lack of credentials, I explained that I did not use PowerPoint and that there would be a mid-term and final. Those exams would be based on the lectures, discussions and the reading, I told them to be prepared because I could call on them at any time and that twenty-five percent of the course grade would reflect class participation. These announcements—particularly the last—sparked commotion.

What I tried to do that day, for the most part, was get a sense of how much English the students could speak and comprehend. The answer to both: not much. My mood sank. How could I teach *in* English to students who didn't know enough of the language to understand what I was saying? Would I be teaching *English* while teaching *in* English? Wasn't UGRU supposed to do that? And how on earth could I evaluate participation if we had no language in common in which to discuss our subjects?

These questions were secondary, however, in view of the basic fact: *Intro* was required for all communications majors. A student couldn't get her degree without passing it. So this class included sophomores, juniors and seniors, with widely varying degrees of preparation. Oddly, it had no established curriculum. My boss for *Intro*, Carol, had suggested I invent my own course. So, I'd combine things I'd taught elsewhere, cherry-picking what struck me as suitable.

"What's suitable for female students at UAEU?" could be a course in itself. The cut-and-paste syllabus I'd just handed out included lessons on the history of language and human communication—verbal, nonverbal, interpersonal and intrapersonal. Other planned lectures included self-concept, social roles, values, attitudes and beliefs, critical thinking, and something I liked to call "thinking styles." I knew I'd be pushing it with the roles of journalism and propaganda in society, and I looked forward to it.

Most students hailed from the seven emirates—Abu Dhabi, Dubai, Sharjah, Fujairah, Ras al-Khaimah, Umm al-Quwain, and Ajman. A third called Buraimi and nearby Omani villages home. One came from Sri Lanka. Unless their families lived in Al Ain, they resided Sunday to

Thursday in on-campus hostels within Maqam's barbed-wire-crowned perimeter wall. Many, I learned, were the first in their families to go to college, even if they had brothers. Some came from large families—three had more than a dozen siblings, and a dozen had eight or more. One, at 19, the oldest of eight daughters, revealed that her mother, age 32, was "very proud" of her for attending UAEU.

I did the math quickly. "Your mother was 13 when you were born?"

"Yes," she said, beaming from ear to ear. "I am the first, and the first in college."

The Sri Lankan, a junior, was the only non-Arab Muslim student in any of my classes. She spoke competent English and was at UAEU on an international scholarship. Her hobbies included reading and watching South Korean love stories on the Internet.

Learning names, normally a big part of my first day in any class-room, presented a challenge. Twenty-one of the students shared the most-popular Arabic given names for women. The two most common honored Mohammed's daughter and Jesus' mother. *Intro* had five Fatimas, four Mariams, and three each of Noura, Amna, Sheikah and Anood.

At a respected co-ed Jesuit university in suburban Cleveland where I'd once taught, many female students had been named Mary. But they dressed individually, not uniformly as part of a flock. No student in this class wore a veil, a *neqab,* for that I was grateful. I noticed that many of their *sheylas* and *abayas,* some featuring fine embroidery, concealed designer jeans, denim skirts, colorful ankle-length party dresses, athletic shoes, and even spike heels. Expressions of self peeked out from under the black fabrics. I took heart. Perhaps what the *abayas* concealed—though not entirely—symbolized their wearers' affinity for modernity, individuality, the West, and new ways of thinking. All the same, here I was in a culture in which conformity and near-anonymity were a major part of the feminine ideal.

I gave in and did something I'd always hated: assigned each same-named girl a number on the seating chart and asked her to sit in a designated seat. That would let me work out face-place associations. So "Noura 1" was the tall Noura who sat in the first row, as "Fatima 1" was the Fatima in that row near the door who modeled expensive jewelry. "Fatima 4," the Fatima in the fourth row decked out in a *sheyla* and *abaya* embroidered with golden thread, traveled to Italy in the summers, and the Sri Lankan was "Mariam 3," in row 3, and so on. The only anomaly was "Anood 2" who sat in the back row. A week later "Anood 3" appeared for the first time and sat in the third row. I didn't change their names. Almost immediately the girls started referring to themselves and addressing one another by name and number.

Fifteen minutes to my next class, but just one floor up. The computer printout said eight students had enrolled in *Writing for Media*. All eight showed up. Seven in black. And the one in pink.

A small class. Maybe I can get to know these students and really teach them, I thought.

The windows of the corner classroom were wide open and the hot desert wind stiffened the flimsy white curtains, as it did the flag outside. Why would I think the a/c would be working in this room, too? Through the windows I watched dust and sand swirl in tight dirt devils. Behind a construction wall the new campus was being built atop the sand.

I lined up all eight students in the first row—Black. Pink. Black. Black. Black. Black. Black. Black—and started learning names. Samah's pink *sheyla* framed a light-complexioned round face with piercing eyes set behind wire-framed glasses. Instead of a black *abaya* she wore a faded pink floral shirt and a floor-length beige skirt. She hailed from Abu Dhabi and there was little doubt she was someone special. I believe in first impressions. I liked what I saw that day.

Of the seven girls in black, all with darker complexions than Samah, several modeled elaborate henna tattoos. Latifa, a tall, slim senior, showcased intricate designs on both hands and forearms. She lived in a small town, between Abu Dhabi and Al Ain, where there was by her own report "nothing to do." Her father, a retired UAE Air Force general, had eight daughters. "I am the eldest and the first one to go to college," she revealed. "My father thinks it's important for us to get educations." It encouraged me to hear that her father was not disappointed to have only daughters in a culture that so revered sons. "He says that daughters are just as good," she beamed.

This class was evenly split between the UAE and Oman. The Emiratis all sat together nearest the door, the Omanis nearest the windows. The seating chart read: Latifa, Samah, Mariam, Hessa ... Reem, Sendeya, Rhouda, Noura. The door-ward side spoke good English. Among the UAE-born, Mariam and Hessa both lived right in Al Ain. Mariam had an identical twin. "We have the same birthmark on our cheek." Hessa was one of seven daughters with no brothers and a deceased father.

The window-ward side struggled with the language of instruction—enough to make me question whether they should have been enrolled in the class. Would they get anything out of it? Reem, 20, also had an identical twin attending UAEU; her family lived just across the border in Buraimi. Sendeya, 19, told the class that she and her husband, her cousin's best friend, had married not through an arrangement but for love. That elicited "oohs" and "ahhs." In a society that favored brokered marriages between cousins her union of love, with a boy not from her clan, was still the exception. Her husband lived in Oman and encouraged her to continue at UAEU, even though her studies kept them apart. She was looking forward to her first anniversary in December. Rhouda, a 22-year-old junior, hailed from a village not far from Buraimi. She understood English the least well.

Noura, closest to the window, was as big and broad as a small-college linebacker. Reinforcing the comparison were her bright green Converse high-tops, a colorful, literal footnote to the black in which she was clad. That jockish touch, so unexpected, made me like her on sight. It seemed daring.

As in *Intro* I handed out a syllabus. *Writing for Media*, whatever that was supposed to be, was in my take heavy on the "five W's" plus lede and nut-graph writing. I'd looked at the textbook and tossed it. My thought had always been if you can write a good lede and nut graph the rest follows. I said clearly and emphatically that I would not give a midterm and that no grade would count until I said it did. Until that time, everything would be practice—and I planned to devote several weeks simply to ledes and nut graphs.

"Your final will test how well you can write the basic elements of a news story and a real journalistic assignment of five paragraphs. If you can do that you can write for media. Any kind of media. Most professionals can't do it well even after years on the job."

Hearing that, Samah raised a skeptical eyebrow. "Professor, that's not how it's done here."

I caught her eye. I could feel fourteen others on me. "Samah, that's how *I* do things here."

She was right, of course. I didn't have a clue how things were done at UAEU. And I wondered—was she correcting me, warning me, challenging me or throwing down the gauntlet? Whatever her aim, the feistiness she showed I liked. Just as much as Noura's sneakers.

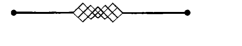

At 8 a.m. on Wednesday I stood once again, both humbled and dismayed, before the Women's Toilet. Room 04. This time I knew this was where I belonged. But it would be my last visit there, ever.

All three *Computer-Assisted Reporting* students showed up. I told them that I hadn't received a new classroom assignment yet and that they should meet me at my office in Building 71 next time. I tried to explain the location of that closet in Outer Siberia. If in doubt, check with Mariam in the Mass Com office for directions. At that suggestion, Fatima Al Falahi rolled her eyes. Dr. Beverly's brief gushing about Fatima's family's *wasta* already had me intrigued and that little bit of wry body language raised my curiosity even more. Another individual among my students? I certainly hoped so.

But chances were the inquisitiveness would prove moot. *Computer-Assisted Reporting*, with only three students and no classroom, seemed doomed to cancellation. What university could afford to keep it?

CHAPTER 6

Noor's Al Ain

AFTER THAT FIRST DAY, WHEN NOOR PICKED ME UP HE'D ASK, "How was class in the women's toilet?"

With the country and university working on a confusing Ramadan schedule, I not only relied on Noor to take me to the university, but also started calling him on non-teaching days to escape my rising claustrophobia at the Intercon. No matter where he was or what he was doing, he always came. "My taxi is your taxi," he told me, adding, "You pay me what you want."

Believe me, I did want, and I tried. Noor got his base rate of 240 dirhams a week, but that was just for taking me to and from school. When I attempted to pay for trips he made just to drive me around, he refused. So I tried tipping—something we'd been told during orientation was "not expected here" by taxi drivers. Noor hardly seemed to expect it, but evidently this was compensation he could accept.

He typically drove fourteen hours a day, seven days a week, taking off just half of Friday, to pray. He paid his Emirati sponsor 1,500 dirhams each month for the privilege of working, which left him a monthly take-home pay of between 4,000 and 6,000 dirhams. Most of that he sent to his wife and family, in their village in North Waziristan. He shared a two-bedroom flat with three fellow tribesmen, in an older section of Al Ain. His share of the monthly rent was 1,100 dirhams. This, and many other things, told me that Noor and I could operate by a natural partnership. I had more money than I needed, and he had something I very much wanted to acquire: knowledge of the terrain and the ropes.

He had lived and worked in Al Ain for nine years, only occasionally visiting home, and knew the city well. When I needed something, he knew where to go among the downtown stores, well off the Westerners' beaten shopping tracks, in which Indian and Pakistani shopkeepers sold the goods I was after, but a lot cheaper than I'd find at the malls. After I broke my eyeglasses, he took me one evening after *iftar* to an Indian-owned optician. I bought a pair of blended bifocals and top-quality titanium frames for 550 dirhams; at the upscale Al Ain Mall, for something comparable, I had been quoted 2,750.

"There are three prices in the UAE," Noor explained at the start of that outing. "The first is for Emiratis, who pay the most. Next is for people like you. Not as much as the Emiratis, but still too much. And the last is for the rest of us. That's the price I will get for you, the Pashtun price." He nodded, and added with gravity, "Do not shop with the Egyptians." I'd learned that with Mohamed.

He quickly added his opinion about Egyptians and their peculiar relationship to Emiratis. "Did you know that Emiratis use the same Arabic word—*masri*—to designate both an Egyptian and a donkey? They think the two are the same." He let out a laugh. "But the Egyptians call Emiratis *metnaakit il-jemel,* which means in English something like 'that which is fucked by camels.' He footnoted this information with the point that Egyptians were widely known to spy for their Emirati bosses. He said his elderly Emirati sponsor, whom he called a "kind, good man," referred to the Egyptians as "dogs of hell."

Noor's Al Ain was not the one shown to us by the university or described on websites I'd visited before leaving the U.S. He preferred the inland desert city to Dubai and Abu Dhabi. The highways between the

UAE's three leading metro areas sketch a roughly equilateral triangle, at the base of the rhino horn crowning the Arabian Peninsula: Dubai sits at the upper vertex; Abu Dhabi to the west; Al Ain midway between the Persian Gulf and the Arabian Sea, tight on the border with Oman. Al Ain boasts a greater native population than any other UAE city, and while it's growing fast, Abu Dhabi's "Garden City"—built around seven oases—remains livable. For urban congestion, skyscrapers and construction run amok, the two dominant Gulf cities aren't far away.

"Not so crazy like Dubai," Noor said. "Abu Dhabi is less crazy. Al Ain is the nicest."

He had arrived in the eastern region of the Abu Dhabi emirate at thirty. His first two years he worked for the municipality and lived in a labor camp on Al Ain's outskirts. He moved through a variety of transportation jobs, taxi driver being his least favorite. His longer-term plan was to buy a sixty-seat Tata bus and get a fat contract from a construction company to transport South Asian laborers. He had already saved 30,000 dirhams of the 60,000 he estimated he'd pay for a used Tata.

I told him I wanted to see his Al Ain and that he should take me wherever he thought I should go.

"You'll spend time with me in Sanaiya, the industrial city," he said. "You will like it."

Noor had seen Al Ain grow into the UAE's fourth largest metropolis, with nearly 400,000 residents. At 900 feet above sea level, with its arid inland climate, Al Ain was different from the humid coastal sprawls of Dubai, Abu Dhabi, and Sharjah. Before oil transformed the economy, those boomtowns had been fishing villages. Of course, they were booming less furiously in the imploding economy in the fall of 2008 than they had been even weeks earlier when I arrived.

Al Ain's name means "the spring," and its plentiful fresh water long made it the center of life in this part of the Arabian Peninsula. It has been continuously inhabited for more than four thousand years. Its archipelago of sources, the largest being the Al Ain Oasis, adjacent to the Zayed Palace Museum, still formed an ancient *falaj* irrigation system, channels of flowing water augmented by nearby mountain runoff, crisscrossing lush farms and date-palm groves.

What gave Al Ain a special panache was its status as the ancestral home of the Nahyan, Abu Dhabi's ruling family, and birthplace of Sheikh Zayed bin Sultan al Nahyan, father of the UAE. Reverence for the deceased Zayed was palpable all over the emirate—his image was everywhere.

Grand palaces, such as Al Maqam and the Shakboot, dominate sections of the city, and scores more are reputedly hidden in verdant landscapes behind tall masonry walls. I never found out if there was any connection between the Maqam campus and the palace. Zayed's predecessor as emir of Abu Dhabi, his brother Shakboot, had lived in his namesake palace. That, fittingly, sat across the street from the building where the other new faculty and I would end up living, once we were booted out of the Intercon.

"Some roads just stop because of a palace behind a wall," Noor told me. "People say some of them have golden elevators inside."

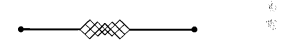

Jebel Hafeet, straddling the Oman border and at 4,068 feet the UAE's second-tallest mountain, also looms large in the local lore. Zayed, in his youth, had famously climbed to the summit. Khalifa, his eldest son and successor as UAE President and Emir of Abu Dhabi, was now king of the mountain. He was building a grand palace, with heliport, at the top. Adjacent to the site sat a cafeteria with a large parking lot offering breathtaking views of the Omani desert.

Noor liked picnicking with friends at the foot of the sacred mountain, the Green Mubazarrah, a verdant park cut in the craggy red foothills, boasting hot springs with Jacuzzis. The manmade oasis stands at the gateway of what Tony called "perhaps the greatest driving road in the world." Bollywood had used the switchback grade for the chilling climax of the film *Race*. With twenty-one hairpin turns and three lanes (two for climbing, one for descent) winding some 10 km to the top next to Khalifa's palace, it's a challenge even for a *good* good car.

Having been almost but not quite to the summit at a UAEU faculty dinner at the hotel on the mountain, I was eager to go back. Maybe Noor read my mind. One evening he picked me up at the Intercon and said that he had a surprise. We drove out of town toward Jebel Hafeet. Noor announced that we were not having a picnic since he had already had his *iftar* meal; he was driving us to the top.

"I just put in a new engine," he laughed, as we passed the Green Mubazzarah, blemished by the summer heat with large patches of brown grass. "It cost five hundred dirham. My friend made it from parts we bought in Sanaiya. *Insha'Allah*, I think we can make it up to see the palace."

With much chugging and gear grinding, we did. A blanket of stars pricked white pinholes in the cloudless dark sky and a partial moon illuminated the dunes lolling off into the distance. We stayed more than an hour alone in the empty parking lot, looking at the wonders of the universe.

Just before we left, I asked Noor, "What does your name mean?"

"Light," he beamed. "'Noor' is light. Why do you want to know?"

"My name, 'David,' means 'beloved of God.' And 'Noor' means light. You told me that your middle name is Islam. So you are the 'Light of Islam.' There is power in a person's name."

His face lit up like the moon shining over the desert and he slapped me on the shoulder. I'm not sure Noor had touched me previously. A handshake at most. "It will be more fun going down," he laughed, getting into the taxi. "I do not have new brakes. *Insha'Allah*, no problem."

The smooth streets of Al Ain were not paved in gold, but might as well have been. The city's annual landscaping budget, at one billion dirhams, matched the total operating budget of UAEU. Narrow, linear gardens lined the city's boulevards, and nightly after sunset clusters of people, most of them South Asian, lined the lawns and flowerbeds to picnic on rugs and kick soccer balls, staying well past midnight.

When I asked Noor about this custom, he said, "Everything else is brown and desert. This is the only green grass and flowers in Al Ain for families." He added that Emiratis stay home, go to malls or drive their SUVs into the desert at night to barbecue and drink. "It's too hot to go out in the day."

He tried to teach me the city by taking me through its twenty-plus roundabouts, whose designs and names form the basis of locals' attempts at giving directions. "Just go straight at the Globe…." "If you get to the Jewel Box, you've gone too far." Especially confusing was "Go right when you're three-quarters round the Zoo," as that meant the roundabout at the zoological park, not the attraction itself. Some of these traffic configurations feature impressive public art, including a large coffeepot and cups, Arabian stallions, and the ornate jewelry box dangling a strand of huge white pearls. The Zoo roundabout, at the south end of the city by the entrance to the Mideast's premier collection of animals, features a grazing herd of sculpted zebras and giraffes. The Sanaiya roundabout, the gateway to the industrial district on the southeast side of Al Ain, was notorious as the most dangerous.

That said, danger is what the traffic circles had in common. Multiple lanes of vehicles flowed into the vortex, where almost mystically they accelerated like colliding atoms. Stories circulated about deadly accidents, and I'd already had a few near misses. But how dangerous were they, statistically? That struck me as an ideal reporting assignment. I'd make my students' job to go to police databases and find out.

Noor navigated the roundabouts without ever looking in his side or rear-view mirrors—or at least I never caught him looking. He floated through the chaos like a Zen master.

He was right about Sanaiya. It became my favorite part of town. A third-world industrial suburb, filled with scores of single-bay auto repair shops, "tyre" shops, paint shops, used-car lots, furniture stores, "saloons" specializing in "heir cutting," Bollywood video renters, perfume shops, spice shops, mobile phone stores, cafeterias, and just about any kind of retail establishment you could imagine—run by Pakistanis and Afghanis, many of them Pashtun and Punjabi.

Burned-out and broken-down cars littered many of the streets, stray cats wandered searching for food, pigeons scratching for anything to eat, overflowing trash containers hunkered down on corners; old couches and chairs filled space on sidewalks where there were sidewalks, and other flotsam and jetsam decorated the ground. I'd spotted almost no litter on Al Ain's streets; did it all blow down to Sanaiya?

During the first *Computer-Assisted Reporting* class at my office in Building 71, waiting for the course to be cancelled, I had bemoaned the sameness of Al Ain's buildings. Everything was brown and white, I complained. Fatima Al Falahi smiled. "My father's buildings are the color of apples."

I tried to think where I'd seen any red buildings.

"Light green," Fatima added. "He does it to honor my mother, who loves everything green."

Of course! A Granny Smith. A Crispin. A Mutsu. Tangy and sweet.

After Beverly told me about Fatima's family, I'd done a little research on the clan, which wasn't easy. The online archives of the country's English-language papers—*The National, Gulf News* and the *Khaleej Times*—turned up nothing. A trip to the university library revealed that there really wasn't any written UAE history that could be considered authoritative in the academic or even journalistic sense. UAE history was apparently oral, not printed. The only chronicles I could find were sponsored vanity memoirs, the most respected something called "From Rags to Riches." But Noor told me his sponsor, an 86-year-old Emirati who during Zayed's reign had gone virtually overnight from laborer in Saudi Arabia to millionaire, said that without the financial support of Fatima's grandfather, Sheikh Issa Al Falahi, Zayed might never have become the Emir of Abu Dhabi and founder of the UAE.

In the days before oil, Sheikh Issa, and his father before him, made their fortune from *lulus*, pearls, harvested in the shallow waters off Abu Dhabi. Then the emirate's capital was a Persian Gulf outpost on a barrier island habitable only a few months of the year—not an air-conditioned modern metropolis of a million people, boasting an architecturally distinct *corniche* lined with skyscrapers. But I didn't recall the apple-green buildings of Al Ain. I just hadn't been on the lookout.

After class one day, Noor drove around so we could scout for Fatima's father's trademark. We ran out of fingers and toes on which to count them. It was true Granny Smith, just short of ripeness—and a refreshing visual break in sunbaked whites, browns, and endless blue skies.

Another afternoon following pick-up, Noor had an informal lesson for me. He drove to an empty expanse of sand and rocks on the outer edge of Sanaiya. We walked a short distance onto a gravelly moonscape framed by a barren, rocky hill.

"What do you see?" Noor asked, as we picked our way amid plastic bottles and trash.

"I see trash and nothing but a lot of sand and rocks. Is this a trick question?"

"That is what you see today. You see nothing. But this used to be where thousands of Pakistanis lived, for free. It was filled with our homes and shops and we lived here for many years without paying rent to anyone. Sheikh Zayed gave it to us because of how Pakistan's leader helped him create his country. It was ours. Zayed's gift to the Pakistani people who came here to build the UAE."

"Did you live here?"

He nodded.

"What happened?"

"9/11 happened. There was a rumor that some Pashtun had weapons. So the government came with bulldozers and destroyed our village. It was very crazy." In Noor's lexicon, I'd come to interpret "crazy" as the equivalent to "seriously fucked-up."

"Did they find weapons?" I asked.

Noor shook his head. "But they knocked it down anyway. Now we pay rent to the Emiratis."

He turned and started back to the Corolla.

I stared out across the aridity. Did *they* want the land or want the people who lived on it somewhere else?

CHAPTER 7

"That's not how it's done here"

CLASSES DRAGGED THROUGH THE REMAINDER OF RAMADAN.
Mohamed's prediction turned out to be true. As the holy month moved
forward the students, all female in my case, became increasingly listless.

Much to my surprise *Computer-Assisted Reporting* wasn't cancelled,
despite its tiny enrollment and lack of, as it were, facilities. Not having
received a room assignment to replace the Women's Toilet, I continued to
hold class at a table outside my office, or when—as happened often—only
two students showed up, the two usually being Fatima and Mariam, in the
office itself. More problematic yet, no textbook ever arrived. I soon figured
out why. There was no way to teach advanced reporting here. None of the
girls had had basic instruction in reporting or journalism.

So I punted, laid out the five W's, and treated each class as a tutorial.
One day I discussed media ethics, another the U.S. Constitution's First
Amendment vs. UAE media laws. We invented the course on the fly; the
syllabus I had been required to file was indeed a work of fiction.

At one class I mentioned having had knee surgery at the Cleveland
Clinic. That grabbed Fatima's attention. "My mother and grandmother
were in Cleveland one winter with Zayed. It was very cold."

The local media had made a big deal of the UAE president's stay at the Clinic. Zayed had gone for a kidney transplant, and his entourage had taken over several floors of the hospital's hotel. Fatima's family had been among them. A hook to explore, which I filed away.

I gave the three students the team project I'd dreamed up while driving around with Noor: find out which roundabouts are the most dangerous. I suggested they look for police statistics, government data, insurance records, and newspaper accounts. I was betting, silently, on Sanaiya.

"Doctor, there are no records like that here," Fatima piped up. "How can we do this?"

"You're reporters," I said. "Your job is to figure it out—together."

Of course, Fatima was almost surely right, but the point was not so much getting the information as determining where and how to look for it. Every journalist needs to know how to deal with an assignment that's doomed to fail. In my experience, many do. As do, for that matter, many careers.

Moreover, there was something about Fatima's confident attitude that said she would not be easily daunted. She'd have a way of handling the futility, *insha'Allah,* and her two colleagues could learn from it. I might learn something from it myself.

Nobody else had wanted to take on the task of teaching this course. I learned why from Dr. Beverly; it had been conceived simply to teach students how to use computers. Word Processing 101, not a reporting course, let alone one that mined databases to achieve in-depth news coverage. No professor preceding me had had the experience to direct such a course, so they didn't. But it was kept on the books anyway. Her chief sin, Dr. Beverly believed, had been trying too quickly to change the curriculum.

In a month on the job, I'd come to understand the mechanics driving failure of this sort. There had been a rapid succession of MassCom department chairs, all invited to the altar to be sacrificed, with Beverly being the latest hapless lamb. Now the university's organization chart listed Dr. Ali from Erie Pee-Ay, originally from Djibouti, as our chair, which, at least in a glad-handing, ceremonial way he was.

The department's undisputed ruler was the not-to-be-messed-with Mariam. Stories about her powerful *wasta,* reaching into the chancellor's office, were as big as she was small. Completing the power structure, or the "coven" as Dr. B once let slip, were two entrenched female professors—an Emirati, the "journalism expert" Beverly had referred to in that email, and her Egyptian factotum. These three decided who toiled where and in what subject. What the triad practiced wasn't black magic, just a drab grey. They made it known they were fond neither of the university's shift to an English language-based curriculum nor of Western expat teachers taking *their* jobs. Beverly suspected *they* were behind her ouster. The Egyptian professor was the one who'd objected that I didn't possess a PhD. Beverly had managed to hire me despite that, but my teaching assignments came after her demotion. This no doubt explained why I was given a lavatory as a classroom, what amounted to a typing course, and two other basic, non-journalism subjects required for graduation.

Had they checked out the box marked "Religion" on my application?

The expat faculty grapevine did inform us by various means what subjects were off-limits for classroom discourse: Darwin and evolution, politics, criticism of the government, criticism of the ruling family, religion. In the UAE this short list effectively ruled out discussion of about half of what would constitute—elsewhere—hard news. Yet here I was supposed to teach journalism and communications.

Legends told of professors who'd said something that offended someone. The stories all ended the same: the teacher was unceremoniously "put on a plane"—unofficially but firmly expelled from the UAE. Completion bonus cancelled, too. There were even rumors that one outspoken expat on the faculty had been detained and jailed. That could give my antagonize-the-employer personality something to aim for.

Whenever I broached a forbidden topic in the classroom, testing the limits a bit, I would look upward and speak to a phantom microphone. Corny *shtick* but it always brought forth laughs. The students knew I wasn't supposed to raise those topics, but did they care? Know something I didn't? I was just making believe there was an "eye in the sky," and an ear, catching everything I did and said. Maybe there were. Was one of the students secretly recording me? Had other new professors tried anything similar, only to find themselves put on planes? Idle questions or not, I wanted to observe the classes' reactions.

Once again I heard Samah's words from that first day. *"That's not how it's done here."*

For *Intro*, on a day not long after Ramadan had ended, I tried out a lesson plan I'd used in the States: nonverbal communication.

I walked in, planted my briefcase on the desktop, and sat quietly. Thirty minutes of silence. Well, not complete silence, but no words. I spoke only through my eyes, gestures, facial expressions, and inarticulate sounds. I had used the same technique at an Ohio community college. I wondered whether it would work here—or would all be lost in translation? To the students, thirty minutes felt like an eternity.

"Why aren't you talking, Doctor?" Fatima 4 asked, frustrated that I wouldn't engage in banter as I typically did until everyone had straggled in. Others piped in similar inquiries.

I smirked and kept mute. After the last students slipped in, ten minutes later, I went to the whiteboard and madly scribbled key phrases about nonverbal communication, in bright colors—Speak with Your Eyes, Facial Expressions, Body Language, Sound, How You Dress, Posture, Personal Space, and "It's Not What You Say, It's How You Say It."

Then I sat back down. And belched. Blew my nose. Groucho-ed my eyebrows.

"What's wrong, professor?" Noura 1 implored. "Are you mad at us today?!"

I glared at her. Stood up, strode over, and planted myself in the seat next to hers, smirked, and batted my eyes. Along with Anood 2, the captain of UAEU's women's soccer team, the class looked up to Noura 1 because of her effervescence and, literally, because of her height. They were *Intro*'s yin and yang.

"Doctor, are you flirting with me?" she giggled.

Smatterings of nervous laughter ricocheted off the walls. I rose and followed the sound to Fatima 4. For her, I frowned. "Why are you unhappy with me, Doctor," she asked, frustrated.

My answer, a shrug. I rose and walked around the room, making eye contact with virtually every student. Long looks. Eye-rolls. A wink. A squint or two. That produced plenty of giggles. What produced squeamishness was close proximity. (Don't get too close to, let alone touch, female students, male faculty had been warned.) Even the flirty Fatima 4 recoiled when I too closely invaded her space. But I expected this reaction. Getting too close is discomfiting in many cultures.

But not for Anood 2, the soccer star. At the end of the thirty minutes, excruciating for many of the students, I stood beside her chair, leaning against the back wall. She looked up at me and offered a knowing smile. "Doctor," she began, as the others watched her intently. "I know what you are doing."

I fixed my gaze on her and cleared my throat.

She laughed loudly. "You are playing with our heads."

And I spoke. "Yes. I am."

A sigh of relief filled the room.

Anood 2 beamed, but shook her head. "We have never seen a class like this here."

Not only did we explore nonverbal communication, that day marked the beginning of an understanding between students and teacher. The six weeks leading up to it had been a prelude. From that class forward performance art became a key component. Carol had told me to invent the class, so I did.

CHAPTER 8

Mutton with Rice...
or Rice with Mutton

NOOR WAS EAGER TO TAKE ME TO LUNCH AT HIS FAVORITE Afghani restaurant in the center of Sanaiya.

It sat next to a smelly truckwash on the main highway.

"The menu never changes," my host told me with a big grin.

At the sink off the dining room near the kitchen we ritually washed our hands, alongside other patrons. Noor spotted two seats at a table beneath a map of Afghanistan and a portrait of the omnipresent Emirati trinity—Zayed, Khalifa and his half-brother, Crown Price Mohammed. The trio's picture seemed to grace the wall of every establishment in the Abu Dhabi emirate. We squeezed in among the Bahtan.

"Today we have a choice of two dishes," Noor explained, laughing. "You get mutton with rice... or rice with mutton. They may also have soup." He caught my eye. "I will buy you lunch!"

"Okay," I chuckled, "I'm in the mood for rice with mutton."

And that's what we soon had plunked in front of us—two heaping dishes of mutton *biryani*. Sides included a big plate loaded with cucumber, lettuce, tomato, mint and raw onion, two large flat loaves of hot Afghani *naan*, plus a liter of bottled water and plastic cups. No soup that day.

After lunch we washed up and Noor paid, explaining when I reached for cash that he would lose face if other Pashtun saw him let a Westerner pick up the tab.

Noor and I had by then developed our own Al Ain version of "taxi-cab confessions"—since our time together revolved exclusively around trips in his old '93 Corolla rebuilt many times over.

He never attached his seatbelt but would yank it out and stretch it across his chest leaving it unbuckled. That way he hoped to avoid a ticket, as there was a new crackdown. Of course, the measure didn't affect Emiratis, most of whom believed seatbelts would kill them in an accident. Noor also worried one would strangle him if he crashed and nothing I could say changed his mind. My own seatbelt was always attached the moment I was in a car. I'd flipped two vehicles, belted, and lived, I told him.

One afternoon, heading to the city center to visit Pakistani shops, we talked about our children.

"I have one son," I said. "I am blessed. He is very smart and goes to a great university. But more importantly, he has a good heart. He's visiting this winter, so you'll meet him."

"Just one?" Noor asked, sounding almost alarmed.

"We tried for another, but there was no luck."

"*Yaya*," Noor grinned, broadly. "Give thanks to Allah for one."

"Yes," I said. "*Al haam doo lielah.*" I'd had learned that phrase meant, "Thank God."

"Yaya," Noor replied. "Allah directs every sperm."

That pronouncement stuck a new pin into the growing bulletin board in my mind. Could Noor really mean it? Literally? Does *He* direct every little sperm that swims? Even those of infidels and non-believers? Orthodox Jews have a thing about not wasting seed. So do many Christians. Is it the same?

We turned onto Khalifa ibn Zayed Street—one of many in Al Ain named after members of the royal family, making the more or less uniform streets even harder to distinguish.

"I have one brother," Noor said.

"Just the one? No other brothers?"

"Just one, *al haam doo lielah*," he said.

"Sisters?"

"Five!"

"I have two, and had one brother. But my brother, a physician and a religious man, died suddenly a few years ago and was buried in Atlanta on my birthday. It was the last big joke he played on me."

"Oh," he moaned. "I am very sorry for you, my friend." Noor's eyes turned sad.

"Now I am the family patriarch."

Noor nodded, took his hands off the wheel, and spun them in the air. "People in my village asked my father, 'Why do you have only two sons? Why not more?'" He paused putting one hand back on the wheel. "And my father said to them, 'A tiger has only two.'"

"So your father is a tiger?"

"*Yaya*. He is old, but he works as a teacher in my village. He is a great man and very respected. A tiger among my people. I miss seeing him and my mother and family."

Another day Noor asked, "How can I go to America? Do you need to show your bank account? That's how it's done in the UAE."

"I think you could come as a tourist to visit. There are many Pakistanis in the US, but I don't know how many from North Waziristan."

As far as Americans were concerned North Waziristan was only a headline, if that. Just another wild, remote tribal enclave where the War on Terror was being fought. Maybe even Osama bin Laden's hideout. Few Americans, it occurred to me, could even tell you the continent on which Waziristan is located. I knew nothing about its topography or its people.

What did it look like? I pictured a great deal of rock, some of it nearly vertical. Google Earth helped fill in the gaps in my knowledge.

"*Yaya*, as a tourist," he said. "But won't they think I will run away and hide?"

"They would probably think you are Osama's taxi driver and send you to Guantánamo."

"Yaya," Noor chuckled. "Osama's taxi driver!"

"Americans think everybody from Waziristan knows Osama."

Not literally, but Noor got the point. "Americans could be right. Some say Osama has been given the 'Golden Word' by powerful men who will protect him with their lives."

We laughed. The Golden Word? I wanted to ask.

But Noor had a question for me. "Where in America are you from? You told me but I forget."

I'd told him about Ohio, where it's cold and snowy in the winter, sitting adjacent to an inland freshwater sea. He listened as I described Lake Erie again, adding that Canada is on the other side.

"My home is a city called Cleveland," I said. "On the shore of the lake. You are from Pakistan, the 'Land of the Paks' and North Waziristan, the 'Land of the Wazirs.' I am from Cleve-land… or as we might call it here, 'Clevistan.'" I laughed at my bad joke. "The land of the Cleves. I am a 'Clevistani.'"

"Ah, Clevistan," Noor chuckled. "A very funny name."

"Trust me. Clevistan jokes are very popular in America."

Noor swerved to avoid a merging Land Cruiser. "Do you know what 'Pak' means?"

I shook my head.

"Our great thinker, the poet Muhammad Iqbal, studied in India and England. He was a philosopher and poet and had the first idea that there should be a separate country in India for Muslims. He said that 'Pak' means the 'pure people,' and that we would be 'Pakistan.' But Iqbal did not live to see Pakistan become a nation for Muslims."

Sometime I'd ask about the poet's untimely death, but right now I was more curious about the name he'd given the country. "So Pakistan is the 'land of the *pure people*'? The spiritually *pure*?"

"*Yaya*, we are the *pure* people." He intoned the phrase with irony, and grinned.

"Well," I said, with a short laugh, "the Clevistanis are certainly not *pure*, spiritually or religiously. Though we still have great faith in the Clevistan Indians."

"You have Indians in Clevistan? Are they Hindu?"

I let out a belly laugh. "They are a baseball team. Christians for the most part. Baseball is a sport like cricket, although a little less boring. The Clevistan Indians haven't won the championship for longer than I've lived, but each year there is new hope." (Yeah, right!) I looked him in the eye. "Noor, there really are no people called the Cleves. I'm just making another bad joke."

"*Yaya*," Noor said, nodding.

Finally, I'm not sure why, it hit me. "Yaya" was not a foreign word; it was simply Noor's version of our informal affirmative, "Yeah." A curious opening presented itself. "Some believe those North American natives, the Indians, are one of the Lost Tribes of Israel."

Noor looked at me with mild astonishment. I had never mentioned anything to Noor about my being Jewish. He knew I was an American and a professor, and apparently figured, as did others, that must make me a Christian. I had just told him my brother was religious, but hadn't cited a religion. I remained unsure when or how to tell him. Or, when I did, what the revelation would do to our friendship. Maybe we were about to find out.

I'd heard many stories about what had happened to some of the descendants of Jacob, who took the name *Israel*. The oldest is that they were deported to conquering Assyria and got absorbed into that people. Another is that they became the American Indians. My favorite is the claim by a 17th-century Portuguese explorer who said they were living way up in the Andes Mountains. How the hell could they have gotten there? For that matter, how had the Portuguese guy?

Noor's eventual reply left me floored. "The Pashtun are descendants of Israel, from the family of Ibrahim, from our holy prophet."

"Some Pashtun are descended from Israel? I didn't know that."

"Yaya, from the grandson of Ibrahim."

"I hadn't heard that they became the Pashtun. Makes more sense than some theories."

Noor's version was certainly more plausible than the Lost Tribes' crossing the Atlantic or Bering Strait to roam the Great Plains, hunt bison, or trek the Inca Highway chewing the coca leaf. They made their way from the land of ancient Israel to eastern Afghanistan about three thousand years ago. One tribe's name, he noted, is the "Sons of Yusef."

"The son of Jacob, known as Israel?"

"Yaya, Yusef ibn Yacub," he said. "Some Pashtun still pray facing Jerusalem. And when Da'ood wanted to tell someone a secret, he said it in Pashto."

"King David spoke Pashto?" I asked, incredulous.

"Yaya, everyone *knows* that."

Everyone but me and every other Jew I have ever talked to.

Yet another lesson from Noor. Maybe he was less a *rabbi* than a *rebbe*, a mentor, teacher and guru all in one. A *rebbe* who had attended a *madrassa*, not a *yeshiva*.

CHAPTER 9

The Story Noach's Ark

PICKING ME UP AT MAQAM AFTER *COMPUTER-ASSISTED* *Reporting,* Noor offered his usual greeting, "How was class in the women's toilet?" We'd gotten on familiar enough terms and arrived at a who's-on-first routine. Sliding into the front seat, I answered simply with a laugh. Noor ejected the cassette of the Koran. As music is *haram,* forbidden, his only soundtrack in the taxi was the scripture, read in the original. Sometimes I listened, too.

We'd come to talking often about religion—more specifically Noor's religion, which he was always eager to share and I was curious about. I remained mum about my own.

What held me back was not anxiety about Noor's reaction—it would, *insha'Allah,* be what it would be. And I knew Noor well enough not to mistake him for a person driven by prejudices, his jokes about Egyptians and Hindus notwithstanding. My hesitation arose in response to the evident fervor with which Noor believed all that he recounted. On several occasions, too, I'd agreed to wait in the taxi so he could step into a mosque for prayer. When had I last prayed? Had I ever prayed with a conviction that Any One was listening? Let alone directing my every sperm. The question of how I "believed" Judaism's teachings had started to nag at me. Noor was as devout as anyone I had ever met, of any faith. A profession of faith from me, barely a committed practitioner of my own, would have been forced. To claim a religion despite my doubts seemed—especially in Noor's taxi—downright blasphemous.

Rabbi or *rebbe*, this morning he was all but possessed, and launched into an account of "Noach's Ark." His inspired transport would take us somewhere unknown to me, and I was curious to explore.

He spoke excitedly, taking both hands off the wheel, the cab doing 110 kmph down Khaled ibn Sultan Street. "The Evil One, Shaytan, sneaked aboard the big boat because he wanted to sink it and kill everything. He pulled a… a…" The non-automotive need of his hands became clear: He had to pull an imaginary something down over his face.

"Mask?"

"Yaya, a mask," he continued, his hands still engaged in adjusting this invisible item rather than gripping the steering wheel.

"A donkey mask because, how do you say, he wanted to be.…"

"Disguised?"

"Ah, yaya, disguised." Noor smiled and finally placed both hands where they belonged, much to my relief. Although I marveled at his driving skills, I was a firm believer in one thing: the nine-and-three grip. We rolled into the notorious Sanaiya roundabout. "So Shaytan disguised himself as the Donkey and snuck onto Noah's Ark… and he pulled a mask over his face to hide from Noach." Noor merged into the current of cars before slipping out the other side.

"Noach is called 'Noah' in my holy book."

"Yaya, we say 'Noach.' You say, 'No-ah.' Yaya. Christians believe that story. We have the same story in the Koran. Everybody is very bad and Allah makes a big flood to kill all of the evil, and Noach takes the animals and the righteous ones on his big ship so they can copulate. But the Evil One wants to kill everything and he hides and he is a Donkey."

He said "Christians" as if he assumed he was addressing one. While I'd done nothing to suggest any fealty to Jesus Christ, his natural inference that I did was reasonable. Noor and I knew each other well enough by this point that my failure to clarify was at least a sin of omission. Possibly an act of bad faith.

I laughed. "Is that why the Emiratis use the same word for Egyptians and donkeys?! They're calling the Egyptian a jackass?"

"Ah, yaya," Noor chuckled, stroking his short, dark beard. "A jackass! An Egyptian. The same." He naturally let go of the wheel. "So," hands flapping in the air, "the Evil One told the Rat to eat a hole in the bottom of the big ship...."

"The Ark?"

"Yaya, the Ark, as you say, so it will sink." This, too, was illustrated with gestures. "But Noach discovered what the Evil One was doing and so he touched the Tiger, and changed the Tiger into a Cat to catch the Rat."

"And the Ark was saved?"

"Yaya, Noach changed the Tiger into a Cat... it ate the Rat... and Shaytan's plan was... how do you say... ruined?" He took a breath. "Is the story of Noach I told you like the story in your holy book? The story of the Rat is not from the Koran, but from another holy book. I study all of the holy books."

Another opening had presented itself. I felt a kind of vertigo. "The story of the Evil One and the Rat is not in my holy book," I answered, though I wasn't sure. "But some of the other parts are similar."

Noor's face lit up. "I study all of these stories and I know the Koran by heart." That I believed. It made sense that he'd have committed a lot of his faith's scripture to memory. How many Jews know the Torah even a fraction of that well? Certainly not this one.

"There are some differences in our stories. In my holy book, Noah had three sons on the Ark with him. You mentioned that Noah had four sons."

"Yaya, Canaan, that was his other son," Noor said. "He did not join Noach on the Ark. Noach pleaded with him to go on the big ship, but he was an unbeliever and he went to the mountains with the idolaters and drowned. God told Noach that Canaan was an evildoer."

"In my book, Noah's son's were Ham, Shem and Japeth. They had many children."

Noor said something about seventy former idolaters joining Noach, his sons and their wives, and the animals on the Ark. I noted that there was nothing in my holy book about seventy converts joining Noah's family on the Ark. The story of the "Curse of Ham," as related in my book, passed on to Noor in the vicinity of the Hilton roundabout, left him confounded.

"Noah got drunk and Ham saw his father naked, and told his brothers, who then covered their father while averting their eyes," I said. "When Noah awoke, he was angry and cursed Ham's son, Canaan, Noah's grandson, not his son in our version, with eternal slavery."

Noor looked appalled. "Noach was drunk?" His voice rose as he went on. "He is one of Islam's five greatest prophets! Noach did not drink!"

Having upset Noor, I wanted to back down, assuage his alarm. The moment had come, organically, of its own accord. Or was it by the mysteries of *insha'Allah*? It wasn't for me to question.

"Our stories are similar, but there are differences."

"Yaya," Noor said, calming. "The sky religions are similar but different."

"Sky religions?"

"Yaya, the ones that pray to God up there," Noor said, pointing through the windshield into the always-blue, always-cloudless sky. "We do not pray to pieces of stone. Or to cows! God sent Jibril to Mohammed to reveal the Koran. He corrected the mistakes in the other holy books."

An assertion I wasn't going to touch, at least not at that moment. Obviously I, being a *Christian*, had it wrong while the Muslims' book got the story right. God had sent a software update by way of Jibril to Mohammed.

"God sent Jibril, his most important angel, to Mohammed to give the Koran. All four of the great books come from God to His prophets. There is the *Torah* to Musef. The *Zabur* to Da'ood. Jibril gave the *Koran* to Mohammed, another holy book to Isa. What do you call yours?" He glanced at me. "The Christian one?"

Yes, Noor knew, or wondered. But for whatever reason, he could not simply ask. "Isa is your prophet, yes?" he inquired, looking me in the eye as he started up the Intercon's lengthy drive.

I took a breath. "Noor, the Christian book is not my holy book. Isa is not my prophet."

"The Christian holy book… the *Injil*… is not yours?" The pitch of his voice rose with each word. "You do not follow Isa?" He slowed as we approached the hotel entrance stopping in front of its large glass doors as South Asian bellmen helped other new arrivals inside. "You... are not... Christian?"

Knowing Noor as well as I did, I still couldn't read his tone—was it incredulity, shock, or possibly some kind of challenge? I looked him in the eye. The taxi idled. "Noor, my holy book is the *Torah*." Getting no reaction, I went on. "My holy book is not the *Injil*. I don't believe in Isa." There, okay, I was waffling some, stating what I *didn't* believe, not what I did. That was as close as I could get to anything I'd accept myself as the truth.

Noor's eyes lit up and he gripped the steering wheel tightly. "The *Torah*!? Not the *Injil*!?" he asked, his voice rising higher. He had known the names of the Christian scriptures all along. Was our Noach/Noah conversation his way of winkling out the truth? "So you are not Christian?"

That was easy enough. "No, Noor, I am not Christian. I am Jewish."

"Oh," he exhaled. "You are *Yehuda*?" He slowly released his grip on the wheel. "You are not Christian? You are *Yehuda*. Not the *Injil*? The *Torah*."

"Yaya, I am Jewish. I am *Yehuda*. The Torah is my holy book."

We sat in silence for what felt like the rest of the afternoon, but could have been as little as ten seconds. "Am I the first Jew you have ever met?"

"The first," he replied. "You're the first. I knew you were different."

"Is that okay with you? Are we still friends?" I opened my door. Was this friendship—and my reliable and affordable transportation—finished?

I slid out, shut the door, and leaned down to the open window. "Will I see you later today?"

"*Insha'Allah*," Noor replied. "You are Jewish, like King David."

Suddenly, what I'd come to hear as a matter-of-fact answer carried massive ambiguity.

I watched as he drove off. I admit to having wondered, as I stood there under the Intercon's marquee, whether Noor would return. Of course, the decision rested not with him any more than with me. Like everything else in this life, it was a matter not of our wills, allegedly free, but of God's.

If need be I would get a taxi from the hotel, and scare up another to get me back.

He returned two hours later five minutes ahead of schedule.

"Hello, my friend," he said, as I opened the front door. "I am early for once."

"Hello, my friend, I thought I might not see you this afternoon."

"*Insha'Allah,* no problem," Noor said, with a smile. "I am early, you see."

From that day, Noor always arrived early, or at least on time. I wonder how my life in Al Ain would have played forward had he not returned. In my heart, though, I believed he would. So, in fact, I did have a capacity for faith. There was more of God's will for my Pashtun rabbi and me to explore. Maybe make some forays into the question of fallible free will, too.

CHAPTER 10

Insha'Allah, bukra

UAEU'S IMMIGRATION OFFICE HAD RETURNED EVERYONE'S passport but mine. It had now been not two weeks, *insha'Allah*, no problem, but six and counting, which I was doing daily at this point. Finishing breakfast one morning at Arabesque with Brian, I mentioned my many fruitless phone calls.

"You're hearing the same rumors I am," Brian surmised. "With our apartments close to being done, they'll be kicking us out of the hotel any day now."

Being expelled from the Intercon and still without my passport? My anxiety ratcheted back up.

A few days before, Brian, Tony and I had checked out our prospective digs, on the opposite side of Al Ain from the Intercon. Small. Cheaply built. Hardly "luxury," especially by UAE standards. Brian and Tony selected units in back. Mohamed refused to come, underscoring his protests. He'd take whatever was left if he had to. Sort of the housing equivalent of a hunger strike, I gathered. I put dibs on a second-floor unit, with a tiny dining room, tinier kitchen, and a row of front-facing windows. For light, my cramped living room had only an airshaft. From the bedroom, though, I looked across the street at a walled villa and a major road leading to the gates of the Shakboot Palace—still home to some relative of the emir the powers-that-be had replaced with Zayed.

One of us, Brian I think, had heard a rumor. Neighbors were angry that *someone* had developed the land for which they had other plans. Someone powerful, someone related to the Zayed. I debated with myself the question of whether *wasta* of that sort was desirable in a landlord or to be feared. The building I noted, was salmon, not apple green.

Brian, often moderately psychic like the 1960's Martian TV character he resembled, was saying as we breakfasted, "You don't want to be without your passport now. Not with the contract tied to it…."

His advice: Go to the Islamic Institute, where the university's immigration office was housed and my freedom of movement and employment status were being held hostage, and camp out.

Naturally, I called Noor. Thirty minutes later he dropped me off at the appointed place. "I will wait for you here. Hopefully, it will be *insha'Allah*, no problem."

His tone of voice was less than encouraging. The Islamic Institute did little to dispel my misgivings. The place gave me the creeps. I had visited the UAEU administration and Sharia Law Center several times, always to deal with HR, and each time I squirmed. This time, I bumped into Moraig, and she directed me to immigration. She would have accompanied me, she said, but the new HR director, a Canadian, had just started. Her tone made that news sound ominous. Maybe it was just my mood.

Immigration was a world within a world, commanded by an Emirati named Saif. To start things off on the wrong note, I asked for "Sa-EEF." This was corrected: the name was pronounced "Safe." Thirty-something, sporting a crisp white *kandura* and *guthra* with a *tagiyyah* sitting like a crown on top, Saif was educated at Ohio State, self-entitled, disinclined to answer his phone, but—lucky for me—in his office. I walked in and took a seat. Three others waited ahead of me. Attending them each in turn, Saif opened a metal box and took out a passport, received a sum in dirhams and relinquished the document.

When it was my turn, I slid to the chair in front of his desk. "I'm Dr. David"

Saif's mobile phone chimed and he raised an index finger.

I waited for him to finish his call and started again. "I'm Dr. David."

"Oh, yes," he said. "You have telephoned."

"I am trying to find out about my passport," I explained, calmly. "I don't have it back, but my colleagues all have theirs. Is there a problem?"

He opened the metal box and drew out the stack of passports. He opened each, slowly, studied its photo and glanced at me. "It is not here. Has nobody called you?"

"Noooo," I said, trying to suppress an onrush of anxiety.

"*Insha'Allah*, no problem," Saif replied. "Let me make a call. *Insha'Allah, bukra*. Come back then. I may have an answer. We will see."

Bukra? I wondered, getting up, thanking him and leaving, mystified.

Back at the taxi I asked Noor what bukra meant. His definition started with, "Not good."

"I gathered. But does '*bukra*' mean something else? I mean literally?" I dearly hoped Saif had not said, "God willing, not good."

"He is telling you, '*insha'Allah*, tomorrow.' But when Emiratis say '*bukra*' it means 'Forget it.'"

"Right. 'Tomorrow' as in 'never.' Or *mañana*. Or 'fuggetaboudit.'"

Two thoughts sprinted through my mind. Had something gone wrong at the health screening? Or did this passport seizure have something to do with the word "Jewish" on my application? It was a dead heat. Noor had dealt with the Jewish Question more than enough in our talk about Noach, Shaytan, the Flood, the *Injil* and the Torah, so I left my two worrisome theories unvoiced. I looked forward to getting Brian's read, but he wasn't at dinner. I gave Tony, Carol and Mohamed an overview.

"They probably want more blood," Tony chortled.

Carol jumped right to my own thinking. "It's not because you're Jewish, is it?"

Mohamed, who by then was in on the secret, said, "They found out, Dave. This isn't good."

It would be hyperbolic to say I felt like Anne Frank behind the bookcase, but the walls were suddenly closing in. Was I actually living in a place in which "they found out you're Jewish" could have so ominous a set of implications? And what even were the implications? Deportation? Dismissal? Or just a variety of forms of harassment? Was that my reward for labeling myself with a yellow six-pointed star?

Carol and Mohamed both looked chagrined. They knew that stoking my paranoid speculations would do me little good. The talk around the table turned to the imminent move out of the Intercon and into our new non-luxury apartments. Carol had secured the best unit in the complex via her *wasta*.

The next day, after my morning class, Noor dropped me off again at the Islamic Institute. I waited for more than an hour to see Saif. He told me the cause of the trouble: I had failed my blood pressure test. "Go and get me a letter from a doctor with your new blood pressure. *Insha'Allah*, no problem. Then bring me your letter and three hundred dirhams cash and I can give you your passport. *Insha'Allah, bukra.*" The payment was the fee for a three-year visa. But he had concluded again with *insha'Allah, bukra*.

My worries were abated, but only somewhat.

Noor took me to Oasis Hospital, the first built in Al Ain, founded by an evangelical British doctor. I entered the third door, the entrance befitting my insurance designation, and had my blood pressure retaken by an Indian physician. "Normal," he said, and provided me a letter to that effect. "You are not the only one who had this problem. It was too hot in August and many people were dehydrated."

The following day I saw Saif, happily, for the last time. I gave him the doctor's note and the wad of dirhams. In return I got my identity back, with a three-year visa stamp. I now had the ability to exit the country and to re-enter. My contract was validated, whatever that really meant.

The timing was propitious as the university informed us that we would begin moving out of the Intercon the next day, a Jewish High Holy Day. I didn't have much to move so I crammed everything into two suitcases and a few boxes.

Noor arrived early the next morning to help with my move. It was Yom Kippur. I felt compelled to search my soul. The three Rs: Remorse? Repentance? Regret? Did I regret being in Al Ain and the UAE? It was a relief to determine that I didn't, but also a reminder that I had yet to find much purpose in being here. And whose forgiveness, in addition to God's, did I forget to seek?

"Today is the holiest of Jewish holidays," I mentioned as I hefted a suitcase into the taxi's trunk. We now talked often, even casually, about both sky religions. The previous day he had come to my room for the first time, and I'd given him an illustrated lunar calendar for the Jewish year 5769, just a week old, and a colorful *yarmulke*. He had beamed in accepting them.

"This is your holiest day?" he asked, moving the bag to accommodate a box.

"Yes, the tenth day of the month of *Tishrei*. I should be in temple, fasting, not moving into a new apartment, but the university's casting us out of paradise."

"You are fasting?" Noor inquired, loading the other suitcase into the back seat.

"No, I'm just supposed to be. I have diabetes, so I really can't."

As he descended the hotel's drive-up, I looked back longingly at the place that had served me as my point of entry. The Intercon had been a decent safe harbor, a good place to hunker down—especially during Ramadan. Brian had been right on that score, as on numerous others.

"On Yom Kippur," I said, turning back around, "Jews ask God to forgive us our sins against Him. But He cannot forgive the sins we commit against other men. For that, we have to ask them."

"Yaya, it's the same for us," Noor replied. "Allah can only forgive us for our sins against Him, not against other men."

"And today, if I were at my temple, I would ask God to inscribe my name in the Book of Life for another year. But there are no synagogues in the UAE, though I have seen a Christian church. And as far as I know I am the only Jew around here."

Noor nodded. "That's because there are no Jews here. Only one crazy one."

Inquiries turned up the information that our new housing complex was called "the Falahi Apartments." Were other clan members investing in real estate? Mohamed's refusal to make a choice had gotten him the worst unit. The accommodations had been rushed to completion and few of us were thrilled with the result. But I was living in the city, at last, even if in a hastily thrown-up faculty ghetto.

The afternoon was devoted to buying a mattress. While I believe the connection was coincidental, Noor's topic of theological discussion for that outing was heaven and hell, via a kind of compare and contrast as we made our way to the Carrefour mega-store at Al Jimi Mall. Every Muslim, he explained, has two angels, one who records the good and the other the bad. When the believer dies, Azreal, the angel of death, takes her or him up into the sky to await Allah's judgment. The deceased are "lined up in one hundred and twenty queues, close to the sun." The image made me think of the old Bugs Bunny cartoon with an angel and a devil perched on Bugs's shoulders, battling for his soul.

"Allah protects the good with a cloud to keep the sun from melting their brains and they are only there for a short time before going to heaven. The bad are not protected and the sun..." Here he took his hands off the wheel to make scrambling motions above his head. "Their brains are... are...."

"Fried?"

"Yaya," he laughed. "Fried... their brains are fried and they go crazy and they go to hell. One day in hell is the same as a thousand years on earth."

"That's a long time."

"Yaya, a very long time in hell." Noor apparently found the thought pleasing. Such a sentiment from anyone else would have alarmed me—taking delight in the torments of the damned. But had I suffered a fraction of what Noor had thanks to the world's legions of assholes, I'd relish the prospect of their brains frying, too, and wholeheartedly believe in a God who would see to it.

His silence I took as my cue. "Jews don't have two angels and we don't have one hundred and twenty lines. We believe that after death the spirit goes to paradise, 'Gan Eden,' the Garden of Eden."

"Ah, yaya, the Garden of Eden," Noor said. "We call it 'Aden.' You are 'Da'ood Aden.'"

Through the ongoing process of getting me settled, Noor gave lessons on Islam's prophets and Armageddon.

"You know Jesus was a Jew?" I asked nonchalantly in the course of another outing.

"Yaya."

"We don't believe he was the Son of God."

"We also do not believe. We believe that God sent Jibril to Mary and he...." Noor pursed his lips and puffed out a breath of air. "Jibril make like that." He puffed again.

"The breath of life?"

"Yaya. God sent Jibril and he made the breath of life." He puffed again. "And Isa was born."

"So you believe like the Yehuda that Isa is *not* the Son of God?" It surprised me that Noor's affirmation of something at least mystical in Jesus's conception prompted me to seek reassurance. Noor's seminars on religion had brought me to something from my past, long dormant. "You believe Jesus was a *man*. Yes?"

"A man," Noor verified, puffing out a final breath. "We do not believe he was the Son of God."

"Jews don't believe he rose from the dead, either. We don't believe he's the Messiah."

"We also don't believe," Noor said, firmly. "He was not God's flesh, but a man, a great prophet. God chose him for the *Injil* and gave him the power to do miracles. He was not killed, but God raised him to heaven. When it's time he will come back to fight the Evil One."

Now we were talking. The Apocalypse. Noor's understanding of the Last Times and all that was one of the things I wanted to hear about. How a Pashtun Muslim viewed the end of this world.

"So, at the End of Days," I speculated, "Jesus will come down from heaven and fight the Evil One, the devil. He will fight what people call the Anti-Christ?"

"Yaya, Jibril will bring him to a tower at a white mosque in Damascus," Noor continued. "He will come down as a man dressed in yellow robes and lead the Mahdi against the Dajjal, the Evil One. And Isa will defeat the Dajjal. Then all the sky religions will be one, and follow Allah."

"So Isa will defeat the devil, and everyone will follow Islam. All three sky religions?"

"Yaya. Then Isa will ask God to take him back to heaven. But God will say, 'No, you live as a man. I am not bringing you back to heaven.'"

We'd come to exactly what I wanted to know. The expectation that all three sky religions would follow Allah was an article of faith I'd learned about. Even if the tumultuous events described in Revelation were to come to pass, that was something I just couldn't see. The Jews and the Christians were both pretty stiff necked, and nowhere more so than in learning about, let alone accepting, the tenets of Islam. Were Revelation's prophecies to be fulfilled would that be any less unlikely? Would reason close the divide—any more than modernity, with all manner of technological magic, had failed to drive superstition and entrenched dogma into retreat? The Crusades weren't so long ago.

"So Allah," I resumed, "says 'no' to Isa and instructs him to stay on earth and live as a man?"

"He tells Isa, 'You are a man, you stay with men and lead them.'"

God ultimately turns away His only Son and tells Him to live as an ordinary guy, albeit a leader. This was not going to play well in the Bible Belt. Noor was undaunted. "When the sky religions are one under Islam, Isa will live forty years. Isa will pray to God to help him defeat the Ya'juj and the Ma'juj."

"Gog and Magog."

"Yaya. Who are destroying the earth. God will listen to Isa's prayers and send worms that will…." He now let go of the wheel to make wiggling motions around his head and shoulders. "The worms will go into their necks and kill them. And Isa will die like a man and he will be buried in a grave next to Mohammed in Medina."

A pretty detailed version, even in a nutshell, of Armageddon. Not the Christians', and not my faith's—well, the faith of my ancestors. But that was a dialogue for another shopping trip.

I'd have to approach the subject carefully and had some brushing up to do. In Israel I had gone to Megiddo, the site where the faithful believe the End of Days, *acharit hagamim,* will be enacted. The part I felt apprehensive—for reasons that weren't so clear to me—about sharing with Noor: the world was slated to end in the Jewish year 6,000. Not so far off, really. It is written.

CHAPTER 11

Too Much Red Ink

"DOCTOR DAVID!" HESSA CRIED. HER EYES BRIMMED WITH tears. She moaned, a solitary drop trickling slowly down her round cheek.

The looks of shock and gloom among her classmates concurred. The young women in *Writing for Media* had just received back the first written assignment I had graded closely. Ink redder than the bloody Nile of Moses's ten plagues engulfed each paragraph of every 500-word paper, and the cries that rose up could hardly have been less strident than the wailing of Pharaoh's army drowning in the Red Sea.

"You cross out so much," Hessa lamented. "You give me a seventy-two!"

"Yes, I did," I said, with a big smile. "Yours was one of the better papers."

Even that was sugarcoating things. All the essays were substandard. With the practice we had put in on ledes and nut graphs I'd been hoping for better results, limited English notwithstanding. Other faces registered doom and despair at the news that Hessa's low "C" was a top grade.

I handed back the last paper, Samah's.

Hessa's tears now threatened to drown us all. "But I never get bad grades. I always get an 'A.'"

I had heard the same line, verbatim, from students in *Intro*. Several had wept openly, blubbered even, after a pop quiz. A mere "B'" engendered distress. My grades had never provoked emotional displays like this in a U.S. classroom. But I was not about to cave in to whining, pouting or tears. A few colleagues had warned me not to give in: "Do it once, they'll never stop."

"Don't worry, this grade doesn't count."

That pledge, which I was reiterating now, had evidently fallen on deaf ears. "None of your grades count until later, remember? This is practice. You'll be graded on how much you improve." Looking from stricken face to stricken face, I couldn't resist. "*Insha'Allah*, no problem."

"But I am worried!" Hessa lamented. "I am worried I will fail."

The others, dressed in black, watched the interchange with visible anxiety. The girl in pink wore a look of worldly acceptance. Even she'd gotten a B-minus.

"Sometimes, to succeed, we first have to fail," I assured. "It's how we learn."

"But that is what I am worried about, Doctor," Hessa whimpered. "That I will fail."

"If you were an expert before you started the course then there would be no point in taking it."

Samah spoke calmly. "Professor Eden, we're not used to this here. Everything we do gets a grade that counts. We never get papers with so many corrections."

Naturally. Just like students in American public schools, these girls were passed up the education food chain even if they hadn't gotten a firm handle on the subject matter.

Samah continued. "Latifa and I are graduating in December. We can't flunk."

With a nod, I stepped back and addressed the room. "I laid on a lot of red ink. For a reason. You're all smart women and can learn a great deal about writing for media—which is what the class is about. If you do the work and show improvement you will get good grades, and graduate."

"*Insha'Allah*," Samah sighed. "From your lips to God's ears."

That semi-blasphemous version of *insha'Allah* I'd not yet heard here. It was one of my *bubbe*'s favorite expressions. I smiled at Samah and when she smiled back I almost thought she winked at me.

After weeks trying to teach the course in English and drilling the girls on the fundamentals—to little effect, as the papers showed—I improvised a change to the curriculum. The students had told me they didn't trust UAE or Arab satellite news channels. I allowed as how virtually every news source is biased in some way, and announced that we would visit, via internet, U.S. journalism resources I thought generally trustworthy. To start, I'd steer clear of news, per se. The students would take turns reading film reviews, aloud. Their next assignment was to write one.

But the class took things a different direction. Noura arrived last, and laid a black artist's portfolio in the middle of the table. She unzipped it and slid out a sketch. That got everyone's attention.

"Please, Doctor," she said, pointing at the drawing. "I need words with it. Help me."

"What is it?" Latifa asked.

"It's a drawing about war," Mariam offered.

What Noura had drawn: Images of war surrounded the figure of a symphony conductor, very Western looking, decked out in a cut-away tuxedo with tails. Jets emblazoned with the Star of David. Exploding bombs. Arabs launching surface-to-air missiles. Tanks firing. Soldiers shooting. Dead bodies scattered on the ground. In the midst of this stood the smiling conductor, waving his baton and orchestrating the mayhem. The cartoon struck a chord, but it was a chord with at least one note of kneejerk anxiety. I'd been diligent so far in steering clear of Mideast politics.

"You're a cartoonist?" I asked Noura. Was this the special talent that had been planted inside those green high-tops? She didn't need to speak English because she could speak through art.

"Yes, Doctor," she said, and smiled.

"Wow!" I exclaimed. Here, one of my retiring, downright reticent female students had in fact found a way to assert herself and her opinions.

Movie reviews could wait a bit. Samah looked at the drawing, and nodded her approval. "Noura's a very good artist but I have never seen this before."

The drawing skills on exhibit were impressive; in fact, they blew me away. But Noura's English skills still presented a problem. For us to suggest captions or titles for the cartoons we'd need to understand their aims. To hear them from the artist, I called on Samah's services as interpreter.

"Can you ask Noura what help it is, specifically, that she needs from us?"

Following their exchange, Samah turned to me. "She needs a caption for this one because she's getting a grade on it for her political science class. She wants your help naming it."

Taking this on would derail the class. It would also likely open another can of worms about my heritage. Perfect. I'd just get the scripted lesson out of the way first. Save the dangerous part for the closing minutes. "Very well," I said. "Let me think about it." That seemed to satisfy Noura.

It hit me that my plan and Noura's request dovetailed nicely. Both were about journalism as a forum for viewpoint. We'd start with the softball stuff.

Online, taking turns, we read an A.O. Scott review in *The New York Times* of "Bolt," the animated tale of a canine super-hero voiced by John Travolta. We discussed the review's lede, nut graph, structure, point of view and how to criticize acting, writing and directing. All, I instructed, were "necessary parts of a good review. A movie review is much more than whether you like the film."

This seemed to register, but chiefly they were impressed to learn that their teacher, who had written movie criticism for American newspapers, had interviewed celebrities. I got sidetracked talking about Robin Williams, "Charlie's Angels," and a few more. To them, I now had special *wasta*.

Near the end of the class I told the girls that someday, I believed, they would be able to write and speak their minds, *insha'Allah*. But, as always when I let myself talk like that, my gut told me I was a fool, a liar, or both. I doubted things would progress that way in the UAE. Like many teachers I harbored a fantasy that I was making a difference. Was I kidding myself? My best hope was making a difference for one, maybe two students. As a mercenary, parachuting in for a few years, I needed to believe

I had a stake in something tangible here. Something more than a tax-free salary and good perks.

Sure, the government provided young women with a free college education, but post-graduation they'd find very few good career opportunities. The oft-cited statistic, that 80 percent of UAEU students were female, was great to run up the UAE public relations flagpole. But enrolling women in college without much for them to do after graduation was smoke and mirrors. That was already apparent.

As I reflected on this weird mix of cynicism and idealism, utterly uncharacteristic of me even a few months earlier, Samah saw me struggling. I wanted to direct us to Noura's political cartoon, but felt apprehensive. That would be a Rubicon crossed. Samah helped me out.

"Doctor," she said. "Noura's drawing."

I nodded, still a bit uneasy. The drawing came back out, and we all admired it again. No one proposed a title, so I hurriedly offered one: "The Symphony of War."

The girls pronounced it good. Good or not, the phrase got me through a sticky moment. I knew it would help Noura earn an "A." But I had, by doing her thinking for her, let myself down. And her, too. Instead of using this teachable moment I'd lucked into, I copped out. My goal wasn't to get her an "A" in her other course with ideas provided by someone else. It was to encourage her to think for herself. She'd walked into the session with the perfect object for that lesson tucked under her arm, too.

Walking out to meet Noor, I quizzed myself. I'd just done a bunch of acrobatics. Why? Was I now a guy who didn't risk breaking the rules? Was I afraid "the Jewish question" would come up? The answer to the first I knew—I *wanted* the question of my ethnic roots and religious faith to come up. Per my don't-tell-unless-asked policy, that would be the way to get the fact out there.

So I'd turned timid?

I was upset with myself, but thought about how there had been something in Samah's manner when she reminded me about the drawing. She might not have Jewdar, but she sensed there was more to the story. Just as a shrewd journalist should, she went for the subject's point of discomfort. If my wild fantasy proved prophetic and things in the UAE did change, the country would surely need people like her and Noura, ready to think for themselves and ask awkward questions. Samah knew how to push my buttons, and on that basis alone I made a pledge not to let my skittishness get in the way again.

I was counting on a second shot. Noura's political cartoons would be back, that much I was sure of. Samah would see to it.

CHAPTER 12

The Death of Brian

A SIZZLING LATE OCTOBER GUST BENT THE PALMS IN THE garden courtyard at the Al Ain Rotana Hotel. Encamped poolside with Carol and Dan in the fading sunlight, I picked up a solitary *frite* nesting alongside a two-inch-thick bloody cheeseburger. We'd frequently have beers and burgers after visits to the Rotana's popular health club, but this twilight was singularly, eerily dreamlike.

My Nokia buzzed and I did a double take. I held the device up so Carol and Dan could read the caller's name: "Brian."

I paused deciding whether to answer. "How the hell can a dead man be calling me?"

"Answer it," Carol implored. "Let's see who it is."

I pressed the talk button.

"Hello?" I said warily.

My greeting was followed by silence.

I had been the last friend to see Brian alive. Noor and I had rushed him to Oasis Hospital at midday. A few hours later a doctor called me, since I was listed as his local medical contact, and pronounced him dead. Brian's name had last flashed on my phone after Noor had deposited me at the Falahi apartments following my morning class. The weather was brutal, well over 100°F. A call came in—Brian. Could I come over immediately? He had just been to Carrefour and felt a shooting pain down his left arm. Every man our age knows what that means.

I was at his flat in a minute. He stood there, ashen. "I didn't know who else to call." He assured me that he was feeling a little better, but I wanted to call an ambulance. Brian noted that you couldn't trust emergency services here like back home. He was right. But I knew who to call—Noor.

We bypassed Al Ain Hospital—it had a grim reputation—and headed across town to Oasis. Noor wasn't aware of a medical center with a bona fide emergency room. The one that might have one—American-branded Johns Hopkins-Tawam—was exclusively for Emiratis. At Oasis I knew the drill, and took Brian directly to Door #3. I stood up tall at the reception desk, telling the young Emirati woman, "My friend is having a heart attack."

She half turned her gaze up from her papers. "Please have him take a seat. We will call him."

"You don't understand," I pleaded. "He's having a heart attack!"

"*Insha'Allah*, no problem."

The phrase, which I'd come to find charming, boiled my blood.

"It will only be a few minutes. We will call you."

Noor stepped up and spoke at length in Arabic. I gave him an interrogatory glance. "I told her that Brian needs to see a doctor right away." He added a half smile. "And a few other things."

"*Insha'Allah*, no problem," she said, smiling. "But first we need to get insurance information."

"I'll be fine," said Brian, listening from his seat. "I'm feeling better. You know how it works around here. Have Noor take you to your afternoon class and we'll have a drink and laugh about it all later. I'm sure it's really nothing."

"Hello," I repeated into the phone.

Carol arched a blond eyebrow. Dan took a bite from his burger.

"Hello," I said once more.

Finally, a thick voice mumbled something incomprehensible, in what I took to be English.

"Who is it?" Carol asked.

I shrugged. I had heard nothing I could understand, and unless ghosts can shift ethnicity, the man on the phone wasn't Brian. "Who is this?" I asked one last time. Surely this wasn't some sick prank.

The voice spoke rapid-fire. "*DoyouknowBrian*?"

"Who is this? How do you have Brian's phone!?"

"*DoyouknowBrian*?!?!"

"Who is this?!"

A momentary silence was followed by a different, more assured voice. "This is the Al Ain police. We have Brian's mobile. Are you Brian's family? We need you to pick up the body."

I stared dumbfounded at Carol and Dan and relayed that information in lip-synch. Then I put the Nokia on the table and turned on the speaker

"We need you to take the body!" the voice commanded.

"I am not taking the body. I am not family. I am a colleague from the university."

"You must to take the body now!" the voice insisted.

At the next table, another Western couple perked up, exchanging troubled glances.

"No, I will not."

"Where is his family?" the voice demanded.

"Canada."

"We need you to pick up the body now. We cannot keep it."

"I am not picking up the body," I said, no less forcefully. "Call the university."

I pushed the red button. It felt odd—and ominous—to hang up on the Al Ain police.

The next morning I called the new Canadian HR director and told him about the police. He assured me that the university would handle everything. "Don't worry about it," he said, which immediately made me worry.

I had been replaying the events of Brian's demise, on a continuous loop, most of the day. Next I called his friend Sasha. She said Brian's family lived in Toronto, his mother had Alzheimer's and his sister had "mental issues." Sasha had the name and number of Brian's niece. More a remnant than a family, but that was all the family she was aware of.

The following day an HR representative called to say they couldn't find Brian's passport and did I know where it was. She said UAEU couldn't do anything about claiming Brian's body until they found the document. The police, she added, were annoyed. A few hours later she reported that Brian's passport had been found, under his mattress. Who, I wondered, had gone to Brian's apartment to conduct the search? That evening my idle question got an answer. Sasha called, distraught, from Brian's flat. "Look at what they've done!" she cried, when I arrived.

The place had been tossed. Brian's ever-tidy living room was a mess; books scattered, pictures askew, electronics missing. In his bedroom, the mattress was propped against the wall, sheets and pillows and clothes were piled in a heap. In the kitchen, drawers had been spilled onto the floor and left in heap. The laptop I was used to seeing on his desk was gone.

"They told me they'd found his passport," I said. "Now I see how."

Sasha related how she had tracked down Brian's niece who requested that only his pictures and a few personal belongings be shipped to Toronto. She said to give the rest away. Brian kept his pictures in his laptop. "Now his laptop is gone," she said. "There are no pictures to send." She fell into a chair at the kitchen table and wept. Along with the laptop, several watches, a camera and other valuables I knew Brian had kept in plain sight were all missing.

The ensuing day I called the HR director and told him that Brian's flat had been ransacked. I reported what had been stolen and noted that the only people who had access were from UAEU. The director immediately became defensive and denied everything. I suggested, strongly, that he investigate.

Sasha called me, again in tears. HR had contacted her and said that Brian's flat had to be cleaned out, within five days. Further, she said, the university said it would sell his non-personal belongings to reclaim some of the 22,000-dirham furniture allowance single professors were allocated.

Together, she, Tony and I hatched a plan. That night we gave away most of Brian's remaining possessions to UAEU faculty. Sasha boxed up some personal items and sent one box to his family. The university took what was left—which, it gave us some consolation to know, wasn't much.

Over the following days, more details found their way to me— thanks largely to Noor, who was outraged over the whole affair and stepped into the role of Columbo. He could do some things I couldn't— not least, speak Arabic and Pashto. From a friend at the hospital he learned that Brian had died on the exam table. Nothing the doctors tried gave him "the breath of life." From Abu Ahmed, our building's friendly and down-trodden Egyptian watchman, Noor learned that the university had sent an unsupervised crew to search Brian's flat. Abu Ahmed was ordered to let them in but had been unable to stay to watch their work. He worked for the building's owner, who it turned out was Fatima's uncle.

At the Islamic Institute where I had gone to confront the HR director with my new information, he disarmed me by admitting it had all gotten disastrously out of hand. I went away with an empty commitment of an effort to recover the missing laptop and other items.

In the end, nothing was returned. *Insha'Allah, bukra.*

No autopsy was performed. The body was kept more than two weeks in cold storage at an Al Ain morgue. When the police released Brian's remains, the university shipped them to the Dubai Airport, accompanied by Sasha, who saw the UGRU teacher off for his last long trip home.

CHAPTER 13

The Big Lie

YOU NEVER FORGET THE DAY, THE FIVE MINUTES, IN WHICH you come to a shocking new perception, a realization that knocks aside cherished, romantic and often naïve ideas. That moment resides in your present, but extends into your future, putting an end-point on your past. Yet there's an irony to all this when your new perception is: "Nothing really changes, does it?"

That hit me, along with the thought that most likely nothing ever will, at the end of a lively session of *Intro*. As a further irony, this was the Wednesday following the historic Tuesday on which Americans chose a black man with a Muslim father as their 44th president. Hope. Hope?

As usual the a/c in my Building 66 classroom was broken and it was hot and stuffy for early November. I'd scrawled on the whiteboard behind me, in a rainbow of dry-erase colors, a quartet of buzzwords: *Propaganda, Seek the Truth, Speak Truth to Power,* and *The Big Lie.* My teaching plan was a lesson and discussion focused on uses and abuses of journalistic influence, not on the U.S. election.

Noura 1 was anxious to get the subversion going the moment class started. "We are so excited about Obama. He is our president, too."

"He is the world's new hope," Fatima 4 exclaimed.

That word again. I'd arrived knowing the students would want me to go off-topic. With their first genuine exam set for the following Wednesday, they weren't going to derail me easily. I stood firm. "We will talk about Obama and the American election another day. Today, we have other things to do."

Noura 1 persisted. "Are you glad he won, Doctor?"

"Yes." I smiled, trying to hide my jaded journalistic doubt. "Keep hope alive."

The class erupted in applause and loud chatter—in Arabic—and I waited for the moment of youthful political passion to subside. That "hope" thing. I'd felt that way once myself when I voted for the first time for president. But Nixon won and my man, McGovern, was crushed. The rest is history.

When the chatter persisted, I raised a hand and reminded the class that the midterm was a week away. That did it. Calm—and anxious calm—was restored. I skipped over to the whiteboard and put big red quotation marks around "Seek the Truth" and "Speak Truth to Power."

As I wrote, I all but chanted: "You trust your government. Your leaders never lie. Politicians are honest and truthful." I pivoted on one foot, with a bit of flair, and faced the students. "Right?"

"All politicians lie," Noura 1 said, with a big laugh.

"All governments lie," added the Sri Lankan, Mariam 3.

The "choir," the majority who seemed to blend together in the background and who by then I had come to see as something between a Greek chorus and a black-clad cheerleading squad, nodded in agreement. Together, we'd just breached the rules and raised the taboo subject of politics. But in a generic way since no government or politician was being identified.

So, I pressed. "Are you saying *all* governments lie?" That drew uncertain stares. "Are you saying that the UAE government lies?"

"Oh, no, sir!" the choir sang. But the answer was shaded with sarcasm, even laughter. This was getting close to a much more dangerous taboo: criticism of the powers that be. Probably vastly closer than most in this group had ever ventured, at least in a public setting, to sedition.

Fatima 4's hand went up. "Our government doesn't lie," she declared, each word dripping with irony. "It always tells us the truth, Doctor."

"Very good answer," I intoned, looking up at the ceiling and getting a laugh. That routine hadn't failed yet. The illicit, in all its forms, is evergreen. Sometimes as I performed my *shtick*—scribbling madly on the whiteboard in colored inks—I reminded myself of Professor Irwin Corey, "the world's foremost authority" on everything and a staple of TV variety shows in my youth.

For the next half hour I ad-libbed, hopping around the room and ranging to the whiteboard to scribble. I drew a big red circle around *Propaganda* and did a pirouette. That brought a wave of laughter. For the first time all semester, I could feel the class's energy. Was it the vaudeville? Was *shtick* the way to go? Rely on my broad, physical material and transcend the language barrier? It worked in the Catskills.

The gleam in their eyes told me something different. It bespoke the thrill of subversion. In a culture in which one cannot speak freely, it struck me that doing so could be a drug. I had one more topic to circle. The one I'd been building up to—*The Big Lie*. Maybe there was some free thinking here. I had seen flashes. Something was simmering beneath all the black and uniformity. The thirty-five young women in this class hadn't just sat there and played with their *sheylas*, as other faculty widely complained.

"Who," I asked, "can give me an example of 'The Big Lie'?"

Nothing.

"A lie told so often, so insistently, that it passes as the truth."

Still silence. Whether it was apprehension, puzzlement or both I couldn't tell.

"So, someone, tell me a Big Lie! Tell me one!"

To get them going, I batted out a couple softballs. "America invaded Iraq to bring democracy to the Middle East." That met with derision. "George Bush always tells the truth. He is one of the greatest presidents in American history and has made the world better."

"No, sir! You are crazy!" Fatima 4 exclaimed, rising to her feet.

The chorus's cue. "No, sir! No, sir! He is bad. Very bad."

Noura 1 took the floor. "But, Doctor, we like Americans. We just all hate Bush."

Anood 2 from the back: "You are just trying to be funny, Doctor."

Thinking back to that interval, I recognize it, somewhat paradoxically, as a "come to Jesus moment" in a Muslim classroom. The wiser choice would have been to shut the conversation down and go to safe ground. Wrap up the hour, say, "See you next time." But I had gone too far, as I saw it, to wimp out. I'd wimped out with Samah and Noura's cartoon and vowed that would be a one-shot. More important, this class had come along with me and it wasn't my prerogative to play the authority card. Even if I was the world's foremost authority on everything! The girls in black were coming out of the shells they'd been raised in. I reiterated my request for a Big Lie.

"Democracy is a Big Lie!" called out Mariam 3, the Sri Lankan, who had asserted that all governments lie.

In an hour already notable for the unexpected, that took me by surprise. "Democracy is a Big Lie? Why do you say that?"

"It is a lie because democracy in America is a lie," she offered, earnestly. "Obama only got seventy percent of the vote, and thirty percent didn't vote for him. So democracy is a lie."

I think I kept my poker face, but my silent reaction to that was, *Huh?* "First," I noted, "Obama did not get that many votes. But are you saying that the fact one candidate didn't get *all* the votes makes democracy a lie. A Big Lie, even?"

Mariam 3 was adamant. "Yes, Doctor. It is a Big Lie."

The chorus concurred. "Yes, Doctor, yes."

In the heat of the moment I just didn't get it. So I glossed over why Mariam 3 and others felt democracy in America was a Big Lie. In retrospect I blew another richly teachable moment, in my haste—only five minutes left in class—to get to a more sensational level of discussion. That evening during my daily debriefing Tony set me straight about how widely I'd missed the point. Democracy, he informed me, for most of the world, simply didn't match the American fantasy. So, because the American fantasy was—it had to be!—a lie, democracy itself was incriminated. Made sense. But my gut said the girls in *Intro* were telling me something more. That in a culture of sameness, with the illusion of consensus, anything short of unanimity was wrong, false, a failure. Uniformity, conformity and unanimity, all in the service of nation building and national-identity-preservation. Japan, I'm told, works that way, and Japan certainly does work. But in the Land of the Rising Sun, I suspect, the key is homogeneity.

Obligatory consensus is going to be tougher for the Emiratis as they become a smaller and smaller minority in their own country.

Making no such open reflections, I pressed on. I had a real Big Lie I wanted to float with this group. "Now I'm going to tell you a 'Big Truth.'"

The chorus rang out. "What, sir?"

"Sometimes there *is* very little difference between a Big Lie and a Big Truth." I paused for a beat. "Now, tell me which one this is."

I took a breath, squared my shoulders. "All Muslims are terrorists!"

The chorus was mute. One count. Two count. Three. Four …

Noura 1 shot to her feet, towering in the first row. "No, sir, it's a Big Lie, a terrible Big Lie!"

I couldn't resist. "What do you mean?! Everyone knows that all Muslims are terrorists. I see them on TV all the time. Blowing things up. Suicide bombers. Murderers."

Noura 1 stood tall. "We are not *all* like that!!"

"But it's on TV," I pushed.

Anood 2, near the back wall, was on her feet as well. "No, sir, that is a Big Lie! We are not like that. Only a very few. They make us all look bad!"

I grinned, pointedly, and refrained from eyeing the ceiling. "Yes, it's a Big Lie. Of course it is. Some infinitesimal minority of Muslims are terrorists. But this unfair stereotype persists. And it persists strongly among many people, especially in America, because it's repeated again and again in the media."

The lesson I was driving at, how journalism has to be vigilant against efforts—including its own—to be subverted into the dissemination of propaganda, which it more and more is, was lost in the shuffle. It took a back seat to a more pressing issue in the students' minds.

"Doctor," Fatima 4 said, "do *you* think we are terrorists? Do *you* think we are bad?"

"No." In the brief pause, as I considered how to elaborate, I sensed the room thirsting for my answer. "I think all of you here are good people. In any group, there are some bad people who do bad things and make unthinking people hate everyone in that group. There are many unthinking people in the world, however, including many people in America, and they think Muslims are terrorists because that's what they see on TV. And, after all, TV is reality, right?"

"No, sir," Anood 2 said, sitting down. "It is not."

"She is right," echoed Noura 1, doing the same. "TV is a Big Lie."

We weren't going to have time to examine that, not today, so I simply shrugged. With two minutes to go, I went for broke. Not once in this class had I allowed my religion to come up. We'd talked about theirs, and just now gotten to prejudices they face because of it. Clearly they had assumed, with nearly everyone else around, that their teacher, as he was an American, was Christian. I had done nothing to make them think so nor had I found any occasion to make a religious declaration—not that I necessarily would have.

But I had the chance now, in the context of The Big Lie, and in a roundabout way that appealed to me, *via* the natural follow-up question. I hadn't anticipated this, but it was obviously the place to go. When would I have another chance to pose *the* question to an ensemble like this? I moved to the center of the room and drew in a breath like a flute player. "Tell me if what I say next is a Big Lie." A pause for effect, and then I spoke slowly, without inflection. "*All* Jews are evil."

This time Fatima 1 jumped to her feet, balancing on her spike heels. "It is true, sir!"

The chorus reached the top of its range. "It is true! It is true!"

Holy shit, I said to myself. Had they misheard the assertion?

"Now, listen to what I said. '*All* Jews are evil.' Are you saying that's true? *All* Jews, *all* Jews everywhere, are evil?"

The chorus, usually so retiring, sang out. "Yes, sir!"

"So not *all* Muslims are terrorists. But *all* Jews are evil?"

Fatima 1 punched the air. "All!"

I scanned my students' faces. These were women I laughed with and who joined me in mocking untruths we'd been fed throughout our lives. Now I could detect not a trace of the irony that had gotten us on this track. Nor could I see a flicker of doubt. I was as desperate for a break in their certainty as they had been for my answer only moments before. Under their definition, I was evil by association.

The reprieve came from Anood 2, my star, in the back: "Not *all* Jews are evil." Noura 1 and Mariam 3 joined her: "Not *all*." Fatima 4 had visited Venice, the city of Shylock, and had a like view: "No, Doctor, not all." Two more voices: "Not *all* Jews" That made six. This sextet hummed in agreement.

But the choir, directed by Fatima 1, countered with one voice. "Yes, sir. They are *all* evil."

"So that is *not* a Big Lie?" I asked.

Fatima 1 rang out defiantly. "No, sir, it is *The Big Truth!*"

The chorus rose to a crescendo. "The truth! *The Big Truth!*"

There were still those voices saying "no," but our time was up, class was over. I'd gotten my comeuppance and been asking for it. Neither the answer I had sought nor, more disconcerting, the one I had, with breezy confidence, expected. My students, the educated elite, the country's rising female generation, maybe even political leaders, simply wouldn't, I had convinced myself, hold such blind prejudices. But that's what they'd been fed their entire lives. *All* Jews are evil. What did I expect?

I auto-piloted through campus navigating toward the lot where Noor would be waiting. I bounced between despair and humiliation— what an utter chump I'd been, certain that all the Stateside friends saying, "But they hate us!" had been wrong. There would be little point in sending home a dispatch with my hopeful finding: "No, guys! Only five out of six of them do!" Sure, the brightest lights in *Intro* had taken a less extreme view—though "not *all* Jews are evil" is about as moderate as "have you stopped beating your wife?" Six out of thirty-five. Not odds I would play at a dog track, even the dollar window.

Have all of the modern hi-tech gadgetry, the smartphones, Internet, Facebook, Twitter, and globalization, made no difference? Can a teacher make any difference? I laughed out loud at my stupidity, the parking lot now in view. Yes, all those wonderful tools made a difference—in service every hour of the day whipping up the blind hatred I'd gone looking for, blithely certain of finding instead what I *wanted* to believe in. Fool that I was. The object of the anger suffusing me came into sharp focus—the hand that had fed me all these years, the news media. Ratings and eyeballs and Google-analytics "uniques." Hatred and violence and the yearning for revenge outsell conciliation and understanding. Probably 29 to 6, on average. The same dark forces that had demonized for Westerners the *Adnan* chanted from minarets had demonized my kind and me. I'd just gotten an earful, here on the other side of the fence.

Noor's look, as I entered the taxi, confirmed that I was visibly upset. Hearing my synopsis, he wrapped the farce up neatly in a box. "They are spoiled and stupid. All Jews are not evil."

Naturally, Noor had a grace note to add, with a smile. "I know you." In a tone less admonishing than imploring, as his smile faded, he tied up the package with a ribbon: "But you *cannot* tell people here that you are *Yehuda.*"

CHAPTER 14

The Tiger's Son

IT WAS HAPPENING, THE THING I'D VOWED WOULDN'T. I VAC-
illated, moving like a twelve-stepper from liberal rage—"oh *why* is the
world the way it is?"—through seasoned resignation—"well, this was
inevitable"—and on to recognition: this had happened because *I'd* let it.
My plan to play-things-by-ear and leave the incidental fact I was a Jew to
filter out to people naturally and organically had been unceremoniously
exposed as the delusion it was. There was nothing at all *natural* about a
Jew being here. The Diaspora had once sent the children of Israel down the
Arabian Peninsula to Yemen, east to Syria, Mesopotamia and Iran, west
to Egypt and all of North Africa, but not to this little corner on the Gulf.

My adult version of running away and joining the circus had cast
me as both acrobat and clown, but the place I'd found refuge was no
glittering Barnum & Bailey. Secular and globalized as were the images
brought to me via Dubai-dominated media coverage of the UAE, what
lay below the shiny surfaces was as dark as Bob had called it—"Tell them
you're Canadian."

To that advice, that admonition, Noor had added his own. So far,
every occasion on which I'd failed to listen to my Pashtun friend's coun-
sel, proceeding per my own half-baked thinking, I'd regretted it. But

acceptance of this prohibition carried another regret, and maybe a deeper one. Contrary to my hopes and expectations, my life in the UAE was not going to be about becoming part of an open, international academic community blazing a trail for journalistic bravery with integrity, and reaching across tribal lines. And if I was going to have a life in the UAE at all, I'd better get out and find one.

But I'd be damned if I was gonna go Canadian.

Boarding the plane in Clevistan, I had identified myself as a member of "a tribe"—the Indians and their long-suffering fans. I even had the hat to prove it. Oh, yeah, right, I was a Jew, too. We're "a Tribe." We even joke about our rituals and bicker about who belongs. But "Jew" was never the front-and-center, tent-pole, primary aspect of my identity. My family, three generations under one roof, kept kosher but wasn't religious. People are the sum of the values they witness and live. They are not brands with a big "J" or a little "j," a big "C" or a little "c," a big "M" or a little 'm" stamped on their foreheads.

Unconsciously emulating my sparsely known father, and the legends of him I'd grown up on, I'd affixed various nouns to myself as I came of age (in ascending order of importance): kid from the Heights, student at Missouri J-School, American, journalist, husband, father. "Jew" was on the list, somewhere between "middle-aged guy in not-quite-retirement" and "onetime Boy Scout." I was a "J." Others who judged me maybe thought differently.

I'd slapped on the yarmulke at the TV station, indeed, when there was a point to be made, and a principle at stake. Now it was more a question of putting on the yellow armband. Hell, a sandwich sign, or a t-shirt printed in big "Frankie Goes to Hollywood" letters: EVIL JEW. Though of course a redundancy like that was hardly the kind of thing a writing teacher ought to go around promulgating.

My life had come to a knotted-up contradiction, an oxymoron, a paradox. To be who I was I had to turn into what I never had been, an adherent of crude identity politics. Here, in the UAE, "Jew" headed my self-conception list. It had become top-of-mind in a way it never really had been elsewhere.

Right there in the incongruity, I sensed, lay the answer. *Insha'Allah*, I'd located it.

For the few days following my solicitation of The Big Lie, I stayed in my soul-searching daze. I was dogged by an unshakable, recurrent sense of picking myself up on my own Jewdar *while* looking over my shoulder. The dismissal from the TV station and ensuing trial had forced me to depths of paranoia I'd never, once it was settled and over, wanted to plumb again. Now I was taking hourly readings. Noor and Tony were both in my foxhole, but neither yet knew me well enough to be my reality check, my canary in the coalmine. What would be the point of asking a friend to gauge my sanity when the consensus was that my being in the UAE at all was the act of a madman? A "crazy Jew."

Each day, letting people assume that I was a generic gentile, i.e., a Christian, I saw how I was digging myself in deeper. I'd read about people like me, in 1930s Europe, and seen them portrayed in movies. I had dreams of being back on the witness stand being accused by the TV station's Catholic attorney of being a phony Jew. By a cruel twist of *insha'Allah*, I was living their revenge: not just the Jew I'd claimed to be, but a tawdry cliché.

As I had at other times of crisis, I attempted what I like to call strategic procrastination. My detractors call it hiding out and other things less laudatory. To me it's StratPro and it always works.

Such a withdrawal does require a place to retreat to and hole up. Wait things out. My refuge after the "All Jews Are Evil" class was the very thing I'd fulminated against: binging on good, old Western media. Shortly before my Ohio exodus, a friend had recommended a SlingBox and I purchased one before I left. Staying plugged into things in the U.S. preserved my sanity one moment, threatened to annihilate it the next. The wind-down—hallelujah—of the Bush era and heady wind-up toward an Obama presidency. Redoubled attention to the financial crisis, now remarketed as "The Crisis," induced panic. I'd only half-paid attention as the sky was falling and the financial tsunami circled the globe. It was then that I realized my comfortable nest egg had taken a big hit. I was fucked like everyone else.

When I'd glutted myself on "whose-fault-is-it" coverage, I ventured outside the faculty ghetto. Nearby there was Pizza Hut, Hardy's and KFC.

Reassuringly familiar in their franchised interchangeability with outlets I knew elsewhere, and popular with most of Al Ain's demographics. There was La Brioche, a French-style patisserie, and behind it was Spinney's, the liquor store Moraig raved about. Both became regular stops. I had been looking for the places Emiratis went and then I realized my error: these *were* the places Emiratis went. La Brioche and Spinney's were as popular as the fast-food chains.

A half-block from my apartment window I looked out at a neighborhood mosque, and the loudspeaker mounted near the roofline that emitted a *muezzin's* pre-recorded chant five times daily. Every morning before dawn it woke me. Near the mosque I also discovered a hole-in-the-wall store.

One evening Noor accepted my invitation to visit. As he passed through the doorway, his eyes almost popped out of his head. On the wall facing the entry I had placed my newest piece of art—a bigger-than-life-size official portrait of Sheik Zayed—one of the variants seen hanging everywhere. The UAE's founder has one eyebrow slightly raised, meaning... what, I wondered? The Indian dealer offered no interpretation, but was happy to part with it, framed, for fifty dirhams.

Noor looked at me in incomprehension.

I shrugged. "When the police bust in to get me, this may give them a moment's pause. Meanwhile, I can go out a window. Zayed may save my life."

That met with a good long beat. Noor's look asked, "Have you already gone around the bend?"

I kept a straight face.

He finally burst out laughing.

There was cut up fruit and peach juice on the table, which drew Noor's approval. I booted up the computer and tuned in to *Morning* Joe as Mika rolled her eyes at Joe, the all-knowing host. It was near dinnertime in Al Ain, almost nine a.m. on the East Coast. The eponymous host, as was his way, was mid-pontification when Noor's phone rang. Taking the call, he spoke in Pashto, looking troubled. He talked often with his wife, but not wearing the face I saw now. He rose from the sofa, paced, and held up his end of the conversation in a way that sounded like questions. His call wrapped up; Noor looked stricken. He was, in fact, wringing his hands. "There has been no electricity in our village for ten days."

"What happened?"

"The Taliban cut the electrical lines," he groaned. "No one can get water from their wells because there is no power for the pumps. So my wife and our children have gone to live with her father in the country." He paced and paused. "There, the government cut the phone lines. So they have no electricity and no telephone. Things are not good for my family."

I struggled for something to say, but settled for a concerned look.

"In the tribal areas, we are caught between the government and the Taliban."

"Between a rock and a hard place."

Noor looked at me curiously.

"It's an American expression."

He nodded and sat back down on the sofa. Reaching to the plate on the coffee table, he picked up a guava, cut off a chunk, and passed it to me with his well-manicured fingers. That simple gesture—a friend accepting my meager hospitality, helping himself to a piece of fruit—let me know it was fine just to listen, and have nothing to offer in the way of insight or consolation.

"Yaya, between the Taliban and the government." Noor chuckled, selecting another slice. "A rock and a hard place. That's the way it is. Yaya."

Joe Scarborough asked Willy Geist, "What have you learned today?"

"Nothing," I bitched at the screen. "As usual!"

Someone among the pundits mentioned bin Laden.

"Some people, many people, think Osama died years ago," Noor said. "Others think he is still alive protected by the Golden Word of powerful people. He is like a phantom, a ghost. It doesn't matter if he is alive. He is a legend, and enough believe."

I reflected on what our conversations, and my inquiries, had taught me. Noor's village lies in a valley inside Pakistani Tribal territory, but less than nine kilometers from the Afghani border. When an American drone targeted the home of Taliban leader Jalaluddin Haqqana, Noor's house—less than a kilometer away—sustained damage, with windows and doors shattered by the blast.

"Haqqana was a big hero, too," Noor said. "In the first war, the one against the Russians, the U.S., Saudis, and UAE give him money to fight. They give him stinger missiles. Now he has gone from being their friend and a hero to being a terrorist. Very crazy. They think we are all terrorists."

Per my wayward riff in *Intro*, Pashtun Muslims, who were our allies in the resistance against Russia's occupation of Afghanistan, were now our enemies, all branded terrorists, too. Had *they* changed? Or had the winds of American foreign policy shifted? We'd retired the Cold War and replaced it with the War on Terror. Our TV screens needed enemies. Who else would sell us the beer, cars, soft drinks, pharmaceuticals, and bargain mortgages that kept the economy going? The old adage "the enemy of my enemy is my friend" holds up only until that enemy becomes my new friend and you become my enemy because your friends are my new enemies. Maybe the paradox burdening my life wasn't so bad. Noor headed into the kitchen and I tried to remember whether I'd even known before I met him, or let alone cared, that North Waziristan was under regular bombardment by drones.

"My wife asked again now for me to return home," he called out. I heard the sigh that followed. "But there is no opportunity in Pakistan."

Between taxi-bound lessons in theology I'd connected the dots of Noor's life story. He had studied engineering at college, but left after two years to become an administrator at the *madrassa* in his home village where his father taught. "Then the Taliban came into North Waziristan. They made it not good and I had to leave and come here for work."

His plan had been to work six months in the UAE, spend six months at home, and repeat. But he had been back a scant four times in nine years. In nine years he had been with his family for just one *Eid Al Fitr*, the holiday following Ramadan, called by some of my fellow Western expats "the Muslim Christmas." His wife ordinarily lived at his father's home along with his parents, brother, sister-in-law and the two couples' eight children. They lived as an extended family in a big house with several houses together. "My wife and children live in one house. My brother and his family live in another. And my father and mother live with my wife. Another family lives like that next to us. That is how we live in the tribal area. Everybody knows everybody." I recalled him telling me that his wife was also his first cousin, his father's sister's daughter. An uncle, aunt and eleven cousins also shared the family compound.

"Did I tell you that we have a neighbor who has forty sons?" he asked, with a grin.

"How many wives?"

"Four, now," Noor laughed. "You are allowed four wives, and one of his wives died, so he married again. He has had five wives, but only four at one time. When he married the fifth wife, his sons said to him, 'Father, how come you marry again when we are not even married once?' They were not happy. They want to be married, too."

Noor had only one wife and five living children. Their first two sons, born breach, did not survive home delivery. A local doctor gave Noor's wife "medicine to make them turn," but they didn't. After that they went to the hospital. Now the family was facing an especially difficult time, without him. Difficult? It sounded more like impossible.

His father, "the Tiger," had been educated at a British mission school and still taught at the village *madrassa*. Noor's Indian-educated grandfather, he added proudly, was considered "one of the three great scholars in our country." He took equal pride in the heroism of his father's uncle, who was a martyr in fighting the British Raj. The Pashtun warrior attacked an English military convoy traveling in the mountains and killed a famous general. "The general was riding his motorcycle and my uncle jumped up from the side of the road and killed him with his knife," Noor related, proudly.

This revelation captivated me. I flashed on images from the 1939 black-and-white classic *Gunga Din*, based on Kipling's tale, with Sam Jaffe in the title role. That's how I romantically pictured Noor's forbears' world—and, for that matter, Noor's world today. North Waziristan, our tutorials had brought me to understand, has "semi-autonomous" status. What that meant, I gathered, was that the central government had thrown up its hands and given up trying to control this territory. Noor called the

Wazirs "wild men." His tribe, the Dawar, numbers about 12,000, and are known among the Pashtun as teachers, businessmen, farmers, and local government officials. In the UAE they mostly drive vehicles.

"The British captured my ancestor. They offered a big reward and he was betrayed. They took him to the fort and they shot them with a big gun—and then they burned their bodies. It was okay to kill my grandfather's brother because he killed a famous British general… a life for a life… but not to burn his body. That is *haram* to Muslims. It was a big insult. In our tribe, we never forget things like that."

A phrase from my own upbringing. "Never forget." Many of my childhood friends were children of Holocaust survivors. I understood the phrase, in Noor's usage, somewhat differently: We kill you, you kill us, but don't disrespect us by violating our ancient burial customs. Civilized men do not insult the dead, and the dead never let the living forget.

All of this, I had become convinced, harmonized perfectly with his absolute commitment to seeking and submitting to God's will, living by *insha'Allah.* In my present circumstances, raging inwardly against contradictions I felt had trapped me, I wished Noor could impart his secret.

He continued telling me the history. With Pakistan's independence, little had changed for the Pashtun. The new government was the old colonial system, with a new name. The tribes still lived by the time-honored code: Stand up heroically against any and all intruders. An eye for an eye. Never forget. The Pashtun and the Jews had one trait very much in common. Maybe we are the same ancient tribe.

The Taliban's rise, however, shifted the tribes' relations with the Pakistan and Afghanistan governments. Having maintained, remarkably well, a balance between the new and ancient orders, the Pashtun were caught in the crossfire—high-tech lethal crossfire—of the War on Terror. At the time of 9/11 the Taliban had the support, Noor said, of no more than twenty percent of the people. "Big mistakes by America" and its Pakistani allies made the Taliban popular. Simply by being the enemy of the U.S., the ousted theocratic regime had won the support of half the population.

Maybe Noor and I were sitting in an air-conditioned apartment watching American TV, but he had taken me a good deal closer to a reality I knew only with heavy media slant. His stories revealed conditions in his homeland on a granular level, that of his people's daily lives that scholars in think tanks, or journalists at newspapers and networks, rarely let themselves imagine. The conflict in North Waziristan, involving the Taliban, U.S.-launched drones, and vast collateral damage, was hardly a War on Terror. We'd like it to be that clear-cut, but it isn't. The region's history means nothing could be that simple. History does repeat; the British and the Russians could have told us as much.

He talked about the army base outside his village. "Every night the Taliban come and shoot at the base, and the army shoots back. In the morning the Taliban are gone. Then they come back the next night. It is very bad. All night they shoot back and forth." Furthermore, he added that many of the informers the army pays are really part of the Taliban. "They tell the army that this person is bad or that person is bad when they are not. The army kills them. That drives *more* people to the Taliban. Then the Americans drop bombs that kill innocent people, and that does the same. The army comes and shoots women in the fields. They don't care who they shoot."

No longer struggling for words, I said nothing. The phrase "War on Terror" hit me, the first time I heard it, with Orwellian force. Like "Homeland Security," with its creepy Josef Goebbels ring, it sent a shiver down my spine. The terror inflicted on Noor's village wasn't countered by our troops and our policies—American actions, decided from afar, brought much of the terror, and kept making it worse.

"People remember. When you kill someone's wife or child you make an enemy for life. Forever."

He sighed. "I want to be home with my wife and family, but I cannot make a living for them there. It is not good." He paused. "My wife is angry with me. She suspects I have another wife here and that's why I don't come home."

For the first time, I heard despair in Noor's voice. Moreover, I saw it in his eyes. His family was caught between the Taliban, the Pakistani government, and my American tribe. I wanted to believe that Americans, had people just known what was going on, would do something about it. Sure we knew, in general, what was going on. We learned daily about weddings blown to hell, families wiped out by bad intel or missiles that sought the wrong kind of heat. Did we believe The Big Lie that all Muslims are terrorists? No. We'd come to a more convenient version of that: *All* Muslims were now the enemy. Collateral damage was just a price to be paid.

Noor's predicament had a gravity beyond anything I'd ever had to face. It was a grim matter of life and death. His troubles, though considerably more fearsome, brought me back briefly to my own. Noor feared that if I made people aware I was *Yehuda* I could come to harm. My anxiety didn't exclude that, but it inclined toward something else. If I told people I was a Jew, what were my chances of making any real contact with the Emirati world—beyond the barbed-wire perimeter of Maqam—outside the Falahi Apartments? But would I claim membership in my ancient tribe only when and where it was felt safe here? The question was so stark in my mind I fleetingly thought what Noor said next was his answer.

"I know my God will take care of my family. He directs everything."

My guest's faith gave him consolation I could never have offered. For that I was grateful—though from whom I received comfort was a question that lodged in my mind.

CHAPTER 15

Stereotypes

THE LESSON PLAN FOR *INTRO* FOLLOWING *ALL JEWS ARE EVIL* coincidentally was headed: *Stereotypes*. At the community college in Lake County, Ohio, where I had taught Interpersonal Communications, it had been my favorite session. How would it translate to UAEU?

At the end of that class in Northeast Ohio, the whiteboard was filled with every nasty, angry, mean, evil, awful, banal, derogatory, brutal, offensive, insulting, clichéd, deprecating, and belittling epithet the students and I could hiss or snarl. We started with religions. The lone Jew, I wrote: Kike, Yid, Christ-Killer, Shylock, Smart, Cunning, Rich, and a few other sobriquets, to get things started. We did the same for Catholics, Muslims, Protestants. Then we moved on to ethnicities: Polacks, Micks, Wops, Guineas (most of the students were Catholics of those varieties), Wetbacks, Krauts, and even a few lame epithets for Canadians. (So lame I don't recall any.) We branched out geographically to Camel Jockey, Raghead, Chink, Jap. Moved on to race: Nigger, Spook, Slope, Slant, Gook and, of course, Honky. Finally, the reliable Homo and Fag. Etcetera. Etcetera. Etcetera. It took most of the hour to exhaust our collective repertoire of hate speech. By then we had exhausted all the supposed characteristics of each group. Shifty, wily, lazy, thieving, etc.

The lesson: Everyone has something bad to say about everyone else, and in that alone, we're all stereotypes. The point wasn't sensitivity, I told myself, but writing every desensitizing word we could think of that breeds insensitivity

At the start of this class, I wrote "Stereotypes" on the whiteboard. To get things started I wrote one word: *Blondes.* Since every student had black hair and dark eyes I wanted to start with something easy. Fatima 4 started it off. "Sexy." Fatima 1 added, "Stupid." The names Britney Spears and Paris Hilton were added.

Next I wrote: Muslims, Christians, Catholics, Hindus, Jews. Of course, the Jews part was easy for Fatima 1. "Evil." I added a few more. Anood 2 offered "smart, intelligent, rich." The girls hadn't heard of the Reformation and didn't differentiate between Christians and Catholics. "The same," several in the chorus sang out. Hindus were cow worshippers, monkey worshippers, red dots, Bahtan. Muslims were true believers, the faithful and I added a few more, including terrorist, Fez, camel cowboy, etc.

Unlike the Ohio class I didn't push for slang that these students didn't know. But soon the whiteboard had lists of stereotypes—the good, the bad and the ugly—under every group.

At the end of class Anood 2 said, "Doctor, I know what you are doing."

"What *am* I doing?"

"You are showing us that there are bad things to say about everyone. That there are hurtful words that everyone can say about everyone else." She paused and added, "Not *all* Muslims are terrorists. Not *all* Jews are evil. Not *all* Hindus are monkey lovers. We are *all* people. The same."

The lesson that day—the same as in Ohio. Maybe a third of the class got it. The others? Well, this time at least there were a few more than six who seemed to be on my wavelength.

CHAPTER 16

The Camel's Kiss

I'LL NEVER FORGET THE FIRST PAIR OF SOFT LIPS THAT caressed my own in the UAE. A golden full moon floated low on the desert horizon, crammed between craggy peaks rising from Oman. Her features softened by the mid-November twilight, Mahasba took a regal step closer to me. I felt her deep, dark eyes study my face.

"Now she will kiss you," Hilal said. "Just wait. Don't move."

Indeed, Mahasba lowered her head, flicked her long eyelashes, moved in, and gently set her lips, her hairy lips, on mine.

"You see!" Hilal exclaimed. "She is very sweet, very gentle. She is my favorite."

His father stood nearby, beside a wood fire burning on the sand, and looked pleased. Around him, other Bedouin men took in the odd scene.

The assignment on roundabout safety or lack thereof had been doomed to failure the moment I assigned it. Yet it had somehow brought me to this romantic moment. That exercise in futility was the closest I'd come to sending students out to do genuine reporting. Journalism isn't simply about official requests, or about *wasta*. As I told the fledgling reporters, it's often simply about not taking "no" for an answer. Fatima Al Falahi proved to be a Cassandra, and my misreading, or rather my latest misreading, became evident.

The Sanaiya roundabout was widely known to be Public Enemy Number One. But a journalist would verify the conventional wisdom and that would entail reporting. The police or transportation ministry had to compile statistics on accidents, injuries and fatalities. Would those stats be available for public consumption? Maybe there were accident reports in the local media? It turned out that Al Ain, although the size of urban Cleveland, had no TV station or daily newspaper, even in Arabic. The UAE's media were concentrated where things were happening, and audiences were big, in Abu Dhabi city, Dubai and Sharjah, so it may have been that UAEU students were in fact the only news-gatherers in town.

Only one student, Fatima, set about pounding the pavement. She marched into Al Ain's Central Police Station. "I asked to see a supervisor. I told him I was there for information about accidents at roundabouts. He told me it didn't exist and tried to shoo me away. Then I told him who my family was."

Put some wasta *into it!*

Fatima continued, as if it were the most natural sequitur in the world. "He quickly apologized and told me he would get me the information the next day." Yet here we were discussing it five days later, and Fatima was still waiting. *Insha'Allah, bukra.* "I told my father about this and he is proud of me for going to the police, but he doubts they will give us anything."

My takeaway was greater curiosity about *wasta* and its applications. If Fatima's family held high cards, how could the police ignore her request? Would her father play an ace to help his daughter? I thought about my son. There were times when he ran into a roadblock and I considered using such *wasta* as I had in Clevistan. I never did, though. It was less a question of whether I had any trump to play—generally, I had little—than the fact that Max would learn more by taking on the problem and finding his own way or not around it. Fatima's father might be looking at this from the same angle.

At any rate, I remade the lesson on the fly. "Part of learning is learning how to deal with failure and move on," I told the three students. "Sometimes you can't get the story and that's usually a story in itself." Thus I pontificated as my preface to cancelling the assignment. Their grades, I added aloud, would now be based on class participation and an individual project.

After class Fatima stayed behind. "My father wants to meet you," she beamed.

Had my lobbying, subtle or not, paid off? My silly asides about camels, dromedaries and anything else I could think of with a hump? Not only was Fatima blessed with clairvoyance, apparently, she was also able to read minds. At least this one. With a smile, she added, "He will take you to see the camels."

A chance like this was not to be passed up. My best—and likely only—shot at getting to know Emiratis outside the artificial worlds of the classroom and shopping mall. To "see for myself." Hell, to see legendary racing camels! Maybe learn more about this thing called *wasta*. I'd been in Al Ain nearly three months, and people back home kept asking me what the locals were like. After hemming and hawing awhile, I'd begun to answer, "They're from India, Pakistan, Bangladesh and the Philippines. As for the actual Emiratis? Your guess is as good as mine."

Of course I told Fatima I would very much like to meet her family. Reaching the door, she turned back. "But please don't tell Dr. Beverly." I grinned and said I'd keep the invitation a secret.

A few days had passed since I'd rescinded the roundabout traffic accident assignment. Like a high-school girl who's been asked whether she'd like to go out on a date, but not yet actually been asked out on one, I waited by the phone—okay, my mobile phone, which was always in my pocket. Late one afternoon, napping at my apartment—bad cough—I'd been awakened by the Nokia's ring. Fatima asked whether I could come and meet her parents and visit their farm. Right then.

My enthusiasm set off a new round of hacking.

She asked whether I was well enough to go into the desert that night. I assured her I was.

"Good, because my brothers and I are on our way to pick you up now."

Although she and I had spent no time together outside class, she'd given me thumbnail bios of her siblings. The two coming, Mohammed and Abdulla, were the youngest of the boys and very smart, Fatima said, adding ruefully, "They think they are funny."

In the shade of the car park, I waited with Abu Ahmed, the ever-present Egyptian watchman. The name he used, "Abu," means "father of," and Ahmed was his oldest son. The man's actual given name I never remembered. To him, I tried introducing myself as "Abu Max." He spoke no English, but understood a little. Our chats, given that my Arabic was limited to ten words, were pretty one-sided.

"The Falahi are coming," I casually told him.

The name of the family that paid his wages made the poor man visibly anxious. He was *masri*—"an Egyptian, a donkey, the same!" Naturally, my news put him on edge. The Falahi controlled his access to the privilege of living and working in the UAE, and with that his whole life. He had served as foreman for Fatima's uncle during the construction and stayed on when the project was completed. That's the way it was done here, and thus each building had its own *masri* overseer. For that his pay was 1,000 dirhams a month and a free, unfurnished apartment. Abu Ahmed sent most of his money home to Cairo to support his wife and their seven children, so tenant largesse got him by. How, given that I understood so little of his language, did I learn all this? I might not be a reporter anymore, but Noor was about the greatest researcher-stringer one could hope for. I'd made a point of learning about Abu Ahmed.

A new Toyota Land Cruiser, white, pulled into the parking lot and Fatima waved from the back seat. The front doors opened and two beefy young men, wearing traditional white *kanduras* and white *ghutrahs* tied in the Emirati style—with the little tail sticking out—emerged, smiling. The driver bounded to me and offered his hand. "Our family owns this building," he declared. "Our uncle built it. How do you like it? The university rents many of our buildings."

"That's Mohammed," Fatima called out. "He's trying to impress you." She rolled her eyes. "My other brother is Abdulla."

All I could tell at first glance was that Abdulla was bigger. The brothers looked, especially as they were attired, much alike. Together they could fill out a side of the Ohio State offensive line.

"Our cousin is the chancellor of the university," the larger told me proudly. "He is Nahyan."

In this brief conversation I had learned more about Fatima's family's *wasta* than she had revealed in three months. She was no *wasta*-dropper, but her brothers made up for her reticence. I felt the kneejerk urge to bring them down a peg, but refrained. The Falahis might think I was just keen on having a snapshot of myself on a camel, but my real motivation—baldfaced social climbing—was probably nothing to be embarrassed about at all.

Mohammed handed me a box. "Open it. I think this *kandura* will fit you. You are big like us. We just bought it for you at Al Ain Mall."

I fixed my gaze on him. "First, I am not *big* like you. But I am big. What do I wear under it?"

"That is up to you," he said, with a glint in his eye as our eyes locked.

Abu Ahmed stood close by, nervously taking in our exchange. Not an opportunity to let go by, I reached over, placed my hand on his shoulder and pulled him close to me. Fatima watched with curiosity. "Abu Ahmed is a good man," I said. "He's always helpful to your uncle's tenants."

Fatima nodded and smiled. She was onto me. If I had any *wasta* with her, maybe I could use it to Abu Ahmed's benefit. Was *wasta* like a food chain? Were there six degrees of *wasta*?

Abu Ahmed grinned, revealing more gaps than teeth. He understood, too. Fatima exchanged words with Mohammed, then he spoke to the watchman. Next, Mohammed turned to me. "I told him that you are his boss here. I told him to listen to whatever you told him because you have *wasta* now."

Maybe I was unfairly discounting the impact of the language barrier in a complex three-party translation. But that all had the ring of the way a person might convey instructions to a donkey. Inwardly, I cringed, but I patted Abu Ahmed on the back. "Then he has a boss who values him."

Mohammed nodded. "Fatima has told us to listen to you."

That sure changed my interpretation of what had just transpired. "We will wait here," he continued, "while you go and change."

On the way out of my apartment, having done just that, I stopped at Tony's. He opened the door and let out a hoot. Before the astonished Aussie stood a Clevistani Jew in traditional Bedouin dress, the two top buttons left daringly open. Tony being Tony, he wasn't flummoxed for long. "You've gone native! David of Arabia. The beard adds a great deal to the effect. You really could pass."

"Bedouin like me," was what came out of my mouth.

The one thing I knew about the Falahi's home was that Fatima called it a "family village." What that meant I was eager to find out. Was it a grand, cloistered palace—to rival the Shakboot, utterly inaccessible behind its walls? Or one of the many McPalaces rising all over Al Ain, built by Emiratis with *nouveau* wealth and *wasta*, which generally went hand in hand. Through Abu Ahmed I'd learned that Fatima's uncle, my landlord, was building a huge McPalace on the city's edge.

Mohammed careened around a residential roundabout as the SUV's tires squealed in front of a two-minaret green mosque. Had their father built it? In the Falaj Hazzah district, near Al Ain's zoo, we passed through an open metal gate. The compound was nothing like what I'd expected, though I'd been pretty unsure what to expect. Certainly no McPalace. In the center of the considerable walled space stood an older, stolid two-story villa with a long front porch, the main house, clearly. Two smaller villas sat side-by-side farther back. Along the masonry wall to the rear was an open-air carport. Under its roof I quickly inventoried two dune buggies, a Chevy Silverado, a flatbed truck, another Land Cruiser, and two Porsche Cayennes. Mohammed parked on the brick-paved courtyard near the main villa adjacent to a pair of immense doors of carved wood.

"Come with me, Doctor," Fatima directed.

I followed her onto the porch. We stepped across a room-sized green silk Persian carpet in front of a long sofa. In the sunlight from the west the rug shimmered like a finely knotted and sheared Normandy garden.

Mohammed opened the door on the right, Door #2, and I entered a dark, musty *majlis*. I guessed it was the *majlis* where the household greeted guests; the other door—Door #1—must lead somewhere else. Fatima grabbed a remote control, pointed it at air conditioners mounted high on the outside walls, and a cooling breeze began to flow. She excused herself, leaving me with her brothers.

To my knowledge, I was the only one among my Western colleagues who had set foot in an Emirati home. Beverly had given it the old college try, but Fatima had always ducked with an *insha'Allah, bukra*. It was killing me that I'd promised not to tell Dr. B. I'd been here. So what had I done to make it beyond Door #2?

The twelve-foot-high walls displayed no pictures or other adornments, which I expected. The lights remained switched off. On a wooden coffee table sat an enormous fruit basket piled high with grapes, oranges, tangerines, apples, lychee nuts, and dates. Abdulla pointed to one of many sofas ringing the large room and motioned for me to sit.

"Abdulla," I said, adjusting my *kandura*. "What do you wear under yours?"

Mohammed sat next to his larger little brother. "Doctor, what are you wearing under yours?"

Now I would bust his balls a little. "Boxer briefs," I answered, coughing. "It was that or letting my boys roam free."

"So you've seen *Seinfeld*?" Mohammed inquired. "They show it on TV here."

Abdulla let out a yelp. "Ah, you are very funny, Doctor. Fatima has told us. She has told us everything about you."

"So, Mohammed, what do *you* wear?"

He had a twinkle in his eye. "Doctor, if I told you, I'd have to kill you."

Fatima had told me Mohammed was brilliant, a UAEU sophomore majoring in chemical engineering. Abdulla was a senior in high school and even smarter. They were, in their way, a decent comedy team. Maybe not Laurel & Hardy, but they did both look like inflated Oliver Hardys, clowning in *Sons of the Desert*. OK, you'd have to be of a certain age to remember that classic 1933 film, just as you'd have to have a certain kind of humor to appreciate the slapstick.

Abdulla laughed. "Mohammed is my brother and my best friend. He is funny, yes?"

I nodded and coughed.

"There is another joke soon," said Abdulla. "You will see."

Fatima returned, wearing a bright yellow-and-green silk sari and matching headscarf. I had never seen her in any clothing that was not black. Three other women, of widely varied ages, followed her. I stood to greet them, keeping my hands at my side.

"This is my mother and sisters," Fatima beamed. "My mother is Amna and this is my older sister, Mariam, and my little sister, Sarah."

"Welcome, welcome, Doctor," Amna said. She was dressed in a colorful pastel silk sari and headscarf like her daughter. She surprised me, not just by extending her hand, but also with the flash of a Rolex on her wrist. I had been strongly warned about touching Emirati women, but I unhesitatingly took her hand. "A pleasure," I said, smiling. "You must be proud of Fatima. She is one of my best students."

Fatima glowed and spoke briefly in Arabic to her mother. "She wants me to tell you that she doesn't speak any English, but that our home is your home in Al Ain."

That certainly sounded like a genuine expression of the Bedouins' legendary hospitality. I looked at Fatima's mother, smiling with kind eyes.

"She wants me to tell you, Doctor, that she can see it in your eyes," Fatima added. "She knows a lot about you already from me, and she wanted me to tell you that she is very happy you are at our home. She also said you looked like a Saudi in your *kandura*."

"A Saudi?"

Abdulla and Mohammed laughed and slapped each other on the back. "That's the other joke," Abdulla butted in. "My brother bought you a Saudi *kandura*."

"It is funny, yes?" Mohammed asked, staring intently over the top of his glasses.

I glared back. Fatima rolled her eyes at her brothers.

"Saudis are funny?!" I asked, covering my mouth and coughing.

"Yes," Mohammed said.

"*Very* funny!" Abdulla chimed in.

I had a feeling that whatever humor the Emiratis see in the Saudis that the Saudis weren't in on the joke. I did a slow burn like Jack Benny. I stared them both down a good ten seconds. Then let out a big laugh. "*Insha'Allah,* no problem. I will be Saudi tonight." I admired my costume. "It's comfortable."

Fatima and her mother looked relieved, and I felt relief myself. Be a Saudi for a night, why not? Anything beat being a Unitarian or Presbyterian or whatever it was I pretended the rest of the time.

Amna motioned for me to sit. I returned to the sofa and Fatima stood with her sisters. "This is Mariam, my big sister." Mariam, dressed like her mother, extended her hand, and said in fine English, "We're so glad you are here. We have been waiting for this day. We know everything about you."

Everything? I said to myself. That can't be good!

A school-age girl, clad in jeans and a blouse, sidled up to Fatima. "This is my little sister, Sarah."

"She's eleven," Mariam added. "I am the oldest. Then Hilal, Sultan, Isa, Fatima, Mohammed, Abdulla and Sarah. She is very excited to meet you."

Amna carefully watched her youngest boldly offer her hand, like a girl on an American sitcom. "I love you," Sarah said. "Fatima tells us *everything.* You are her favorite teacher."

I took Sarah's small hand and pumped it three times. At that moment a slight, dark-skinned young African woman entered. She carried a tray with two white thermoses, six porcelain teacups, and a metal bowl. She placed the tray on the table beside the fruit basket. As she leaned down, I caught the flash of a gold cross hanging from a chain around her neck.

"Doctor, would you like Arabic coffee or chai tea?" Mariam asked. "Please, let us serve you."

I selected chai tea. Her mother poured the steaming liquid into a cup and handed it to me. "*Shukrun,* thank you," I told Amna.

Fatima handed Sarah a plate filled with fruit—a peeled tangerine, grapes, slices of a red apple, a few lychee nuts. She put it next to my teacup and sat on the sofa next to me.

"Try the chai tea, Doctor," Sarah implored, pointing to the black servant. "Layla just made it fresh. She is from Ethiopia. It is our family's special recipe."

I sipped the hot creamy brew, smacked my lips, and tipped the cup at Layla. She smiled.

"Drink, Doctor," Amna implored. "Eat fruit."

After one cup of tea, Hardy & Hardy excused themselves. When I finished that first cup Mariam immediately refilled it. I passed Sarah an apple slice. "Doctor, I love you," she said again, smiling like a girl with a crush. "Fatima talks only about your class."

I glanced at Fatima, who gave me a sheepish shrug. "I tell my family everything we talk about. We talk about interesting things. They have been waiting to meet you."

"Drink, Doctor," Amna reiterated. "Eat more fruit."

I peeled a lychee nut, popped it in my mouth, and made quick work of the sweet, velvety flesh. But now I had the big pit to contend with. Should have gone for the grape. Fatima looked at me, suppressing a laugh. "Just spit it out, Doctor." She pointed to a small plate. With what little dignity I could manage, I complied. I turned to Amna, and asked, "Fatima tells me that you are *fond* of camels?"

Fatima rolled her eyes—but duly translated. Amna spoke animatedly as I peeled another lychee. When she stopped, Fatima said, "Doctor, she said what I told you in class." What Fatima had said in class was that her mother would not allow her daughters to marry a man with camels because they put the camels ahead of their wife and family. "If they have a choice to be with their wife and family or with their camel, they choose the camel," Fatima reemphasized.

"I remember your telling me that," I laughed. "That's why I asked."

"My father will be home soon and he will take you to the farm where we have the racing camels," she said. "Hilal is there. We have another farm where we have more camels, Saudi sheep, and many goats. My mother and father want you to spend a weekend there with us."

The comedy duo returned, toting a box. "Doctor," Mohammed said, "this is for you."

"It's not Saudi," Abdulla noted.

Inside was a *ghutrah*. I unfurled it like a flag to reveal a white-on-white gossamer silk cloth with a light-blue stripe border framing a large field of blue cable-ringed stitching.

"Do you like it?" Abdulla asked.

"I like it very much," I said, holding the *ghutrah* over my head like a *chupah*.

Abdulla and Mohammed slapped each other on the back. Sarah grabbed hold of a corner. "I love you, Doctor."

Abdulla and Mohammed slipped away. Layla returned and spoke softly to Fatima.

"Doctor," Fatima said, "my father is waiting for you outside now. He just returned from Abu Dhabi with his new car and is ready to go to the camels. He will tie the *ghutrah* on you before you leave. My brothers are not that good at it."

Mohammed shot his sister an annoyed look. Fatima guided me quickly out of the house and onto a back porch. Layla was climbing the stairs to a kitchen outbuilding. Across the way by a white Land Cruiser stood Mohammed and Abdulla talking to a man I took to be about my age with a closely cropped beard and wire-rim eyeglasses framing a round face. He was dressed very much like a sheikh and supervising two workers securing a dune buggy to the back of the flatbed truck.

Fatima's two brothers kissed the sheikh on the crown of his head. As we approached, she took the *ghutrah* from my hand. "Father, this is Doctor David." She handed the garment to him. He bent forward and Fatima kissed him on the top of his head.

"Our father's name is Faraj," said Mohammed.

"Doctor," he said, extending his right hand, "welcome to my home. We are glad you are here. Fatima has told us *everything* about you."

There was that *everything* again. We clasped hands. Faraj moved closer and kissed me on one cheek, then the other, as I had seen Emiratis do in greeting. The kids watched, nodding their approval.

"My father will tie the *ghutrah* on you now," Fatima said. "He will do it in the traditional way."

Faraj folded the cloth several times, until it looked like an over-sized cowboy kerchief, and faced me. We stood belly-to-belly, he reached up, as I was a few inches taller, and wrapped the *ghutrah* around my head.

He tucked in one end and formed the tail of cloth hanging out the side—Emirati style.

"Your head looks like one of us now," Faraj said. "But your *kandura* is Saudi."

His sons laughed.

"That's what I have been told." My chuckle gave way to a cough.

Faraj shot them an irritated look and turned back to me. "A Saudi *kandura* has two buttons, like a Christian priest, around the neck," he said. "Next time we will get you an Emirati *kandura*."

My colleague Mohamed had told me that each nationality had its own twist on a *kandura*. In Yemen they are called *thobes*. The variations, he explained, provided a simple way to distinguish people from different countries, all wearing similar cultural uniforms. The Emirati version had a string tie.

"Doctor," Fatima said, "my father would like to go to the camels now."

In Faraj's brand-new Land Cruiser, in the obligatory white, the thick protective plastic still covering its seats, we hit the road. Faraj jigged and jagged through neighborhood streets. McPalaces, newly built or seemingly so, rose up behind pastel walls. By comparison, the Falahis' family village was not just traditional, but understated. Along the highway, Faraj pointed at other buildings, all in the trademark green, and poked his chest. "Mine… Mine… Mine."

"Yes, your color."

That seemed to please him. "True, Doctor. I pick the color. I pick the design. I decide everything. Apartments. Offices. In Al Ain. In Abu Dhabi."

Seeking, I wondered, to impress his daughter's teacher? Why would he need to?

Passing Al Ain's modern soccer stadium and then the Intercon, we were soon outside the city, going almost due east. Oman's jagged mountains rose far ahead. From Google maps, I had an idea what was out here: desert, more desert, and the long, angling fence that demarcates Abu

Dhabi from Oman. Out on the open road we sped by the national falconry research center, built to resemble a Bedouin fort, and angled south, on the road running hard by the eastern border.

"I picked up this car in Abu Dhabi today," Faraj said, pushing 180 kmph. "A diesel. Good, yes?"

I nodded, shifting in my seat and crinkling the plastic under my butt.

"Doctor, I am sorry I don't speak English well." He held out his right hand. "I speak Arabic, Pashto, Baloosh, Hindi, a little German," he said, raising a digit for each tongue. I was a bit distracted by the gold Rolex hanging from his wrist. "And a little English."

"I'm sure you're much better at languages than I am. I know a little Spanish and a little French. As for Arabic, all I know are *hammam, khallas,* and *insha'Allah,* no problem."

He roared and flicked the *ghutrah* away from his right cheek. Had my Arabic pronunciation of the words "bathroom," "enough" and, of course, "*insha'Allah,* no problem" been that off-key?

"That is all you need!" Faraj declared. "But in addition to '*insha'Allah,* no problem,' there are also '*insha'Allah*, problem' and *insha'Allah,* big problem,' and '*insha'Allah, bukra,*' the biggest problem!"

The last part I had already learned. I laughed, which brought on another coughing jag.

Faraj looked genuinely concerned. "Doctor, are you sick?"

"I have a bad throat. Many of the new professors have had it."

"It's the desert. I will fix you later."

Fix me? It's a bit disconcerting, when you're driving to a farm, to hear that you'll be "fixed."

We passed the easternmost border checkpoint. Buraimi and Al Ain were both well behind us. Oman's capital, Muscat, sat somewhere out ahead, a five-hour drive across one of the world's ruggedest landscapes. Recalling Fatima telling me her family had a villa in the coastal city of Salalah, where Oman's sultan lived, I wondered how they went back and forth.

Faraj slowed and pointed to a string of camels being exercised on the side of the road, a tender on the first in line, wielding his stick and reins, guiding the whole group. Each animal in the camelcade sported, over its hump, a blanket. And the color of the blanket? Granny-Smith green.

"Doctor, did you know the Falahi and Nahyan share the same brand for our camels? We are of one family. Zayed was my uncle. Our name, Falah, means farmer. We know camels for centuries."

We passed another string, likewise adorned in green blankets. Out of the blue Faraj said, "You have no family here. So you are now part of my family. What is your family name?"

That caught me by complete surprise. "Eden," I answered, with a cough. Was it too much to think my host would recognize the name as, most likely, Jewish?

Whatever associations Faraj made with my surname, he said simply, "Very good, we will call you 'Eden Al Falahi.' If you need anything, Doctor, you call me. You now have *wasta*. I am your brother. Fatima tells us *everything* about you. I know."

Wasta could just be handed out? Like an honorary degree or signing privileges at a country club? Was this another dose of Bedouin hospitality, graciously served up to a daughter's professor?

Two voices spoke to me simultaneously, like in that old bit from Looney Tunes. I went with the one wearing angel's wings. It said, "Why ask? Why doubt? Go with it." Had there been a way to work it in idiomatically, I'm pretty sure the voice would have added, "*Insha'Allah*."

The darker doubt kept silent.

I met Faraj's eyes. "I'm honored to be part of your family. It's not easy being a stranger in a strange land." I couldn't resist the silly sci-fi quip, and wondered whether Faraj could have run across Robert A. Heinlein. His works must be translated into one of the half-dozen tongues that had been cited.

"*Insha'Allah*, no problem," Faraj said. "Anything you need, you come to me." He paused, as if considering whether he had finished. "I do not speak left or right. I only speak straight." He tapped his index finger against his mouth and pointed forward, and then touched his heart.

That combination of gesture and pronouncement oddly put me at ease. A bold thing to say to someone you just met. Almost like some cheesy buddy-movie dialogue. In other words, Faraj was talking my language. The problem I've found is that few people lived up to the declaration for long.

"I do the same. I tell you what I think, from my heart and head. What I tell you will always be what I think is true, even if I think it is not what you want to hear or what I'm pleased to say."

After those words popped out the inner voice with horns saw fit to assert itself, asking how my being up front about my ethnic and religious identity fit into that bold claim. For good measure, the devilish voice tossed in, "And isn't saying what you think is right what always gets you into trouble?"

Faraj eased up on the accelerator. "*Insha'Allah*, no problem. We will be true friends. Fatima trusts you. She says you are different. She is the most like me."

"She is very smart."

"Yes, Doctor, I know," he said. "She has a good head for business. You will help her be smarter."

Tall grass fencing screened off large sections of desert along the flat stretch of rocky road. Faraj took out his phone, a state-of-the-art Nokia, made a call, and turned off onto a rutted track in the sand. A Bedouin opened the heavy metal gate, and I entered another new world. Through the tinted windshield I saw a dozen single-humped camels, a few tied to metal poles and near a back fence in metal holding pens a huddle of young Arabian camels of varying sizes and colors.

As we exited the Land Cruiser, I watched two Bedouins squatting by a fire in the sand, poking white-hot coals with red-hot branding irons. Two other men wearing dirty *kanduras* stood nearby. Another calmly guided a young camel toward the fire and pulled down forcefully on the rope tied around its neck. The animal howled as its front legs collapsed onto the ground, followed rapidly by its hind limbs. Two more men rushed over and tied red ropes around the camel's folded legs. I noticed blue lines drawn in marker on the immobilized camel's neck, legs and belly.

"Hamood!" Faraj shouted to one of the men overlooking the fire, and turned to me. "He is 'Dr. Hamood,' the *jemel* doctor. He is the boss of this farm, with Hilal, my oldest son, next to him."

Hamood and Hilal left the fire and greeted Faraj with kisses to each cheek. Then, like Eskimos, they touched noses. "This is Doctor David. He is now one of our family. He is your uncle. He is Falahi!"

Hilal clasped my right hand with both of his, leaned forward, I met him halfway, and we touched noses. "Fatima has told me all about you, Doctor," he said. "Do you know why we touch noses?"

Faraj had peeled off to inspect what was happening by the fire. What exactly did Fatima tell Hilal? Did everyone know everything about me? What did they really know?

"No, I do not."

He touched the tip of his nose with his right index finger. "The nose is the center of our strength. Bedouin touch noses to show our strength." I wondered whether that was the Eskimos' thinking as well.

"Doctor," Hilal continued, "do you know that you look Saudi?"

"Yes, your whole family has told me." That gave way to a coughing jag.

Faraj beckoned us to join Hamood and him near the bound camel. "They do fire now."

One of the Bedouin pulled a small, L-shaped iron from the coals, red hot, and stepped to the camel, restrained by four men holding ropes. A fifth man held a line tied around the camel's neck. Hamood pointed at two blue marks at the base of the neck. The man with the branding iron applied the hot iron to the spots. The camel kicked and howled, struggling against the ropes, but stayed down. Another hot iron was brought over, and then another, and another until the blue spots on the neck were seared and the stench of burnt hide filled the air. Faraj kept a tight grip on my arm. "Oh, this hurts me. They are my children, my family. But the fire helps them."

Hamood supervised applications of fire to blue lines on the animal's front legs, both above and below the knee. The hide sizzled and the camel lurched and howled, trying to get to its feet but flopping on the sand. Unlike horses, I recalled—something to do with their peculiar gait—camels can't buck, which may be why they bite. The fire was repeated on this camel's hind legs and other points on its body.

"Why is it they apply the fire to these spots?" I asked.

Hilal answered. "They put the fire on the neck because when the camel runs its head is down. Hamood says this will make it run with its head up."

"It has trouble breathing?" I asked, voicing a wild guess.

"Yes, yes," Faraj said, looking at me with surprise. "You understand. It has trouble breathing with its head down, so Hamood puts the fire there."

"We put the fire on the legs to help the blood flow better," Hilal continued. "If we didn't the legs could break. When we do this it helps to make the bones stronger."

Faraj said something to Hamood, then added for me, "I said that you are a *jemel* doctor like him."

"So this is how the Bedouin have kept their camels healthy for centuries?" I asked.

"For that long and longer," Hilal said. "It has always been done this way."

"How old is that camel?"

"This camel, he is two," Hilal answered. "This will make him better."

Finished with the fire, Hamood ordered the camel's front and hind legs untied. The animal rocked quickly to its feet and strutted away, as if nothing had happened. Soon it stood tied to a metal pole with three other young camels. Near them were two adults, much larger, one black and the other brown, both kneeling calmly. Hilal pointed at the largest of the animals noting that the dark one is a Saudi camel and the other is Emirati. "They are worth millions of dirham each," he noted.

"Doctor," Faraj interrupted. "Hamood asked me why you look like a Saudi."

Faraj chuckled and I looked at Hamood. "I am a Saudi-American."

"Very funny, Doctor," Hilal said. "You are Saudi-American! Every American puts something before their name. You are Native American, yes? Fatima tells us about how you joke all of the time."

As a second-generation Clevistani, I could say I was "native" American. I contented myself with answering, "My jokes are very bad."

"Hamood is from Oman and already is a grandfather at age thirty-six," Hilal offered. "He has worked with *jemels* his whole life, like his father and father's father. He also works with me at the Palace Museum as a Bedouin guard. He thinks you have a heart for the *jemels*. Now, follow me, Doctor."

Hilal took my hand and we strolled to where a majestic, light-brown camel stood tied to a pole. The beast stood eight-feet tall, with a strong, slender neck and a small-for-a-camel nose. It lowered its head when Hilal neared and he reached out to stroke its smooth neck.

"This is my love," Hilal cooed. "I come here every night to see her. I know Fatima told you that I am a lawyer of *sharia* law and have a big job as the manager of Zayed's Palace Museum. But I come to life here where the air is fresh and I can see all the stars." He petted the camel's long, muscular neck. "This is the traditional way of life. As we become part of the world, we are losing our Bedouin heritage."

Despite the solemnity of what Hilal had just said, a quiet elation came over me. After three desiccated months, the UAE was offering me what I had come for—people from whom I could learn. Well, that was a silly thought—from Noor, I learned things every day. *Emiratis* from whom I could learn. I gazed across the open space toward Faraj, in conversation with his farmhands.

Hilal continued stroking the camel's neck. "Her name is Mahasba," he said. "She is a champion, but her leg is hurt. Watch how she kisses me." He whispered to her. She lowered her head and nuzzled his cheek. "Now she will kiss you."

And that brought me to my first, and only, camel kiss.

Al Ain holds a similar esteem in racing-camel circles that Lexington, Kentucky, does among thoroughbred aficionados. Few would dispute that the Al Falahi family breeds the finest racing camels in Al Ain. I had seen plenty of ranches and farms—from the Bluegrass State to Texas—but this was utterly unexpected. An all-sand farm.

Hilal took pride in his city's heritage of champion camels. "If a camel comes in fourth, fifth, in our races in Al Ain, it will come in first in Abu Dhabi and Dubai. That is how good the camels are here."

There are 14,000 racing camels in the UAE. He described Mahasba as a champion racer, the fastest camel in Al Ain, which made her the fastest camel in the UAE, which has the fastest camels in the Middle East, and probably in the world. She was said to be worth six million dirhams—which worked out to more than a million six hundred thousand US$.

Hilal's cousin had recently paid eleven million dirhams for a male. That dromedary, a single-hump Arabian camel like Mahasba, had bettered her best time over a certain distance by three seconds, but not in a head-to-head match. The cousin could afford the beast. He was Sheikh Khalifa bin Zayed al Nahyan, first-born son of Zayed, who had succeeded his venerated father as the Emir of Abu Dhabi and President of the UAE. As a small boy, Hilal unabashedly told me, he had often sat on Zayed's knee.

Beverly had been right about the Al Falahi *wasta*. Had I not been so completely captivated by the landscape and people among who I found myself, I'd have been gloating. There'd be time for that, later.

"I have been resting Mahasba," Hilal told me. "She hurt her leg. I care about her. I do not care about winning races. She is part of our family. She will race when she is ready. Now she needs to rest."

Following Mahasba's kiss, Hilal guided me through an open gate, bypassing an empty car shed with a blue corrugated roof. Two men crouched over a short metal box and fed small chunks of scrub wood into a nascent fire. Around the corner was a single-level white-block house, a satellite dish dominating its roof. Hilal took off his sandals and I did, too, stashing them on the porch. Martial music spilled out of the open front door. Flies buzzed in and out.

Inside, we found Farah, seated in a black leather recliner. He motioned me toward the matching chair next to his. "Doctor, Professor, sit, sit. I will fix you soon."

Couches and more easy chairs ringed the walls of the *majlis*. A flat-screen hooked up to the satellite dish blared music as elite soldiers in the army of an Arab country performed extraordinary commando actions, all choreographed to the thrilling soundtrack. Ah—leading the soldiers, handsome, charismatic, in a fancy uniform bedecked with medals, was King Abdullah II of Jordan.

The screen was filled with heroic images. Invincible Jordanian Bedouin warriors in full modern battledress rappelled down cliffs, jumped out of helicopters, and shot big guns, all under the watchful eye of their sovereign. I hadn't come out here to reflect on such matters and I was the only one focused on the TV. The men around me didn't come here for war-preparedness videos. They had their own version of a cabin in the woods, only this one was in the desert and camels—not deer or ducks— were what to bond around. I couldn't picture Dr. Beverly fitting in here.

"Doctor," Faraj said, pointing to his throat. "I will fix you now." He whispered to Hilal, who disappeared and returned a moment later with a liter-sized glass bottle. Inside, at the bottom, sat a small disk of golden liquid. He handed the bottle to his father, along with a teacup and a teaspoon.

Faraj poured the thick gooey substance into the cup. "Special rare honey from Jebel Hafeet. It cost three thousand dirhams. It will fix you." He stuck the teaspoon into the half-full cup and handed it to me. He pantomimed dipping the spoon into the vessel and then licking it. I did as instructed, making a quick calculation. Assuming the bottle had been purchased full, I was consuming a good forty bucks' worth of this rare elixir.

"The mountain honey cures everything," Faraj said, assuredly.

The honey gave me a good excuse to sit back. I listened as the Bedouin chatted among themselves, understanding not a word except the frequently used *khallas* and *insha'Allah*.

"Doctor," Hilal asked, pointing to a man seated nearby. "He wants to know how old you are. He thinks you are, maybe, forty-two. Something like that."

Well, I could be King Abdullah's big brother. I smiled in the man's direction and we locked eyes. "Tell him that I thank him for making me much younger than I really am. How old are you, Hilal?"

"I am twenty-six."

"You are twenty-six and have a powerful job," I said, warmly. "That is very impressive."

Faraj beamed with pride and touched his index finger to his temple. "Hilal is very smart up here. But *insha'Allah*, big problem. He has a big job with Zayed, but he loves camels the most. He is torn."

Hilal was still intent on an answer to the other man's question. "How old are you, Doctor? Maybe forty-five. Something like that." Faraj laughed wholeheartedly. "Doctor, you are now part of the Falahi family. I am forty-seven and the oldest son in my family now. You are my brother. How old are you?"

Faraj's age surprised me. I'd gathered he was at least my age. I chocked up his weathered look to living in the desert. I licked the last of the honey off the spoon. "You are my little brother. I am fifty-six."

Hilal sat straight up. "My uncle, you do not look that old! Do you color your hair and beard?"

Noor had admitted to me that he colored his hair and beard, as did many men here. They had to—to support all those "saloons" staffed by their compatriots.

"What hair I have left, I do not color."

"Do you smoke or drink?" Faraj asked.

I shook my head and said nothing about how, almost immediately on arrival in the UAE, I had started drinking a lot for the first time in my life or about my fondness for Cuban cigars, which I'd found at what I'd coined a "sin shop" near Al Ain Mall.

He liked that answer. "Good, very good. I do not drink or smoke."

Hamood knelt on a wool rug next to the small metal firebox with white-hot coals under the carport. He pulled a chunk of dough from a metal bowl, rolled it into a small ball, and placed it on a metal tray. He ripped off another doughball and handed it to me. Faraj knelt between us. "Now you cook Bedouin bread with Hamood. This is our dinner tonight."

Hamood tore another piece of dough and rolled it rapidly between the heels of his hands, forming it into the shape of a personal-size pizza crust. I did the same. "The ingredients are simple," Faraj said, ticking them off with his fingers. "Flour, water, and plant oil. In the old days it was a meal."

Hamood leaned over the fire, blew gently on the coals lifting the gray ash revealing the hot embers. He grabbed the dough, flipped it on the heat, and motioned for me to do the same. A minute later he picked up two flat sticks laying on the carpet and flipped the bread. He gave me the sticks and I repeated the exercise. Less than a minute later he flicked both baked crusts onto a metal tray, using the sticks to scrape off any charred spots. He tore off a piece, handed it to me, and another portion to Faraj.

Faraj took the first bite. "Good. Even better with Jebel Hafeet honey."

I broke off a chunk of the hot bread and put it in my mouth.

"Good?" Faraj asked.

I nodded. "There is nothing better than hot bread or pancakes cooked on an open fire." That was punctuated with a cough.

"Doctor, you still are not fixed," Faraj moaned. "Hilal will bring more honey."

"*Insha'Allah*, no problem. I'm sure I'll feel better soon."

Faraj rose and disappeared around the corner, back toward the farmhouse. Hamood reached into the metal bowl, broke off another doughball, and handed it to me. Thirty minutes later we had stacked a round metal tray high with fresh Bedouin bread. Finally, somewhat to my surprise, we tore it all up, into small pieces. Those went into another large metal bowl.

The full moon was higher in the sky, no longer trapped between two rocky cliffs. The brisk night wind felt like a refreshing late-summer Ohio breeze. Away from the city, stars popped like pearls out of the night sky; I hunted for the Dippers and other constellations I'd learned to identify as a Boy Scout. Since my arrival in Al Ain there'd been a few ferocious cloudbursts, followed by flash flooding in the streets and *wadis*, and sandstorms that blotted out the sun. A cloud floating above was about as rare as a white buffalo. Every night was a stargazer's dream.

At the side of the farmhouse a room-size silk carpet had been placed over the sand. In the middle sat Faraj, cross-legged, two big pillows stacked behind him. More pillows were piled near the back fence, creating a bed. "Bring Doctor a chair," Faraj ordered. A moment later an armchair appeared on the carpet.

Faraj patted his knee. "Fatima told me it is not good. Problem?"

Obviously it was one piece of *everything* Fatima had told him about me.

"*Insha'Allah*, no problem," I said, taking my seat.

Hamood placed the bread bowl next to Faraj. Hilal appeared with a full bottle of Jebel Hafeet honey and handed it to his father. He sat down cross-legged between us and produced a small bottle of oil. A Bedouin carried a tray with two white thermoses; another held a tray with a metal bowl filled with water and teacups. They placed the trays near Hilal, who poured steaming liquid into a cup.

"It's chai tea," Hilal said, handing it to me.

Sipping the sweet, creamy tea I watched Faraj empty the full bottle of mountain honey onto the bread. In ancient times honey was "the food of the gods," a sign of status and wealth. Surely the bees of Jebel Hafeet have been making honey since then, and the Bedouin have been harvesting it. It occurred to me they had, from time immemorial, used it as folk medicine and mixed it with hot bread baked on an open fire under the desert stars with their *jemels*. And, obviously, they still used honey as well to measure prominence. I wondered what a liter had cost before the Emiratis had struck oil.

"This is our hospitality," Hilal said, as his father added the oil, pale amber, to the bowl. "It is part of our Bedouin culture. We like to come out here in the evening and drink tea and coffee. Sometimes that's all we do. Sometimes we barbecue meat. We talk and tell stories and look after the camels. When we have special guests, we offer them what we offer ourselves." He paused. "Do you like the tea?"

I nodded. "It's as good as the chai tea at your home."

He smiled. "It is the same. It is black tea, condensed milk, and sugar. Our special recipe."

Faraj washed his hands in a fresh bowl of water held by another Bedouin and slid them deep into the bowl kneading the bread-honey-oil concoction.

"If you want more after you finish," Hilal said, sticking his cup out, "hold it like this and you will be served another without having to ask. If you are finished and don't want more, then shake it like this."

He shook his cup from side to side, the Bedouin serving the tea took it, rinsed it in the water bowl, and placed it upside down on the tray. I held mine out straight, he took it from my hand, put it on the tray, refilled it, and handed it back.

Faraj rinsed his sticky hands in another fresh bowl of water and dried them with Kleenex. "This is our traditional dish. Before we had so much, this was our dinner." He reached into the bowl with his right hand and popped a piece the size of a donut hole in his mouth. "This was what the Bedouin ate."

He reached again into the bowl and offered me a sticky ball. I tossed it in my mouth. Hamood knelt next to Faraj, pinched off another ball, and handed it to me. Hilal declined to eat.

"I have sugar in my blood," he explained. "My family has that problem. Our country has a big problem. We have the second most diabetes in the world. Did you know?"

"So do I," I said, chewing. I had it under control—but probably not after tonight, I thought.

I finished my tea, held the cup out, and it was refilled. After serving everyone else, Hamood finally ate. A small, thin man with a graying beard, yet only thirty-six, yet already a grandfather. Hilal poured a cup of tea and handed it to Hamood. I reached into the bowl and took another chunk. The Bedouin around me ate sticky bread, drank tea and coffee, and chatted in Arabic, all sitting cross-legged on the carpet. I sat perched on my throne drinking in the moment.

Here I was in the desert with Faraj, Hilal and Hamood. In the friggin' desert, under a full moon, surrounded by camels and Bedouin! I was just so happy to be here. For the first time since I'd hit the ground in Dubai, I felt at peace. Sitting under the stars, halfway around the world from home, with a chilling breeze flowing down from the Omani mountains. In savoring the moment, and despite that breeze, I felt a rare, complete stillness. Even my coughing had stopped. Was it the insanely expensive honey? Was it that I'd met people I felt instinctively I would admire and could trust? Or just that for an hour I'd shut off all my internal chatter?

I heard Noor's soft laugh, and his answer. "No, my friend, it had nothing to do with you. It was the will of the One who directs everything." That One, he had told me, had ninety-nine names.

Faraj rose and moved to the bed of pillows near the fence. "It's cold tonight," he said, taking a shawl from atop one pillow and wrapping it around his shoulders. "You are not cold, Doctor?"

I shook my head. "I am from Northeast Ohio. I don't get cold until it's well below freezing."

"You are not coughing," he noticed. "Has the honey helped?"

I nodded and checked my watch; it was past eleven. "You fixed me. *Shukrun.*"

That pleased him. "Doctor, if you need anything you call me. In Al Ain, you have no family so we are your family. You are Falahi. Anything you need, you call me."

This time I let his gesture touch me, in the spirit in which I knew it was made. No longer did I think he was merely being ingratiating, hospitable to his daughter's professor. My aversion about being told the price of camels and honey lifted. What would I expect in a very old world so newly yanked into the one in which everything is measured in money and brand names? Hadn't everyone around the world been promised that status is something one can purchase? And who had popularized that idea?

Faraj wrapped the shawl tighter around his shoulders, reclined on the pillows, and closed his eyes to everything around, even the stars overhead. Hilal and Hamood moved next to my chair. Hamood offered me a fresh cup, filled this time with Arabic coffee.

I savored a slow, bitter sip. "At what age do camels start racing?" I asked.

"Camels used for running start before one year and stop at *hali* or *fahtal,* at seven," Hilal said.

"In the first year, they run only one kilometer or so. The furthest they race is six kilometers."

I finished the coffee, held the cup straight out, and Hamood took it. "What happens to a camel when it's done racing?"

"When it no longer races," Hilal replied, "we take it out to our other farm. Or we keep it here and use it to lead other camels like you saw on the road. Or for breeding or milk. My father told me that he wants you to spend a weekend with us at our other farm soon. We will barbecue meat then."

Faraj was dozing and I could hear his heavy breathing "Do you sell them for meat? Or eat them?"

"No," Hilal said. "Our camels, we don't sell for meat. We don't eat. You know, it's like your child. You raise it like your child. You can't eat it."

"I have read that camels can live to be fifty years old." Hamood handed me a fresh cup of coffee.

"They can live to be very old," Hilal replied. "Some twenty-five to thirty-five years old. If they have good eat, good food, good medicine, they can live a long time."

I asked Hilal how he knew if a camel was right for racing. He turned to Hamood, I sipped the coffee, listened to them talk in Arabic, and watched Faraj slumbering contentedly on the pillows as Bedouin had done for ages—before oil gave these tribes "the sugar" and a soft life. Among the things clawing at me since my arrival was seeing a country consumed by Western materialism. The government had even started a campaign to save the national heritage, called "Emiratization," but many thought it was already too late. The number-one activity in the UAE, the media proudly reported, was shopping. Number two: eating in food courts. Only a small Pacific island had more diabetes per capita than the UAE. The natives were eating themselves to death, largely on fast food. Quick affluence only fueled the epidemic. It was like giving whiskey to American Indians.

Hilal preferred hanging out in the desert with the camels. But his conflict between doing that and his job in the city could only end one way. The past was the past. Camels were no longer a way of life, just an expensive hobby.

A stiff breeze stirred the air and Faraj pulled the shawl tighter.

"Hamood said," Hilal broke in, interrupting my thoughts, "that there are two things: the first is that the mother is a winner or the father is a winner. Or the grandmother is a winner or the grandfather is a winner. If the mother or the father, or the grandmother or grandfather, is a winner, that is the first thing."

"So it's just like they do with racehorses. It's breeding."

"Yes," Hilal answered. "The first is breeding. We have a book with all of it. It goes back a long way." He said a few words to Hamood, who nodded. "Hamood agrees it is like with racehorses. The second is if the baby camel gets more milk from its mother. Sometimes that makes it a winner. But a racing camel does not give much milk. A camel with big… big…"

"Udders?" I asked. "Underneath its belly like on a cow?"

"Yes, with big ones they do not race well. With small ones it races better."

"So males are better racers?"

"No, Mahasba is a champion. Male is not better. The same."

I asked what else?

"If the foot is small and a circle, it is good for racing and they run faster. A bigger foot is not good; they run slower. If its nose is big, no good for racing. No big noses. If it has a small nose, short and beautiful mouth, soft and beautiful hair… if the coat is brown and white, or brown and brown… it is good for racing. Like Mahasba. Dark camels are not for racing, only for milk."

"You mean Saudi camels?"

"Yes," said Hilal. "Only for milk or other work, not for racing. It is rare."

He turned to Hamood and they chatted. My bladder was ready to burst. The other men had melted away and it was now just us. "Hamood wants to know if you have another question," Hilal said.

The natural, or at least predictable, follow-up questions passed through my mind. "How long has Hamood been a *jemel* doctor?"

"He has always been a *jemel* doctor," Hilal said. "His father taught him. And his father's father taught his father. It is like that as far back as anyone can remember. He is teaching his son now. As a boy he rode camels for Sheikh Mubarak and won big races. These races were not around tracks like today."

Hilal related that beginning at age five Hamood rode camels in cross-country races for Sheikh Mubarak. If you fell off the camel, or if you didn't steer your camel the right way, it could run into a tree and the jockey could be injured or killed. He added that Sheikh Mubarak made a lot of money selling winning camels Hamood rode.

"Today, everything is different," Hilal said. "We don't have boy jockeys any more. Now we have robots we glue onto the back of the camel with super glue. We make them from power drills we buy at Ace Hardware, and we use a remote control. We follow the camels around the racetrack in our Land Cruisers with the remote control and talk to them through a microphone as they race. In the old days, with a jockey it used to take fifteen days to teach a camel to race. Now, with a robot, it takes only three."

"Only three days?"

"Young camels learn fast. We have to teach it what to eat and not eat, and the right ways to do things. We tie it to a post for three days so it understands it needs to listen to us. They are very smart."

"Fatima has told you about Noor?" I asked.

"She tells us everything," Hilal replied.

"He told me a story that if you hurt a camel it will wait for the right moment to exact its revenge, and maybe kill or injure you. He said camels never forget a good deed or bad."

"He is right. If you harm a camel, it never forgets. Like an elephant. And if you are kind to a camel, it will always be your friend. "

"Like Mahasba."

"Yes, like Mahasba. The Falahi keep the best camels for our family. The others we sell to other sheikhs for three, four, ten million dirhams. That is how much racing camels cost. We have about six hundred camels. You will see for yourself."

"Now I see why your mother doesn't want your sisters to marry a man with camels."

"Yes," Hilal said, "she knows Bedouin men would rather be in the desert with the camels than in the city with their families. This is my love. My father and I are always here."

"Yes, Fatima has told me," I said, standing up. "I think it's time for me to go home."

Hilal pushed up from the carpet. "I will drive you. My father will sleep here tonight."

Abu Ahmed watched the white Hummer pull to a stop near my entry. It was after one in the morning when Hilal dropped me off, and it was Abu Ahmed's job to observe, and sometimes to report. I'm sure the Egyptian watchman was more than curious about when his "new boss" would return and who would deliver me. I waved to him as I opened the vehicle's door

On the drive back to Al Ain, as the city's lights sped toward us, Hilal confided that he intended to never marry. "Uncle, I don't ever want to. I like to be with the camels too much. I like the old ways. I love my job at the Palace Museum, but I love the desert more."

He had stopped me at "uncle." He had used it earlier that night, but in front of his father. He said it in such a natural, familial way that he reminded me of my nephew, Ethan. Faraj had pronounced me "family" and his eldest son immediately took it to heart. Is that how it worked here? That Hilal was so open, honest and accepting pushed that darker voice deeper into the recesses of my mind. Tonight had been about being open and accepting and, I must admit, about opening the mental walls I lived within and letting *insha'Allah* guide the way. The evening I'd just relished—one I would surely remember forever—I owed as much to Noor's teachings as to Fatima's and her family's generosity.

Something had happened to me—or between Hilal and me—on the drive. I felt for him, hearing what he'd just said, knowing he was straddling two worlds. The old Bedouin traditions he professed to love, endangered by the sinkhole of oil wealth and its numbing effect on his people. I was trapped between two worlds myself, but didn't face Hilal's dilemma. Mine was something far different.

Inside my apartment, I peeled off my Saudi *kandura,* tossed it over the chair in my bedroom, and looked out my open window at the lights of the Shakboot Palace. My cough had ceased and I wondered if the cure really had been the Jebel Hafeet honey. Why not? Was it the magic of the sacred mountain honey that had made me feel for the first time in the UAE that maybe, just maybe, a little bit of *insha'Allah* living—for once in my life—would do me good, too?

CHAPTER 17

The Family Farm

A WEEK AFTER AN UNPLANNED THANKSGIVING FORTH-AND-back to Ohio— the reason being emergency surgery for my mother, not the holiday— I sat at the Falahi's long wooden dinner table, after being admitted through Door #1. They wanted to host me sooner but I'd slipped away from UAEU for a week, unnoticed and without the permission of the administration. There were no university rules for family medical emergencies back in the U.S., so I followed Rule Number One. I cancelled classes and left. I'd done the yo-yo routine before, but never on so long a string. But nobody at UAEU seemed to miss me.

The Falahi's fussed over me like I was nobility. It made me a bit uncomfortable, but I understood. That evening produced an invitation to overnight at the family farm—a place distinct from the racing-camel farm—the following weekend.

Where that farm was located, I never in fact learned, though I visited it repeatedly. All I know is that it's somewhere in the middle of the red sand dunes along the Abu Dhabi Road, and nothing like any farm I've seen elsewhere. When I was little, our family lived on the last road on the edge of a small Ohio town, and my brother and I often played in the high cornfields and woods behind our house. This farm was nothing like that.

As the camel facility had led me to expect, it was a farm of sand. There was no farmhouse as such. There were two single-story block buildings fronted by a patio of brick pavers. Behind sat a kitchen outbuilding. Down the way was a fenced-in barnyard filled with flocks of goats and Saudi sheep. Behind the block buildings spread irrigated vegetable fields covered with plastic sheeting. Tomatoes, cukes and various greens popped right out of the desert. I had heard Emiratis boast that, with enough water, Al Ain's red sand could grow anything. Apparently, even in the early winter.

That chilly winter night we barbecued. Kebobs of chicken and lamb sizzled on three small grills. The family sat on a carpet spread on the slab. I was put, in deference to my knee, at a small table again in an armchair. A platter with more than a bit of everything was placed before me. Amna, with no less authority than my Jewish grandmother, directed me mono-syllabically to "Eat!" It made me laugh. After dinner Faraj asked the young Yemeni expat who worked the farm to sing. He asked me to dance with him and I did, in my way, like Chubby Checker. That made the family laugh. "Doctor, you're a lot funnier than we are," Mohammed and Abdulla chimed in.

Faraj peeled off in the dark and returned in a dune buggy. "Now we will see the *jemels*," he said from the driver's seat. Under the dim light of the crescent moon he aimed the headlights into the dunes and sped off. Guided by genetic Bedouin radar, he seemed to float above the sand. I held onto the roll bar to keep from being bounced out. I sensed he was laying the groundwork for a conversation.

After ten minutes—which takes you a long way in the desert when you're doing upward of 100 kmph—I spotted the outlines of a fence. From the dim moonlight emerged another block structure with a corrugated roof, a water trough… and more camels than I could count.

A lone attendant appeared, a ghost in the headlights, waving. Faraj remarked that he had lived out here tending hundreds of camels for years, residing in a cement-block hut with a metal roof, open windows, no electricity or running water.

"Now we continue your education about *jemels*," Faraj said. "He will show you how to milk."

I didn't drink camel milk that night. I'd heard too many stories from those who had about "stomach problems." I knew how to milk a cow, but wouldn't think of drinking raw cow's milk.

We parked near an open-air shed with a corrugated roof. Nearby stood a female camel, tied to a pole. Faraj handed me a metal bowl and I hopped out of the buggy. From a pen the Bedouin pulled out a baby *jemel* and led its mother. He let the infant suckle briefly at its mother's teats, then pushed it away. He motioned for me to hold the bowl beneath the teats as he yanked and pulled, extracting the frothy milk. When the bowl was nearly full, I took it to Faraj sitting in the dune buggy. He produced a funnel and an empty plastic liter water bottle. I poured in the raw milk, watching it foam up.

On the ride back Faraj grinned from ear to ear. Approaching the farmhouse, he turned to me. "Doctor, I need you to help me make a plan." I nodded. Where was this going? "For my children. You are their uncle now. I am concerned about their future." Another nod. "Later, we can talk about this."

He hadn't asked for a response, but I gave one nonetheless. "*Insha'Allah*, no problem."

After we returned to the farmhouse, we sat in the family *majlis*, admiring Russell Crowe's gladiatorial prowess. I mentioned that my son would be visiting over his school holiday. Faraj immediately announced that we would all return to the farm for Christmas. He would host a party for us.

This was a generous, gracious gesture. The kind I had long ceased questioning, and even took somewhat for granted. The Falahis embody, effortlessly, the desert hospitality we've all heard about.

But there I was again, in a staring contest with the increasingly tedious dilemma. An invitation to celebrate Christmas presupposed that my son and I were Christians. How should a Jew, albeit a non-practicing one, who always bristled at Christmas trees put up in fellow Jews' homes, respond to the invite, let alone when his new Emirati family wished him "Merry Christmas"?

I had a little more than two weeks to come up with an answer, and it had to work for Max as well as for me. What was more, I had not a clue about the sort of "plan" Faraj wanted me to devise for his children. He hadn't mentioned it again during that first stay at the farm.

CHAPTER 18

"We call it Palestine here"

THE PENULTIMATE SESSION OF *WRITING FOR MEDIA* BEFORE I was due to stand in as a Christian at some camel-draped nativity scene in a genuine desert, Noura arrived before the other students toting her portfolio. She laid it on the desk, unzipped it, and pulled out a stack of drawings. On top was a caricature of an old, weathered Arab man wearily climbing a ladder that reached into the sky. The ladder had several broken and missing rungs. The cartoon was more than timely. Things had been bad in Gaza, but now looked ready to explode into out-and-out war as missiles rained down on Israel. What would the Jews do?

Mariam arrived followed by Latifa, Rhouda and Hessa. Sendeya and Reem entered, followed closely by Samah, dressed in that pink sheyla and floral pink blouse.

Hessa asked, "Doctor, is this the day we are going to talk about politics?"

"Are we?" the Girl in Pink inquired.

The week before, Samah had given her graduating class's valedictory address. Not one for graduations, including my own, I had been shopping in Dubai with Tony and missed it. That irritated her. She wanted me there to hear how she made fun of my butchery of Arabic.

Mariam helped change the topic. "Noura wants your help with these like with the other one."

I welcomed the opportunity to redeem myself; my failure over "The Symphony of War" cartoon gnawed at me. This time I planned to do better and the first drawing on the stack showed promise. Moreover, I'd said all I had to say in the class, most of it more than once.

"Yes, Hessa. Today we will talk a little about politics." I pointed to Noura's drawing.

The Arab on the broken ladder, sandaled feet planted firmly on the bottom rung, reaches up grasping two rungs above his head. But the next foothold is missing. How does he climb? Does he have the strength to pull himself up? He's on a Zeppelin-esque stairway to heaven, a Jacob's ladder, but this climb is fraught with missteps; there's no clear path to paradise. He's an Arab Sisyphus pushing an immovable rock. Finally, with the semester nearing its end, these students had the opportunity to engage me on the 800-pound gorilla in the Middle East. Hell, I felt as if I were the gorilla myself.

"I like the simplicity of this," I said. "It has a powerful message and is very good."

Samah translated and Noura beamed. "She said that the Arabs can't seem to find a path to peace, because steps are missing."

"What do you think?" I wanted to hear her thoughts. If this discussion was to go anywhere, I had to persuade Samah to buy in and help direct it.

"I think she's right," Samah said. "The Arabs cannot climb out of their hole."

I looked around the group. "Is anyone here optimistic about peace in Israel?"

Samah, Mariam and Latifa went around the horn in Arabic. Noura said something to Latifa. Mariam said something to Samah. I watched, not understanding a word. They shook their heads.

"To answer your question, Professor Eden," Samah said, "no. And it's *Palestine*."

My inner radar perked up. "None of you are optimistic about peace in Israel?" I should have known better than to ask after "All Jews Are Evil." But I hoped this group was different.

"We call it *Palestine* here, Professor Eden," Samah reiterated, "and, no, we are not."

She'd caught me. At that instant I saw something in Samah's eyes that I had missed before—not so much defiance, which was in her tone of voice, but despair. Why? She was from Abu Dhabi and had spent her whole life, most probably a privileged one, in the safety and prosperity of the Emirates. Yet she said "Palestine" with a bitter resolve I hadn't expected. That sent up a red flare.

"OK," I said, calmly. "So now we each know what the other's referring to."

In the pause that followed we locked eyes. Of course she was right, but I couldn't bring myself to say so. Say I also believe the Arabs and Jews *could* reconcile their differences—but won't? That the fanatics and politicians on both sides will never let it happen? That the children of Abraham can't live under the same tent? They will war forevermore? That would be a bomb of utter pessimism I didn't want to drop. It wasn't my place, I told myself, to inject my despair about the future of the Middle East—all the more so because they had just expressed their own. This was not going as I had pep-talked myself it would. In a way I was blindsided, but I knew, one way or another, what had been coming.

I blinked first. "What should we call Noura's drawing?"

Mariam jumped in. "How about 'The Ladder to Peace'?"

We settled on "Path to Peace" because there is always a path, even if the ladder is broken. Noura proclaimed that she'd earn another "A."

OK, right. As I struggled to push through my hesitation about discussing Mideast politics, what mattered most to Noura was getting an "A." Here was a student who had a rare gift for editorial cartooning and she couldn't appreciate her own raw talent. The next drawing featured a large caricature of Uncle Sam wearing his tall stovepipe hat standing on a rocky shoreline tugging an anchor attached to a listing ship with Arabic writing on its hull.

"What does the writing say?"

"It says, 'The world's economy,'" Latifa translated.

Looking at Noura. "So you are saying that America has ruined the world's economy?"

She nodded. She had a good point.

"You're probably right."

Hessa looked hopeful. "Maybe Obama can fix it."

The theme-*du-jour* was "hope and change," and many students here felt like Hessa. "He isn't president for another month. One man can't do everything."

Samah picked up the ball. "Professor Eden, you have to admit that George Bush and America have really messed things up."

The subsequent drawing sent chills down my spine. It was a body of a man with a globe for a head holding the leash of a small, snarling dog. The dog's head is turned and it sneers contemptuously back at the man with the leash. On the dog's body is a Star of David.

I held the drawing to eye level, blocking my face and not saying a word. I had seen my share of images of the Jewish dog or the Jewish rat. A deep resentment welled up and I fought to keep a poker face. I placed the drawing on the desk and said nothing. The dog is not, to these young women, the Jews, per se. It is Israel—the nation, not the people—even though Jews are complicit.

Samah broke the silence. "So, Professor? What do you think?"

Hessa's turn. "Yes, Doctor, we want to know what you think of this."

I thought, *"No, you really don't."*

But they did, and insisted. I stuck to the professor's response, avoiding the Jew's. "I can see this two ways. First, the world is trying to keep Israel on a leash, holding on, maybe pulling back. Or the dog, Israel, is leading and controls the world."

"Yes, yes," Noura said, joyfully. "Both."

Samah again. "Professor Eden, I think she means that the Jews control the world and that the world is trying to hold them back."

Hadn't seen this coming. "So the Jews control the world?" I let uncertainty inflect the question.

Samah had no doubt. "Yes, they control the media, the banks, business."

At that moment, again, I felt like I did in that *Intro* class. Though Samah wasn't asserting that *all* Jews are evil, simply that the Jews constitute a conspiracy of some sort. "I've heard that, often," I noted. "It's been said by many people. Does that make it true?"

Samah was too smart to fall into that trap. She believed it was true, and—yes, logically—that really had nothing to do with how many people asserted it. She voiced this with a look, one that said, *"You and I know what we're talking about."*

I asked her to translate to Noura for me. "First, there are only about fourteen million Jews in the world. How does one minority of fourteen million people control the world? Doesn't that seem unlikely? That the Jews exercise a coordinated malevolent global power? Rupert Murdoch is one of the people who control the media, and he isn't Jewish." I wanted to get to the point that there was something *tautological* in this whole Jews-control-X thing. But *tautological* was a word few of my students in the U.S. would have known. I needed a different tack. "Do minorities—and for that matter, majorities—have fair or proportionate influence in media, government, business? Some do, some don't. Do the Jews have more influence than others?"

Samah nodded, seeing I was getting what she meant.

"Yes, more than some minorities, for sure. But more than the British on their tiny little island? The Vatican? The Saudis with their oil?" I asked.

No one answered. I wanted to underscore it with, *"So, it's more complicated, this question?"* But my objective here was, first and foremost, to encourage these students to think for themselves.

"Now, talking not as teacher but as an editor." I returned to Noura's cartoon. "I can disagree with you and with what you have drawn, but still support you in putting forward your view." Seeing how troubled the cartoonist looked, I smiled at her. "As well as appreciate your craft." Back to the group. "An editor doesn't always agree with all of his writers', or cartoonists', opinions, but that doesn't mean he won't print them, as long as they hold together. Opinion, however, is different from news, which is at least theoretically anchored in fact. There are no facts to back up the notion that the Jews 'control the world.' That's simplistic." Now a slight turn toward Samah. "I think you know that."

Time to get focused on the cartoon. "Noura, you are talented and courageous. In the society I grew up in, expressing opinions is generally pretty easy. Not so here. While I disagree with your point of view, because to me it's about the *Jewish* dog, I believe I understand why you hold it."

I was looking at Noura, but knew the reply would most likely come from Samah. Waiting, I asked myself whether I did in fact understand, as I'd asserted. Because Noura had heard this notion voiced all her life? Because it was The Big Lie? Or because, yes, we Jews are pretty disproportionately represented in the corridors of finance, entertainment, business and news? Were I an Arab, would I also think the Israelis' and Jews' greater power in such spheres was unfair and aimed at keeping me down? Samah had essentially questioned the very idea of an "Arab people"—there are Arabs with oil, and Arabs without. Mohamed of Yemen had said the same. So had Tony, a former oilman.

I went back to Noura's drawings. The last in the set shot off rockets. Two small boys faced each other, one holding an Israeli flag, the other a Palestinian flag. The English headline: "Once Upon a Time in Rafah." The speech bubble above the Israeli: "My father told me that YOU Arabs are evil terrorist animals." The bubble above the Palestinian: "My father told me nothing. He was murdered by yours."

I said nothing. No one said anything. But all eyes fixed on me. And I wasn't smiling. Suddenly, this wasn't about teaching journalism or editorial cartoons. How much farther would I have to push to give one of these young women the motivation to ask the obvious question?

In a simple image with few words Noura had captured the anguish and hatred of another lost Palestinian-Israeli generation. The cartoon moved and disturbed me. This time, the two voices spoke in unison. Samah was right. There was no hope. There is no hope. I resisted. "This is very powerful. It expresses your point of view clearly." Samah translated without being asked. "I see the irony. But I have to say, Noura, I disagree with your politics."

I asked the students to take their seats. We'd been standing around the desk nearly the entire class. I sat on the front edge of my desk. There were only a few minutes left. I took a deep breath and steadied my eyes on Samah. "I believe that both sides, Israelis and Palestinians, kill each other needlessly. It has to stop. Noura, in your drawing you say Israelis murder Palestinians. But many Israelis say Palestinians murder them. Where's the truth?"

Samah erupted. "Which side kills more?!"

"Both sides kill too many!"

"So, you don't think that the Israelis kill more!?" The pink of her *sheyla* highlighted the shade of red her face had turned.

"Both sides kill too many!!"

It was then I knew that Samah wasn't going to let that go, and good for her. She was the reporter at the press conference, and I was the spin master for the contrasting point of view.

"So do you agree that the Israelis have killed more?!"

Mariam and Hessa squirmed uneasily in their seats. Latifa watched respectfully.

"Anyone can find facts that will support their opinion," I replied. "But what is behind the facts? One fact is that there has been too much killing for too long."

Samah was seething. "How would you feel if someone took your land, ripped out your olive trees, and destroyed your homes?!"

I said something about how it wasn't that simple. But what was Samah getting at? A knowing look flashed across her face. "Where is your family from?!"

And she'd done it. Since our earlier near head-to-head, I'd figured she knew, or had a good inkling. I had repeatedly said that they should feel free to ask me any question without reservation or fear. Would she be the first Muslim in the UAE, in all these months, just to come right out and ask? I'd have to see, but first I had to answer her question.

The answer Samah expected to hear was Eastern Europe, which was one right answer. My father's parents traveled to the U.S. from Russia and Germany in the early 1900s arriving at Ellis Island. They would not have left what they considered their homeland had it not been for the pogroms. At 15, my mother's father, Benjamin Plotkin, the unwanted son of a *shochet*, a ritual slaughterer of cattle and fowl, followed the railroad tracks from his home of Klentzi, Ukraine, to Hamburg, with the $25 he needed to board a ship. He landed at Ellis Island, too. He worked as a New York subway conductor and farm laborer, served as a doughboy in World War I, and was a WPA laborer before ending up in Youngstown with a small candy store, and then Cleveland. My mother's mother hailed from Minsk, one of six offspring of a tailor, all of whom immigrated to America. Samah was pretty sure that the descendants of these bedraggled immigrants and many like them somehow "controlled the world."

My parents were the first from their families to graduate high school. Both served during World II and attended college under the G.I. Bill. Otherwise they could not have afforded it. My father became a chemical engineer and finished two years of night law school. My mother, widowed with four young children at 36, had a degree in nursing and supported us by teaching others how to be a nurse. Like my family, I'm from Ohio, USA, and a variety of other places. All I offered was, "My grandparents came to America one hundred years ago from Russia. I am a second-generation American."

At "Russia," her eyebrows rose. "My family is *from* Palestine. I *am* Palestinian. It was *our* home forever." That statement should not have taken me by surprise. She had reacted passionately the first time Noura brought a sketch to class. Had I been that blind? Or, better to ask, had I been willfully that blind?

"You are from Palestine? But you told us that you are from Abu Dhabi."

"I was born in Abu Dhabi, and have lived there my whole life," she replied. "But I am not *from* Abu Dhabi. I am *Palestinian*. We have family there still. Have you been? Have you seen what it is like?"

"Once. A few years after the first *Intifada*. Things were better then." On a "mission" sponsored by an Israeli investment group. The mission's hosts took us everywhere, except everywhere they didn't want us to go. I met Ehud Olmert when he was mayor of Jerusalem, before he became prime minister, and Uzi Narkiss, the Israeli general who had led the troops into East Jerusalem and captured it during the '67 War. To us, a liberation.

I tried meeting her halfway. "I have been to Israel, not Palestine." I paused. "I've been to Tel Aviv, Jerusalem, Haifa, and Ashdod." That got her attention. "I've also been to the West Bank, Bethlehem, Hebron and Jericho. And to all the tourist destinations. Masada, the Dead Sea and to Petra."

"Have you been to Gaza?" I felt the heat of her X-ray vision.

"No. The closest was Ashdod. Lots of Russian immigrants."

A despondent look emanated from her eyes. "I've never been to Palestine, but most of my family is still there. Gaza is my home and I want to live there someday, but we can't go. We're not allowed."

Gaza as it is had never made sense to me—a gaping wound in the side of Israel that threatened to destroy the patient. Still, I couldn't see how combining it with the land-locked West Bank, with only a secure highway or tunnel connecting them through Israel could create one unified Palestinian state. All of the maps being bandied about as solutions seemed like complete delusions created by kindergartners posing as politicians who could care less about reality on the ground. This wasn't a case of the Lower and Upper Peninsulas of Michigan. A Palestinian state in two slices, Israel sandwiched between like pickled tongue? No Mackinac Bridge could overcome that divide. And then there is Hamas and Egypt.

I heard commotion out in the corridor. Thankfully, the class period was over. I was ready to deal with Christmas, as ready as I'd ever be. But there was one more thing I needed to say to Samah. "I believe that you will be able to live there someday." When I concluded I felt suddenly like a heel.

She scowled. "I don't think I ever will!"

"It's not as bad as you think." As if I could ever know what she thought. Maybe I would have the chance someday, but this was not that day. "I believe by the time you are thirty that you will be able to live in Palestine." I'd said it—Palestine. Didn't kill me. "I believe that with a new president there will be new hope for peace in Israel and Palestine, and that there will be two countries living side-by-side."

She showed no hesitation or lack of emotion. "I don't think Obama will make any difference!!"

I truly wished that Obama could make a difference. That anything could make a difference. Wishing and believing aren't the same. Hope? Only if you believe in *insha'Allah*, and try as I might, I didn't. But I still wanted to believe in *Something*, if not *Someone*.

Samah echoed my desperate thought. "*Insha'Allah*. But I don't think it will happen." She took a deep breath. "It won't happen until the end."

I was taken aback. "Do you mean 'The End of Days?' The Apocalypse?"

"Yes. Then. Only then."

At last, I had something I could say without being a gross hypocrite. "I believe it will happen well before the end of time."

I told the students that I would see them the following week, to hand out the final exam.

Samah exited the classroom silently.

"Merry Christmas," said Hessa as she left.

I doubt that even in my own college years I'd ever so longed for a semester's end. And yet wished I could have a "do over." Correct some of my errors. Not repeat the same mistakes.

CHAPTER 19

Wittgenstein

RELIEF, AND PERSPECTIVE, ARRIVED JUST BEFORE CHRISTMAS in the form of Max. When my son emerged from Passport Control in the newly opened Emirates Airlines Terminal 3, Noor greeted him like long-lost family. I wanted to introduce Max to the world I now inhabited, for how long I didn't know, maybe even open his eyes to the world a bit more, as the blinders on my own were being shed.

On Max's second evening Fatima arranged for him to spend it with her brother, Mohammed, who was the same age. The report I got afterward was that they ended up in the café at the hotel on Jebel Hafeet where locals and tourists toke away on hookahs filled with *shisha*, a fruit-flavored tobacco.

Max returned a bit shaken. I took that at first for a symptom of jet lag and his end-of-semester fatigue. Not of *shisha*, as he said he hadn't smoked any. But he was soon relating the conversation—at moments, confrontation—that had ensued up on the Emirate's sacred mountaintop and during the white-knuckle drive down. He confirmed Faraj's worst fears to me about Mohammed's driving.

"I thought we'd go over the edge of the road in his Cayenne and crash at the bottom."

I had to pick myself up off the floor when Max told me Mohammed was "one of the five most intellectual people my age" he'd ever met." This from a Yale man!? Was Hardy #1 of the Hardy & Hardy comedy team an intellectual? In the course of the evening, Max and Mo had discussed subjects ranging from Sun Tzu and the virtues of the "Five Tiger Generals" of the Shu army, to the ethos of the Persian Immortals. Even homosexuality in ancient Greek military culture. "We almost came to blows over that. He didn't believe the Theban Sacred Band were one-hundred-fifty pairs of homosexual lover-warriors."

That blind spot in Mohammed's learning didn't greatly surprise either of us. Nor did his alternative understanding of the Pope, Catholics and Protestants—it was similar to the grasp expressed by many of my students, who had never heard of Martin Luther. What had provoked the heat was Mohammed's reaction to Max's take on *jihad*. Mo had protested angrily that *jihad* is not political. That argument had been put forward with such vehemence that he nearly drove them over the edge.

"He quoted Wittgenstein!" Max said, with a mix of wonder and chagrin. "Fucking *Witt*genstein."

"OK, so, *jihad*'s not political. Then what is it?"

"Under Mo's definition, I said the Iraq War could be called an attempt at democratic *jihad*."

"And Mo flipped out?"

"By throwing Wittgenstein in my face. 'Whereof one cannot speak, thereof one must be silent!!' In case I was too dense, he paraphrased it: 'Shut up'!!!"

All this was amusing on one level, disturbing on others. I tried to react on neither, but just sat back and let my son give me a lesson in Mohammed Falahi 101. Possibly the most fascinating *Intro* course so far. Most of it I'd heard from my students. *Bush is an idiot and puppet. Others pulled his strings. Obama won't be any different. The same people who controlled Bush control him.*

So far, all PowerPoint.

"'Never draw a line connecting *jihad* with politics,'" Max quoted. "'*Jihad* and history is okay, I guess. But never connect it with politics. It's religious. Not political. Don't mix the two.'"

This was among the most helpful information I'd gotten all year, certainly the most illuminating from a native Emirati. Mohammed—who, in his way, is representative of the best educated and thinking among the young people I was trying to get to know—was saying "Religion. Politics. Between them, a firewall." I knew he was sincere, but all I could see in the world around me was religion and politics so completely bound together, stirred up in one pot, there was no distinction at all. Which, in fact, might prompt Mohammed Falahi to exclaim, "Exactly!"

Still I wanted to holler, "Oh, come on, Mohammed! There's not even a *principle* of separation of church and state—in your country's politics, or its faith!" But Max was doing the talking, and channeling my internal interlocutor. I kept quiet.

"Here's the part that blew me away. When he was angry, really beside himself, he said, 'We are a people. We are not nation-states.' Then he pointed at me and said, 'You'—meaning, I think, the West—'made us into nation-states, and we've been sick ever since because of it. That, if you truly want to know, is why this region has so many troubles. We are a people. We are not nation-states.'"

Why would Mohammed choose to lecture Max, of all people, about this? Was he indirectly lecturing me, his elder? Was the real message, "We are not a tourist attraction?" Or was Mo drawing a line between himself and his family's new "Christian" friends?

On two counts, Mohammed had a point, and had given me some things to think about. Clearly, Max had reacted the same. But on top of that, I realized how much smarter my son is, in various ways, than me. Maybe it's generational smarts. I could not have this talk with Mohammed or get into all that in-depth discussion about such matters without having to dodge the "J" question.

I looked at Max. *Wittgenstein*!? I would have said I was impressed, and proud of him, but he knew that. I'm sure my face said what I was thinking: I can learn a lot from this kid. He was pushing the envelope, and we hadn't even been called on to sing "Away in a Manger" for the Falahis yet.

Thank *Whomever* that he was here to help me navigate my First Noël, on a Muslim family's farm, no less. It sounded like a Currier & Ives print, with sand in place of snow. Max was excited about it, and that was enough to get me through. We discussed the incongruity of spending Christmas in the desert with a Muslim family, the hosts thinking the guests were garden-variety USA Christians. The "JQ" was gonna be there, hovering.

Was it possible Mohammed had a notion of that, and his suspicion I'd been less than forthcoming was coming out in his harangue to Max? My wise son posed the follow-up question I was avoiding. "What happens when—not if—they wish us 'Merry Christmas!'?"

I probably looked at the floor.

"Do we tell them?"

Only if "Merry Christmas!" came at the right time for that revelation. And my gut told me that those moments were not going to coincide. When that time would come was not just still problematic, it was increasingly problematic. The revelation couldn't be plunked down as a "Surprise!" for those hosting us for what they took to be the big family holiday on our religious calendar. That wasn't kosher.

Max's feeling was the same—or at least he let me think that. We'd play it by ear.

And meanwhile, though we'd go to the farm in two days, on Christmas Eve, we weren't there yet.

CHAPTER 20

A Christmas Miracle

TO BELIEVERS, CHRISTMAS IS A SEASON OF MIRACLES. I'M NOT a believer, but Christmas with the Falahis nearly changed my mind—that miracles do happen.

A lot of American Jews, while not believers, celebrate Christmas. I've heard a variety of explanations. So the kids feel as if they "fit in." In *what* do they "fit" is never made clear. Some Jews celebrate *both* Christmas and Chanukah. They're double dippers as well as red-white-and-blue fitter-inners. I was brought up on the idea—it was a more innocent era—that conformity for the sake of conforming was what being American *wasn't* about. Then there's the simple fact that the Jewish "tradition" of dining on Christmas Eve at a Chinese restaurant and catching a movie is a tired cliché.

That wasn't, back in the Sixties, something we did. As for our own calendar, we were something of a "Chanukah-shmanukah" family. There wasn't much discretionary money so it was never the "Christmas that goes on for eight days" you might hear about today. The extended family got together on the first night, the kids each got a silver dollar as *gelt*. The other nights saw the Menorah candles lit and chocolate coins. My brother, a coin collector, was the only one who cherished the silver dollars. I traded mine to him for a paper buck, and snuck his chocolate *gelt*.

Fatima, Mariam and Sarah rushed out of the kitchen outbuilding as Sultan, our evening's chauffeur, pulled up to the farmhouse in his new white Hummer with plastic on the seats. In the twilight, the Yemeni farm-hand tended three fires in low metal boxes feeding in small bits of scrub wood. Amna, too, emerged from the kitchen and waved.

What sticks most vividly in my recollection of that arrival was how quickly the family drew Max in, and how naturally he flowed into their embrace. Mariam took a fast liking to him. Something clicked right away. Sarah, of course, told Max that she loved him. Fatima was more cautious. She watched me watch him interact with her siblings and parents. They escorted us into the main house and saw to it that our bags got deposited in the boys' bedroom—a dorm with nine queen-size beds and a bathroom. That's where we'd sleep along with other male family members staying over. The girls had their own dorm. Both adjoined the *majlis*, as did the bedroom reserved for Faraj and Amna.

Faraj, I was informed, was "visiting the camels" and Mohammed and Abdulla had disappeared down the road in the other dune buggy, no doubt off to comic exploits. I broke off briefly and made my way to the top of a nearby red dune. All I could see were more dunes rolling in waves off into the horizon in the waning light. I wondered how much of that landscape belonged to the Falahis. The sun dropped quickly, dusk descending into darkness, and with it the temperature. Back at the house I discovered Max in the kitchen outbuilding with Mariam and Amna, who was pinching his cheek.

"My mother loves Max!" Mariam exclaimed. "She is adopting him."

Max shrugged and shot me a sheepish smile. His uncertain look told me what he was thinking—this Emirati matriarch was going to adopt an American Jew boy for Christmas!? Once the fires were ready, the women assembled on the large carpet on the patio of pavers. They wrapped themselves in *Kashmiri* shawls against the winter air. The men joined us and, as had become the custom, I was given an armchair and table while they all sat cross-legged on the carpet.

As exotic feasts go, it would be hard to top the banquet Amna and her daughters presented. There were more dishes served up than at a twelve-course banquet on Chinese New Year—and the food was every bit as tasty. The wood-fired grills produced roasted kabobs of chicken, lamb and beef with sauces involving yogurt, tomatoes, onions and eggplant. Hot Arabic bread was abundant, passed with trays of fresh vegetables. Bowls of basmati rice and platters of hummus and baba ganoush, also offered three ways. Different baklavas and a chocolate cake Fatima had made from scratch. Amna played the Jewish mother. "Eat more!" she exhorted Max. She piled his plate with at least one of everything. "To try!"

I laughed out loud.

After dinner Faraj disappeared. The women cleaned up and Max went into the house with Mohammed and Abdulla. Hilal, Sultan and Issa piled into the Hummer to drive back to Al Ain. The stars overhead pricked white holes in the dark desert sky. One in particular seemed unusually bright. But it wasn't shining in the east. More to the north, I judged, though I had no compass.

Faraj pulled up in his dune buggy. I knew the drill. We sped beyond the dune where I had walked earlier and into the lightless, trackless sands, our way illuminated only by the four-wheeler's headlights. We followed that star and when we approached the outlying camel farm the leather-skinned Bedouin stood waiting. Tied to a metal pole in a long shed under a corrugated roof was a tall female Arabian camel. A very young one lay tethered nearby. Faraj parked with the headlights illuminating the camels and called out to the Bedouin.

The baby *jemel* was brought near its mother. By then I was positioned next to it holding a metal bowl. The Bedouin brought the baby to its mother and it began to nurse. He let it suckle a bit and then led the baby away and upon returning took the bowl from me and held it under the camel's teats. I grabbed two gently between my fingers and thumb using both hands, squeezing and pulling. White, frothy foam sprayed into the container. It was like milking a cow, one of my unheralded skills and something few Ohio Jews, or Ohio gentiles for that matter, likely know how to do. As I tugged on the teats, the words that came to mind were, "*Insha'Allah*, no problem." I couldn't remember when I'd last milked a cow.

Faraj looked impressed with my animal husbandry. We filled six empty one-liter plastic bottles with fresh, warm camel milk. On the ride back to the farmhouse, I expected him to mention once again something about a plan for his children. He didn't that night. But when he did I would be ready.

What happened back at the farm is the stuff of legend. Faraj dropped me off and I found the women in the *majlis*, watching a Sandra Bullock movie. In the boy's dorm Max and Mohammed were watching something on a laptop and laughing to bust a gut. No arguments tonight about *jihad* and gay Greek warriors.

"What's so funny?" I asked, eager to wash the sticky camel-milk residue off my hands.

"We're watching *Harold and Kumar Escape from Guantanamo Bay*," Max drawled.

"It's very funny!" Mohammed chuckled, with a squint. "You know it?"

I almost thought he'd add, "Dude?" Two college sophomores from virtually opposite ends of the earth had found common ground. Stoner comedy is universal, even though neither was stoned. No more than fifteen minutes later, once we were all seated in the *majlis*, Faraj entered with a tray. On it he bore a pitcher filled with white foamy liquid and several tall glasses. He placed the tray on a table ceremoniously, and poured two glasses. He lifted one to his lips and took a long sip. "Ah," he exclaimed. "It is very good." He lifted the other glass. "Doctor, this one is for you."

This was working out. No eggnog, no mistletoe, but a nice secular substitute, right here in a tumbler, offered graciously to me. Fresh camel milk cocktails.

Fatima scowled, though, and tried to intercede. "Uncle, do you know that the first time someone drinks camel milk that they have 'the problem'? You do not have to drink it. My father says it's safe to drink without boiling within one hour of coming out of the camel. He has strained it several times."

All the newbie expats had by then heard about what happens when you got your first taste of camel milk, let alone raw camel milk—a night and a day within four seconds' trot—no pun intended—of the toilet. After that, the lore went, your body had some kind of magical immunity to "the problem."

"*Insha'Allah,* no problem," I chuckled.

Faraj extended the glass, I accepted it with a tip of my head and took a healthy gulp. The warm, sweet liquid, surprisingly richer than cow's milk, went down easily. I wiped the froth from my lips with the back of my hand and chugged the rest.

"More?" Faraj asked, with a smile.

Fatima rolled her eyes, Mohammed and Abdulla rocked with laughter and Max's eyes bugged out of his head. I held the glass straight out as if I had finished my final cup of tea.

Fatima piped up. "Uncle, everyone has 'the problem' the first time. I hope you sleep."

So did I.

At midnight, as my stomach was gurgling, Amna stood up and proclaimed, "Merry Christmas, Doctor! Merry Christmas, Max!" Her daughters added their voices, "Merry Christmas! Merry Christmas!" Hardy and Hardy chimed in with their holiday wishes. I didn't know whether to laugh, to cry or to apologize. As far as I was aware there wasn't a Christian soul within twenty kilometers.

Faraj joined in the holiday cheer. "Yes, yes, Doctor. Merry Christmas!"

Any minute, Bing Crosby would be crooning from the TV, "I'm dreaming of a…."

Faraj patted his belly and looked at me. "Any *problem* yet?"

I was grateful for a reason to laugh, and did heartily. "Not yet!"

Faraj had cut through the unintended, and I hoped unperceived, holiday discomfort. I glanced at Max and nodded. In unison, as if we'd rehearsed it, we said, "Merry Christmas. Thank you for the party." My son knows how to "read a room," and our answer felt right to both of us. There would be another time, a better time, to reveal the truth.

The next morning I awoke feeling as if the angels had guided my sleep. Christmas Miracle Number Two: there was no "problem." The Falahis, to a one, couldn't believe it. What made Doctor David different? I believe my iron gut's performance, like my milking skills, increased my street cred.

After a late breakfast that included visiting cousins, we took two dune buggies and eight people to the camels. The Bedouin and I saw to the milking, but I abstained from imbibing another drop. Why tempt fate when you're surely committing blasphemy against the three sky religions?

Later the five males—Max, Mohammed and Abdulla in one dune buggy, Faraj and me in the other—took off once again over the desert. Faraj left the boys in our dust, laying on speed in the flat stretches of sand. As we bounced along and the speedometer climbed Faraj glanced at me and smiled. "Can't this thing go any faster?" I asked. He saw me and raised me. We beat the boys to Faraj's cousin's farm, a McPalace atop a dune. The cousin, maybe in his late thirties, met us outside with his young sons. When the topic of Texas came up, he told me he had been there, at "the big air force base." It turned out he was the commander of the UAE's jet fighter wing. We all posed for pictures out on the dune.

I drove back, with Faraj goading me to go "faster, faster." I don't think I matched his speeds, but I didn't roll the buggy, either. Another test I think I passed. The test I was staring down, the final project on which I was taking an "incomplete," was the one I'd put myself to. I had to find the way to come clean with Faraj, Amna, Fatima and the rest of the family. The holiday with Max seemed in some ways to have opened the course, in others to narrow it.

CHAPTER 21

"I am not Christian"

TWO DAYS FOLLOWING CHRISTMAS THE MEDIA DECLARED A new Gaza War.

I followed two competing versions of the coverage. One via American TV, thanks or not to the SlingBox. CNN, Fox News and the legacy networks squeezed their "balanced perspective" into a flavorless product that came out of the package pre-staled, like Wonder Bread. The "he-said-whereas-*he*-said" approach purported to show the reasons *both* sides had fallen into the new round of the endless conflict. I wasn't even sure what the two sides were. Israel and Gaza? Israel and Palestine? Israel versus Hamas and Iran? My tribe versus another tribe? The Arabs versus the West? I stared at the screen, racking my brain for a set of premises I could buy into. Without those, how could I put any faith in a narrative?

The competing channels, Arab-world satellite, had the virtue of being more engaging visually. As I'd told my students: If it bleeds, it leads. And it bled, so it led, around the clock, in what rapidly became stock images of horror—like 9/11, with twin towers falling on an endless loop. Was that the first tower going down? Or was it the twenty-first? Random violence and unchosen martyrdom as wallpaper. The language barrier actually helped, as scene after scene hit full force, with no need of words.

The versions were, as far as I could see, equally true, equally propagandistic, and equally numbing. Why this Gaza War now? In retaliation for Hamas rocket attacks? Was that the real trigger?

Al Jazeera's approach to news taught me something. AJ, out of Doha, Qatar, a state supporter of Hamas, filled the screen with screaming, sobbing Palestinian women cradling bloody children. But instead of those screams and sobs, viewers heard pulsating music. The first time I tuned in, I searched all around the frame. Where was that music coming from? Oh, it was coming from the studio. Even Fox News hadn't thought of this—war footage enhanced by a dramatic soundtrack. MTV does New Wave Mideast War News. This is what Samah, Noura and the others had grown up watching. The Arab network was telling me what to feel. They had their market to feed. Fair enough, I understood the bottom line. U.S. networks were telling me not to feel a thing, or if I do to favor Israel—although war is "*terrible*" and "*tragically, innocent civilians die.*" War was pure programming, put out different ways to different markets. Not news but a *news show,* not to be taken seriously, except it is.

Maybe "All Jews Are Evil" was a simple corollary to a larger fact: That the whole world is evil. Rather than fall prey to those darker voices, I turned off the Slingbox. As repulsed as I was by the war, that was nothing compared to how repulsed I was by seeing it turned into spectacle. I would have given a lot to have Samah, several Fatimas, and a Noura or two with me. We'd have had a lot to talk about.

When I was fifteen, an earlier Arab-Israeli war had flashed by. It took all of six days. A modern miracle of biblical proportions. That war deeply affected us Jewish Baby Boomers. My Cleveland Heights neighborhood, an American *shtetl* with its dozen *shuls* centered on Taylor Road, was home to scores of Holocaust survivors; many tried to play down their accents and hide the numbers tattooed on their forearms. We revered them and whispered about the horrors.

War brought many things, from diverse eras in history, to a head. The new Jewish homeland hadn't yet survived two decades. Israel achieved a swift and decisive victory. Our teenage chests puffed out with pride. Don't fuck with us! The narrative it spawned created a new mythos of invincibility and swagger. Jews as victors, not victims. For some, those six days fulfilled biblical prophecy. For others, it sounded the call to make *aliyah.*

The war produced a number of famous pictures. The most famous of all features two figures known to many people even today: Moshe Dayan and Itzhak Rabin—at the time, the defense minister and military commandant. The picture is generally titled, "At Lion's Gate, Liberated Jerusalem, June, 1967."

There's a third figure in the photo, far less famous. The third of the Three Tenors, the one no one seems to be able to remember. Uzi Narkiss, general of the Central Command, struts alongside his superiors, entering East Jerusalem after leading the assault and capturing it from King Abdullah's father. A bloody battle that produced a moment of triumph! Jerusalem, unified, is finally *ours* again. I had met Narkiss on my only trip to Israel. A small man, he reminded me of my *zade*. Something the old soldier told me about that day in 1967 stuck like an ice pick in my mind. Halfway to Jerusalem, he said, an order had come from Dayan: "Halt. Do not enter East Jerusalem."

"I decided to ignore it," Narkiss recalled. "I thought he was wrong."

Was Dayan right to tell a Jewish general not to attempt to unify Jerusalem? Was Narkiss right to defy the order? A forty-year-old question, but the world was still living with the outcome. People were still dying because of it. Would things be different if Narkiss had just fallen in line? What would Jerusalem and Israel be like today? Would there be a Palestinian state? Would there have been 9/11 and two Iraq wars and the War on Terror? Would Israel even exist today? What if?

Twenty minutes later, no answer having come to me, I focused on things I could do something about. My son and a friend from Yale who had joined us, Parker, were with me in the heart of Arabia, with a new war heating up in Israel. Noor, who was constantly with us, I could see was tense. The phrase "not good" had been more or less his mantra.

Everywhere we went in Al Ain, screens played and replayed the damning images: bloodthirsty, cold-eyed Israeli soldiers and defenseless Palestinian civilians. Whatever Samah might point out, and however much I might squirm so as not to concede, the local coverage presented storm troopers massacring non-combatants. No one on the civilian side wielded a weapon higher-tech than a rock. Palestinian Davids up against Israeli Goliaths. At Al Jimi Mall's second-level food court, Emirati families sat eating KFC and McDonald's, ignoring the war and bloodshed on the flatscreens all around. These Arabs didn't seem to care. But why would they? Their lives were not the Palestinians'. Hell, they had American fast food and everything else money could buy. Samah would have looked at me and nodded, not even needing to say, "See? It's just what I told you."

Leave it to Noor to put things in perspective. On the second day of the war we were standing inside what he called the Famous Chicken Cafeteria. "Its chicken is famous for being the best in Al Ain," he'd told me the first time I accompanied him there. He was, of course, right. I'd become a regular, and so had many of the expats in my circle. Noor enjoyed that. He was trusted and welcomed by my friends and took pride in being so. In ways neither of us had intended, we each had made the other known in select expat circles. My expat tribe all followed Noor's exploits and quoted his wisdom. Many Bahtan recognized Doctor David. We might not be as celebrated as the chickens, but we got around.

While Noor ordered two whole, particularly famous birds, I turned to Max. "You and Parker picked a good time to visit. Israel's at war and as far as I know you and I are the only Jews in town."

"Not good," Noor said from the counter. "It's not safe here now for you, Max and his friend."

Max and I had talked about this on our own. His thinking was straightforward: We're here, and we're not hopping on a plane and going home. "At least now I have a sense of what it feels like," he'd said, "being a Jew in an Arab country when a war starts."

"When Israel is at war all Jews are at war," I pronounced. "Whether we want to be or not. This *isn't* Kansas. Noor knows what he's talking about."

Noor did indeed. His family lived in a land made a hotspot by the War on Terror. A war that increasingly looks endless, that might look as if it started on 9/11/2001, but has roots going back to the Russians, the days of the Raj, and Alexander the Great. A war that Noor and his people really have almost nothing to do with, and yet they're trapped on the front lines.

Noor stood next to me holding two white plastic bags. I took one from him, but kept talking chiefly to Max. "It's pretty safe being a Jew insulated from it all in America," I said.

Noor looked at me, unsmiling. "This is not good for you." Yes, he was a worrywart.

The next day I gave the *Intro* final, without incident, to thirty-six young Muslim women. None of us mentioned the Gaza War. That was equally a relief and a disappointment. Not one student knew, not Anood 2 or Fatima 1, after an entire semester that their professor was a Jew. I didn't know what I thought, but that only added urgency to my desire to hear what they thought.

But I already knew that answer: *All* Jews Are Evil.

There was no time to linger because I had to go immediately to *Writing for Media*. Seven of the eight students were present. Samah was absent. That decided it: I'd hand out the take-home final, talk for fifteen minutes on whatever topics came to mind, note that the final and course project were due via email by midnight January 1, and wish them all well.

Ten minutes after class began, still no Girl in Pink. My curiosity got the better of me. "Where's Samah?" She wouldn't blow taking the final. Would she, the class valedictorian? Latifa knew. "She's driving in from Abu Dhabi. She'll be here soon, *insha'Allah*."

Hessa asked me what my son and I had done on Christmas. I was about to launch into an account of the visit to the farm when Samah entered. No pink today. Dressed all in black, the class's sole Palestinian—the only Palestinian I knew here—crossed the classroom as if she were arriving at a funeral. I focused on her as I continued. "We spent it at the sheikh's farm in the desert."

That amplified Latifa's curiosity. "What did you do?"

I kept my eyes on Samah. "We drove four-wheelers over the dunes. Barbecued. I told bad jokes. Ate too much good food. Watched American movies late into the night. I milked camels and drank fresh milk." Several girls giggled at that, but it elicited no reaction from Samah.

Hessa needed to know. "Did you have *the* problem?"

"My stomach was fine." Probably the most impressive claim I had made all semester.

Samah sat glumly near the open window paying scant attention.

Mariam spoke from her heart. "Then you had a nice Christmas?"

Not the "nice Christmas" question! Where would this go?

By the window, Samah stirred. She waited—without looking at me, but I felt it—for my answer.

Latifa persisted. "Did you have a nice Christmas, Doctor?"

I looked at Samah and felt the weight of the world on her shoulders. I wanted to walk to her desk, but I stayed where I was. A weight almost as great was tumbling off my own. "Latifa, I do not celebrate Christmas. It's not my holiday. But we had a nice time."

Samah's eyes met mine. She knew. Her look was a challenge, full of outright defiance, and yet I sensed she was nearly as relieved as I was. Mariam asked, "But you went home for Thanksgiving?"

"Thanksgiving is an American national holiday. It's got religious roots, but it's become a secular celebration. People from many religions, and even from no religion, often celebrate it together. But I don't celebrate Christmas."

Mariam looked confused. Samah not at all.

"So..." Mariam asked. "You... are... not... Christian?" She said it just as Noor had in his taxi.

"I am not." Pause. "I am not Catholic." Pause. "I am not Protestant." Pause. "I am not Baptist... Methodist... Greek Orthodox... Russian Orthodox." Long pause. "I'm not Hindu... Buddhist..."

Samah stopped me. "So you are not Christian!?!"

Didn't I just say that!?! I held her gaze, willing my question into her mind. Why won't you ask directly what you want to know? Are you afraid of the answer? I repeated, "No. I am not Christian."

Samah's eyes went lifeless. "I see."

That wasn't how I wanted to end the year, but that's how we did. I handed out the finals and Latifa and Mariam asked me to take pictures with them. Hessa gave me a notebook and asked me to write something and return it later. Noura stuck out her hand for me to shake. As I walked out of the room, I turned and glanced over my shoulder. Samah was staring out the window.

Noor was waiting, as usual, in the parking lot. What stopped my students from asking, "What are you, Professor? What is your religion?" Or from putting it as bluntly as, "Hey! Are you a Jew?"

I knew only one thing. Whatever was stopping them wasn't what was stopping me from simply coming out with it. War or no war. Whether they asked directly or not. But when I told Noor he remained adamant, "You cannot tell anyone you are *Yehuda*. Especially not now."

Events were conspiring around me, to make me the kind of Jew I'd never been. The kind who defines himself first and foremost by his faith and ethnicity, if not religious ritual. Not by things like education, career, friends, love, marriage, parenthood. Or by a contemporary moral "Jewish ethos." Those had been neatly stacked where they belong—behind the Jew, American-Style, in me. Being a Jew in the U.S. was relatively safe and easy, and in some ways that's a shame because it makes you too soft.

The clarity of my new take on being a Jew I owe largely to hindsight. I was there, sort of, but not in my conscious thinking. In the moment I was still resenting the ridiculous predicament I'd made for myself, and showing it by acting out.

Noor and I headed out to get a few Famous Chickens and fixings for a late dinner as the Yalies went on a jog around the Shakboot Palace. It was the first time all day that my friend and I had been alone. Out of the blue, lifting his right hand off the steering wheel and in a voice as pure and devoid of guile as any man could muster, he said, "Tonight I give you my *Golden Word*. In Waziristan when someone gives his *Golden Word*, it means he will defend you with his life. It is very serious. I give you my *Golden Word*."

His *Golden Word*? Defend me with his life? Like he said some Pashtun may be doing for Osama bin Laden? Whether the look on my face gave me away or not, Noor never let on. What I felt was utter surprise. Was he serious? His eyes said he meant it. My heart told me he did.

"I give you my Golden Word. I think of you as my elder."

We were near the Pizza Hut roundabout approaching the Famous Chicken restaurant.

"Noor," I asked, "I am the first *Yehuda* you have ever met?"

"Yaya, the first and only, until Max."

"And you give me your Golden Word. Why?"

"I am inspired by your manner," he replied, without any hesitation. "You do not try to tell me what to believe. You told me that Jews don't try to change any person's beliefs. I have met many Christians and they say too much that Isa is God and the Son of God, and that we must believe in him. Christians do not inspire me."

I was silent thinking he'd finished.

"You do not act like you are better than other people. You show everyone respect." He glanced across at me with a conspiratorial look. "You are not afraid of anyone, either. And when you act like a fool, you say so and apologize. Most men I've known don't do that."

What he'd said, and how gently, humorously he'd said it, pulled at my innermost ideal. Noor, in his words and actions, defined what a man should be. What I still struggled to be, a *mensch*. There were moments Noor made me feel like both Don Quixote and Sancho Panza. I couldn't imagine navigating the UAE, tilting at windmills of sand, without him at my side. In the truest sense a *kemosabe*.

What could I say in response to a golden compliment like that?

"My people say that the tongue is the spoon that dishes out the true words of the heart," Noor continued. "Your tongue dishes out your true heart. We have much in common. Our sky religions have much in common."

We pulled into the parking lot in front of the chicken restaurant. "Noor, I have a question for you." He turned off the motor and looked directly at me. "Have you told your friends about me?"

His face erupted in a huge grin and he laughed. "Yaya, I have told them that I have an American friend who is a professor. They said, 'Are you crazy? You are from Waziristan. America hates us. Americans kill us. How can you be friends with an American?'"

"You're crazy because you are friends with an American?"

"Yaya, they think I am crazy," Noor laughed. "I told them, 'No, my friend he is a good man. He doesn't hate us. He wants to understand.'"

"Have you told them that I am *Yehuda*?"

"No, I told them only that you are an American and a professor."

"So you haven't told them that I am Jewish?"

"No," he laughed, flashing his big, toothy smile. "If I told them that you were *Yehuda* they would *know* I was crazy."

CHAPTER 22

Dubai Cancels New Year's

WAR OR NO WAR IN GAZA, ALLAH DID NOT SEE FIT TO CANCEL the UAE's Islamic New Year's celebrations. But Dubai's Sheikh Mohammed bin Rashid Al Maktoum did use the war as an excuse to issue a last-minute edict cancelling Dubai's 2009 multi-million dollar secular New Year's Eve bacchanalian blowout. I'd already prepaid a three-day New Year's package at a fancy hotel and there were no refunds. Thousands of people had paid millions of dirhams to celebrate here and the Sheikh had pulled the plug, by decree. There were to be no fireworks and all parties with music and alcohol were closed down, too.

Rumors had surfaced that the Sheikh had been shot and killed, by his own son, the day before. Noor, on the drive up to Dubai, had reported hearing this on the "Pashtun grapevine." After Zayed died his death was kept secret for forty days and forty nights while his heirs could divvy up his portfolio. But Maktoum, a very public figure, was eerily not visible. Was it the War in Gaza? Or was he dead?

Whether the Sheikh was alive was not, at the moment, my problem. New Year's having been cancelled, the boys and I did the B-roll runaround of Dubai over several days. The one seen on CNN and in every fawning story about the Middle East's Miracle City. It all looks great from thirty thousand feet, or on a thirty-second video clip, or from atop the Burj Arabia, the self-proclaimed seven-star hotel made to look like a six-ty-story *dhow* at full sail. We visited Atlantis built on a faux-archipelago of stone and sand in the Persian Gulf. Hit the Mall of the Emirates with its indoor ski mountain and the Burj Dubai, destined to become the world's tallest building. We hit Jumeirah Beach, the sky blue and cloudless, the air seventy degrees Fahrenheit, the sand white, the blue water looked crystal-line although pollution was widely known to be a big issue as sanitation trucks dumped their human waste directly into the Gulf. As to the Sheikh being shot and killed by his son, on our final day there Noor reported that the Pashtun grapevine had given an update: He was alive but had been wounded.

The third day of the New Year I found myself in my Al Ain apart-ment, briefly alone. Noor and the boys were out on the near-nightly chicken run, and soon to be back with famous roasted birds. I contem-plated Parker's prayer rug, red and blue, rolled up and ready to go back to New Haven as a carry-on. I peeled back a corner, and admired the color, pattern, the density of the pile, and how the thick Afghani wool had been blended so expertly the carpet felt like one perfectly luxurious fiber.

Noor had insisted that we stop at Global Village on our way back to Al Ain. At the annual winter "World's Fair" held at Dubailand, he led us right to the Afghani pavilion where he did the negotiating, in Pashto, with rug merchants. I sat and drank tea, played the non-speaking white-man role, and simply complied when told to produce dirhams. At a nearby restaurant he treated us to a meal of "mutton with rice" and "rice with mutton" before departing and we drove south with several handmade top-quality carpets purchased at a Pashtun price. Alas, that MO—Noor negotiating this world for me—couldn't serve me everywhere. I could have been happy every day in the UAE if it had been possible for Noor simply to mediate everything. I took stabs at Arabic, but I'd never speak it. I tried to be a good, liberally educated American cultural relativist and go with the flow of customs I found baffling, contradictions, and double standards that struck me as downright oppressive. The only place I felt on firm footing without Noor was at the Falahis' various houses and compounds.

In a short time, I'd be back in the classroom. Unless Fatima enrolled in my upcoming *Writing for Media* or *Intro* courses, I'd be on my own. I didn't yet see how, but I was determined that the second semester would not be a retread of the first. There were a bunch of questions I intended to attack head on, even if it meant forcing the issue. "So you are not Christian?" would likely come up, but I couldn't leave it at that. Spend another four months vaguely defined by what I am not? No way.

Meanwhile, there was still unfinished business from the fall term. I switched on the laptop. My inbox showed seven finals and projects turned in. The eighth girl, whichever of them she was, had already flunked. That alone made me wince. A failure rate over ten percent? Ouch! I thought about taking the vodka out of the freezer and mixing in some fresh watermelon juice before the crew returned. Instead I slid the cursor to the first email in the batch. Nah. I looked down the list. Midway, I saw Samah's name. That was the one I clicked. That would be the tough one, so tackle it first.

Thursday, Jan 1, 2009 at 7:05 PM, via email

Prof. Eden:

How are you? Hope everything is good. Attached are the final project (movie review), the final exam and a little thing I've been working on for a while. You might not like it though and that is okay. I have to say it's a little honest, or should I say blunt, I don't know, but I wouldn't write it any other way. Hope it helps. I also wanted to remind you of the recommendation letter (which you might not want to write after reading what I wrote. I'll understand.). Anywho thanks for a great semester, and let me know if you still want a copy of the picture we took together. — *Samah*

I was intrigued. "A little thing I've been working on for a while?" A bit less apprehensive, too. I clicked the second attachment, called "Diary."

28th December, 1:27 AM

I spent a very pleasant day with Dina, a friend that I haven't seen in ages. I came back home wearing a smile on my face, only to find my whole family sitting around the TV, which doesn't happen often. I knew something was up; they were all fixing their eyes on the news. As it turned out there was another Israeli attack on Palestinian territories. I kissed my smile goodbye and joined my family in their misery. The usual sense of guilt started kicking in as I watched dead bodies lying indifferently in the street like a giant rug. I bet none of those people thought their time was up as they were walking down the street earlier, and again that is the kind of life people lead in Gaza and the rest of our occupied land, always looking over their shoulders, never knowing what tomorrow carries.

Sometimes I get a very weird thought, I feel different, and not in a good way. I spend 55% of my time feeling guilty, the other 45% wondering if anyone else does. I feel like I have it all, a wonderful family, loving parents, a roof over my head, a bite to eat when I'm hungry, a car to drive when I'm bored, money to spend, friends, education, a sense of security. I can do anything and everything without fear or regret, yet nothing tastes as sweet as it should be. Why can't my family back in Palestine have that?

It kills me when I hear stories about people dying under the siege. What kills me more is that the rest of the world doesn't seem to care.

Mr. Eden, my *Writing for the Media* professor, told us about this book he may write. It is supposed to be about his experience in the UAE. He told us we can participate in the writing process if we wish; I remember the first thing I thought was: ok, so I can chip my tooth then wake up the next morning and decide to write a book about it. Those Americans, they have no story. No offense, Mr. Eden, you know I love you, but I'm just trying to be honest. What is your history? You found a piece of inhabited land, decided to make it yours with no regards to its original people, sound familiar??

I don't hate Americans, and however opposite to popular Arab/ Muslim opinion, I don't despise Jews. I just loathe the people that came in and kicked me and my parents out of our homeland, pulled out our olive trees, knocked our homes down.

31st December, 9:30 PM

So the war on Hamas continues, or is it the war on every living breathing Palestinian? I can't really decide. With almost 400 victims, 2000 wounded, mostly civilians, Israel had been nice enough to allow trucks full of medical aid to enter Gaza.

We have a saying in Arabic, "Murder someone then attend his funeral."

1st January/3:01 PM

I'm a very delicate person, I get depressed quite easily, and sometimes I cry for no reason. So when we had our last class of *Writing for the Media*, I was in a lousy mood. Israel bombed the Islamic University in Gaza and my friend's sister goes there and they couldn't contact her, so everyone was freaked. And my best friend's cousin was martyred, and I had to find out about all of this in the same day.

To top it all off, I had to find that one of my favorite teachers was Jewish!!! Talk about bad timing.

OK, this might sound Anti-Semitic and all, but I don't care. Prince Harry wore a sweater with a [swastika] on its arm sleeve, the whole world went nuts. But when an insulting cartoon regarding Prophet Mohammed came out and we got a little mad, "What's wrong with those Arabs?!"

I'll take Anti-Semitism; at least I'm being true to myself. I should have known. We had a conversation in a previous class where he said that he'd been to Israel, and his family descends from Jewish roots. There was this student who draws political cartoons, and there was one about the Palestinian/Israeli conflict that he didn't care for. He thinks both sides did a lot of killing, and that is very sad.

Give me a break!!!

If four Israelis die in a bombing, thousands of Palestinians are killed every day.

The world calls these four "victims of suicidal bombing," whereas those thousand are worthy of what had come of them. Israel is just defending itself!!!

One word, Hypocrisy.

I wanted to say look at Israeli then look at Palestinian territories (and he saw both). The blind can witness the difference!

People in Palestine have poor education, they're starving, there is no electricity, they are under siege, crossing in or out of borders is out of the question. People had to smuggle sheep so people could have proper Eid Al Adha celebrations. Every day they knock down more homes to build more Israeli settlements. And hey, let's not talk of the separation wall!

Who can endure such a life? And who decided that on top of occupying over half of our land, they get to live like kings, while the rest are caged like animals—yes, indeed both sides are equally responsible.

And by the way, if I had to go through what they are living now every day, I would be more than glad to bomb myself. Call me a terrorist!

I wanted to say all of that but I choked. I felt my tears nearing and I struggled to keep my composure. I never let anyone know of my vulnerability.

I wanted to feel deceived finding out like this. I needed an outlet for all this rage I've been carrying around lately. I wanted to dump it all on him, but I couldn't.

When the class was finally over, he got up to leave, I tried to bulk my courage to go over and ask him if it was really true, or is it all the work of my imagination.

The funny thing is I also wanted to say that Jewish or not Jewish you will forever remain my professor, a man I admire greatly. I wanted to tell him I will always look up to you, and that I don't hate Jewish people, and that you should have been honest with us, but I understand your concerns.

But I didn't. I let my hesitation stand in the way, and again there was the possibility of him telling me to bugger off (I know he is not British, I just like using this expression) it's none of your business.

Now I know this is not exactly what Mr. Eden asked of us. He said tell me what it's like being you, a Muslim woman living in the UAE. I don't think he expected one of his students writing a raging political diary instead of "Hi, my name is Samah, I'm 22 years old, I like swimming and riding ponies, I like going to the movies and hanging out with my friends."

What can I say, this is what I believe in, that is who I am, and I'm damn proud of it. Probably none of this would end up in a book, I don't know, and I can't say I really care since I might not have the chance to read it. But what I'll always have is this chance I got to speak up, and I seized it. It doesn't matter if anyone else reads it. I'm contented with just that. — Samah

I stared at the screen. It had never occurred to me that any of my students would "file" a piece to which I would be moved to respond. But what the hell was I going to say? I started typing, doing my damnedest to transmit from heart to fingers to screen. My head could only get in the way. Once I ran out of things that came unbidden, I hit send.

By luck, I heard Noor's and the boy's voices, bouncing off one another in the stairway, which pulled me away from the screen. I couldn't read what I'd said and start second-guessing it.

"Look at this," I showed Max, once Famous Chicken had been devoured. I handed him the MacBook. "Remember Samah? It's what she wrote in her diary the first few days of the war."

"The one who asked if you're a Christian, right?"

"Yes, I confirmed that I wasn't. Read this and tell me what you think."

A few minutes later he told me. "This is amazing stuff, Dad. You were worried that you blew it."

"I'm not sure I didn't, but at least one thing, *insha'Allah*, worked out. If Samah had known I was a Jew, I believe she would have quit the class. We never would have talked at all."

"And she figured it out herself in the end—which in many ways worked out better."

I nodded.

Max noticed the sense of relief in my body language. "How you gonna reply?

"I already have. Take a look in my sent emails."

Saturday, January 3, 2009

Samah: Your "little thing" was brilliant and from your heart. I didn't want to hear stories about UAE girls riding ponies; I wanted to hear stories like yours. You have every right and reason to feel the way you do. As to my religious heritage, nobody in class ever asked me, "What is your religion?" You asked me, "So you're not Christian?" If you asked me directly I would have told you. In fact, many of my friends in the US told me I was crazy to come to the UAE because "they hate us." I said, " I don't know that and I'll find out for myself." And I am. This story helps explain a lot. So, regardless of what you may have thought, or do yet think, I wish you all of the happiness and peace you and your family deserve. And I do wish for peace for all and that my prediction that you will be able to live in your homeland will come true. You are one of my all-time favorite students, and you will always have a special place in my heart.

I added a note: Samah's grade for the course was an "A."
— Professor Eden

I re-read Samah's diary entry more times than I could count. I stared at some specific things I wanted to address. The faithful of a religion will find, quite reasonably, the mockery of their great prophet offensive and objectionable. That's an important thing to discuss, but that doesn't make it the same as the mockery of millions murdered in gas chambers. Prophets, for the most part, can stick up for themselves. Cartoonists and members of royal families have—*al haam doo lielah*—different jobs to do in our multi-polar world. I wanted to put that forward not to "rebut" what Samah had said, but to engage with her wholeheartedly in the discussion of a subject I was grateful to her for putting on the table.

But I refrained. The truth was I don't see—and I think Samah would concede the point—moral equivalence between Prince Harry's sweater and a cartoon. Much of what Samah pointed out, in contrasts between how Israel is regarded *vis a vis* Palestine, reflects a double standard by "my" media that's just as egregious as those I'd been bitching about in the UAE. Samah had made those points, and she knew their truth—my affirmation of them would just sound condescending. She had achieved something powerful. I was forced to acknowledge, at least to myself, that when I stuck up for Israel, I was sticking up for my tribe, which, whatever our political disagreements, was the thing Samah and I had in common. We stood by our people, right and wrong.

Maybe I wasn't so out of place in a world like the UAE. I thought about Max's conversation-slash-confrontation with Mohammed. Nation-states versus peoples. I'd have to talk more about that.

Two days later this came from Samah:

Monday, Jan 5, 2009 at 11:55 AM, via email

Prof. Eden,

Your words brought tears to my eyes. If the world had more of your kind, no one would be dying anywhere. You know if I had known what I know now three or four months ago, my reaction would have been totally different. I like to believe I had grown, your class, no wait... let me rephrase that, you, have taught me a lot.

I am not going to sugarcoat it; people do have certain feelings toward Jews around here. Think of 9/11 and how Americans wanted to blow every Muslim off the continent, it's the same thing. I personally would have pulled out of the course if I had known earlier, fortunately I didn't, and I got the chance to know you and see how wonderful and understanding you are. I wouldn't hesitate to take another course with you, you know... if I wasn't graduating and all. The thing is, people tend to get superficial sometimes, especially when they're hurt and can't find someone to blame, I guess what I'm trying to say is, I see you as an example of what I'd like to be when I'm 50 something, your religious heritage doesn't change that.

It was an honor to get to know you, your tolerance and kindness inspired me to never again judge a book by its cover. You had tremendous respect for me and what I believe in, when someone else in your position probably wouldn't. I admire your boldness for coming here and I also thank you for it. I would love nothing more than to keep in touch with you.

What I sent you were excerpts from my own personal diary, and I'm glad you liked it. I want to believe I helped you get a glimpse of what it's like to be a Palestinian Muslim, and I hope that when you go back there someday, you will see things differently, maybe remember me, and pray that someday I might get the chance to stand where you stand and see the things you got to see.

Thank you for the A, hope it's not a bribe so I wouldn't tell on you. (Just kidding.)

As for the recommendation letter, thank you in advance and sorry for the trouble, just please let me know when and where to go to pick it up. Regards, S.A.

Once again, I started typing wanting to assure Samah that when 9/11 happened, only *some* Americans "wanted to blow every Muslim off the continent." In fact, a small minority but they were the Americans who dominated the airwaves and Al Jazeera. But I stopped. Samah had brought our conversation to a fine, sound completeness. If there was more to say, we'd keep in touch. And something told me that exchange would only grow better now that it was no longer teacher-student.

CHAPTER 23

"My God will take care of me"

A LONG HAUL RETURN FLIGHT TO DUBAI FOLLOWING A TWO-week winter break in a frozen Ohio was a great chance to take stock and look at that distance I had to travel—those blessed hours when one is no longer there nor yet here. I had a three-year contract that brought with it a free place to live, and basically no taxes. The only hardship was the distance from family—something I hadn't thought would weigh as heavily on me as it did, and that divorce? Yes, it had to be concluded.

Like many others I had lost, on paper, a good chunk of my assets. My cushion had thinned, but I was OK—and Max's tuition had been paid for the year. I could conceivably hide in the UAE until my contract ran out, waiting things out until the world economy recovered. Sure, Dubai had ground to a halt. But Abu Dhabi really ran the UAE, still had the world's largest sovereign wealth fund, around six-hundred-billion U.S. dollars, as well as a gazillion gallons of oil and natural gas in the ground, and I had friends with *wasta*. I was getting plugged in.

We at UAEU had all heard that budget cuts were coming, but that wouldn't affect me much. I might teach an extra course. No big deal. I confronted what I was thinking: Talking myself into rationales for staying in the UAE. My main motivator was that my alternative reality back home was basically a non-starter. Thanks to the lawsuit against the TV station, my U.S.-based job prospects fell in the slim-to-none range. Nobody hires a troublemaker, especially in a tight job market. Whenever I went back, I would once again have to reinvent myself. I had doubts whether I still had it in me. In Northeast Ohio? At my age? The region had been in a steady, decades-long decline as its population and heavy-manufacturing base eroded, and now seemed frozen in permanent depression—economic, political and psychological.

Other parts of America no longer promised greener pastures.

In some ways I felt displaced, like Noor—though of course I was much luckier. I could afford to fly home at will, something he couldn't, and I wasn't caught between the Taliban and the Pakistani army. Compared to my friend, I had lots of options.

After fourteen hours of such maunderings, interspersed with surprisingly fine Emirate's Airline meals and halfhearted naps, I hit Dubai feeling almost refreshed. I hefted my bag off the carousel. Stepping out, I welcomed the blue skies and soft morning air over and around the gleaming new Emirates Airlines Terminal 3. Had life in Al Ain and teaching at UAEU really become my new normal? Or was this buoyant feeling just relief at having ditched all that bad stuff back in America?

Noor called as I waited by the curb. He was driving up E-66 from Al Ain and said he'd arrive in "maybe, *insha'Allah,* ten minutes, maybe twenty minutes, something like that." I was fine waiting, and happy just to hear his voice. Noor didn't have a fraction of what most of the people moaning back home still had, whatever bath they'd taken—he just hadn't been swindled out of it by banks and Bernie Madoff.

Just before he signed off Noor piqued my curiosity. "I have a very big surprise for my friend."

"What is it?"

"If I told you, it wouldn't be a big surprise," he laughed. Click.

Noor pulled up to Terminal 3 in his cousin's white Camry. Where was his taxi? Noor popped out of the car, grabbed my hand and pumped it vigorously. "Your trip was good?" He hefted my suitcase, tossed it into the open trunk, slammed the lid, and a moment later eased into airport traffic making easy small talk. The longer he held back the big surprise, the stronger my hunch it was not good.

I took the bait. "Where's your taxi?"

Noor suddenly looked forlorn. "That is my big surprise. Abu Dhabi cancelled my taxi." He watched for my reaction. "I no longer have to be a taxi driver! *Al ham doo lielah.*"

This was the big surprise?! He actually thanked God?! I was speechless. He had lost his taxi and livelihood. Abu Dhabi, which meant the emirate, was accelerating the plan to phase out old taxis and independent Pashtun drivers like Noor and replace them with uniformed drivers working for taxi companies controlled by Abu Dhabi's royal family. But I thought he had another six months?

We drove past the same repetitive series of banners featuring that wheelchair-bound boy wearing a Superman shirt that greeted me on my arrival. As we crossed the floating bridge, Noor explained in more detail. "The government cancelled my taxi early. The Sheikh wants his new taxis in Al Ain sooner." He said all this as if it weren't the world caving in under and around him. He'd purchased the old taxi from his sponsor and it was in Sanaiya, being painted white. More important, Noor's Emirati benefactor agreed to keep sponsoring him so he could stay in the country.

A big smile rippled across his face. "I am looking to buy a Tata bus."

Right. That had always been the plan.

"But that might not be a good idea now," Noor continued. "There are no jobs. Maybe I'll buy a tipper truck. *Insha'Allah*, everything will be fine. My God will take care of me."

He turned his eyes from the road and looked at me. "I can still drive you but it would be illegal."

Right, and would risk having him jailed or put on a plane. No way I would put him in the line of fire. Bahtan who broke the law were jailed, had their visas cancelled, and kicked permanently out of the country. There were other ways Noor could make money, and Tony and I would help. He had told me countless times that he hated driving a taxi and wanted his own business.

I put my hand on Noor's shoulder. "My friend, I think it's time that I drive myself." I paused. "You are more than my driver. You are my friend. You have given me your Golden Word."

Noor took me directly to EuropCar in Sanaiya. I rented a 2009 white Toyota Yaris for 2,000-dirhams a month, which included full insurance. Then on the way home I followed him and we stopped and bought a couple of Famous Chickens and the fixings for dinner. In my flat we popped open cans of peach juice as we devoured succulent roasted bird.

Over the following days Noor spent more time at my apartment, doing online searches for vehicles he might buy. He reported cash in hand of 35,000 dirhams and needed at least 60,000 dirhams to purchase a Tata bus.

"But my family also needs money." He sighed. "*Insha'Allah*, if it is meant to be, I will find it."

I spoke without thinking. "I can lend you the money." Even blurting it out, I wondered at the impetuous statement. Yet my next thought was, "Why not? I've lost that much in the stock market in a blink. Noor is less of a gamble than all the 'investments' to which I entrusted my future."

Noor beamed. "I thought you would say that. If it is meant to be, *insha'Allah*, I will ask you. We would write a contract and I would pay you back with Islamic interest, of course."

Islamic interest, I had learned from Mohamed of Yemen, meant no interest at all. But that's what friends do for friends. I tossed out another idea. We had kidded about it after a few more trips to buy carpets at the Global Village. Noor negotiated effectively at the Afghan pavilion with other Pashtun for hand-knotted kilims and carpets that I bought for a song and shipped to Ohio.

"We could buy rugs together in Peshawar," I offered. "And we'd ship them to America to sell."

He liked that idea, and we chewed the bones of numerous Famous Chickens discussing it.

I considered how to pledge my support. Noor would certainly never take a handout nor would I insult him with the offer of one. The loan for a bus or truck made sense—but what about just day-to-day living expenses and money to send home? I looked into Noor's eyes for a moment. What was I thinking? He knew I was his friend, and he did not need any promises. He had his God, and knew *Allah* would not let him down. What was my assurance compared to that?

CHAPTER 24

Boys and Girls

MY SPRING SEMESTER TEACHING SCHEDULE WAS A MESS. I had more than twice the number of students I'd had the previous semester. The all-female *Writing for Media* section had three times as many pupils as Samah's class. I didn't teach *Computer-Assisted Reporting* but instead taught two sections of *Intro*—one all "boys" and the other all "girls." The all-girls class, which was supposed to be capped at thirty-six students had forty-five. Word had gotten around about "Doctor David" and every one who wanted in got in. The all-boys' *Intro* class totaled thirty-six students— two-thirds Emirati, rounded out by cliques of Omanis, Jordanians and a single Syrian and Nigerian.

Tony had insisted I needed to teach "boys." The Mass Com department would go for that because few Arabic female faculty wanted to deal with male students. That young men were commonly called "boys" around UAEU was another *non sequitur*. Some were husbands and fathers. It was similar to young women always being referred to as "girls." Some were wives and mothers.

Who knew? Maybe I'd meet another Samah or Fatima.

My classes were now conducted on two campuses—Maqam for the "girls" and Falaj Haza for the "boys." That campus was a single-story building with an open-air courtyard and resembled a small high school in the American Southwest. I had just fifteen minutes to travel three kilometers from the "boys" to the "girls" campus. But I could make it work, and more importantly I'd retained my four-day weekend.

This time she wore green. Samah greeted me on the second-story promenade of Building 71, opposite my classroom. The start of spring semester's *Writing for Media* class was overdue. Only one girl in the new crop, Hana from Jordan, wore pastels. The others wore black—and this time a half-dozen hid behind *neqabs* covering their faces. I handed Samah an envelope, the lime-green *sheyla* framing her face. It was the first time I'd seen her since our last class in December, after I'd read her diary.

"This is your letter of recommendation. What are your plans?"

She shrugged. "I don't know. These are not good times."

"Are you thinking of going to graduate school?"

"I am thinking about it, but my family isn't rich. We are Palestinian, remember?"

As if I could forget! "I think you should try to come to America for school."

"You will help me?"

"If you want. Of course, I'll help you."

Here came the punch line. "And you will pay for me?!"

I let out a hoot. "That I can't do! I am already paying a lot for one student."

She did have a plan. "First, I need to get a job. Then I'll think about school."

I looked at my watch and saw the class period had been underway for five minutes. Two girls wearing *neqabs* belatedly approached the doorway, one wearing long black gloves, saw me standing nearby with Samah and stepped into the lecture hall.

"We are always late to class," Samah said, watching my new students straggle in. "You have girls with veils this time."

"Six." Then it struck me. "Would you like talk to the class? I have twenty-six girls and I'm afraid it won't be the same as your class. There are too many students."

Samah nodded and followed me into the lecture hall. Surprise—the a/c was broken. I called the class to attention. "This is Samah. She took this class last semester and graduated. I asked her to say a few words about me so you know what to expect in this class."

Samah stepped in front of the teacher's desk. A few girls nodded in recognition. She turned and looked at me. "First, you must know that Professor Eden will mark up your papers with a lot red ink. Don't worry. That's how you will learn." She grinned. "He tells a lot of bad jokes and may look strangely at you. He also butchers Arabic, but at least he tries." She chuckled a tad. "He isn't like other teachers here. You will learn something. Oh, and he doesn't use PowerPoint. So stay awake."

As Samah continued, holding sway over the class, I stepped outside. A warm afternoon breeze fluttered the red-green-white-and-black UAE flag atop its pole, stuck in a sandpit. Beyond, the relentless sun sparkled off the reflective glass of a new academic building, my likely home in the coming year. That was if I decided to stay, which would be somewhat affected by what I would be teaching.

After five minutes, Samah joined me.

"You told them everything you wanted to tell them?" I asked.

"Yes, Professor Eden. I told them everything they need to know about you." She broke out in a big grin. "But don't worry. I haven't told anybody your secret."

On that note, we shared a hearty laugh.

"Samah," I said, "please feel free to tell any one you wish. It's not a secret."

"I know that, Professor Eden. But they should find out in their own way. As I did."

"Do you know if any faculty know?"

She shook her head. "No, but I do know some don't like you. Not for that. *They* are jealous because we all talk about you and want to be in your classes. Like we did with Dr. Beverly. That's why you have so many this time. *They* don't like that."

It all made sense to me. Samah had confirmed what I had come to believe.

That was the last time I saw Samah, although we exchanged emails.

For the first weeks of spring semester the "boys" and I got acquainted. They ranged in age from nineteen to twenty-six, sophomores to seniors. Three were married with scraggly beards. Everyone else was clean-shaven—or had closely cropped facial hair. Yusef, who I quickly nicknamed "Funny Man," bragged he was getting married after graduation in June. Or at least he still hoped so. If he graduated.

The young men self-segregated according to nationality. The five Jordanians sat in the back by the windows facing the parking lot and they always wore Western clothing. Six Omanis sat in front of them all wearing white *kanduras* and *kummahs*, that country's traditional many-colored round cap.

In the first row near the windows in front of the Omanis sat three Emiratis—Mohammed Saif, Munther, and a big, beefy sophomore I nicknamed "Abu Dhabi." He earned his moniker by boasting that "almost one out of ten of the world's millionaires" live there. He wasn't one of them but dreamed large.

The Syrian sat next to the Nigerian by the door and they both wore Western clothing. Funny Man—everything he said just came out funny!— and his best friend, Ali, the oldest student in the class, at 26, completed that row. He quickly earned the nickname, "Handsome Ali," because of his model good looks; he planned to graduate in May with a degree in urban planning. Handsome Ali had dropped out to work, but realized that for a young man with little *wasta*—one who drove a Corolla, for Christ's sake!—a diploma was his best option for a better future. Others drove SUVs and, at the worst, Camry's. One of the Jordanians, Qais, drove a Mercedes S500. Young men could have cars at UAEU and could come and go from their hostels. Not so the women. The barbed wire at the boys' hostels was for show.

Everyone else on that side of the room was Emirati, all wearing traditional white garb. That included all three married men. Few of these students actively participated.

Like I did the semester before with the girls *Intro* class, I spent time listening to each student talk about himself. In English. Language once again would present a major obstacle, as it did with the girls. Several protested that they "never had to do this before." Funny Man wondered the loudest. "Why, Doctor?" he asked, scrunching his thin face. His English was just so-so, but his comic timing was spot on. "Half of us won't understand what he's saying."

He had a point, but I had a quick answer. "That's why. Because you have never done it. You're graduating soon and need to learn to speak English in public." I paused. "I need to size each of you up and see how well you comprehend English." *We teach in English, as Tony said, we don't teach English.*

Several themes emerged from these talks. The first was that *Intro*, or a class that taught public speaking and interpersonal communications, was extremely important for these students. Nearly all, both the "boys" and "girls," lacked self-confidence in expressing themselves. I told that to Carol and gave her suggestions about what I thought the curriculum needed—if it could get approved and implemented, which was problematic from what Beverly had told me about her efforts to change courses.

Another theme: Everyone has a hero. It was an easy icebreaker and if a student didn't mention his hero during the talk another student prodded him. Zayed topped the list. Not one student mentioned his sons. Or Dubai's sheikh. Several said their fathers. The Jordanians said King Hussein and Queen Noor. None said Jordan's current ruler, King Abdullah II. One student, a married Emirati from Sharjah, whose skin was as dark as the Nigerian's, announced, "Martin Luther King." That came as a complete, and most pleasant, surprise. MLK was an inspiration to a black Emirati. Did he feel discrimination here, too? At least a half dozen Emiratis said Saddam Hussein. That raised my antennae. As one put it, "He knew how to keep his people in line and was strong." Another added, "Kuwait got what it deserved." Two, one an Omani and the other the Nigerian, said Barack Obama "because he gives the world hope." One said Superman.

That was Handsome Ali. I put a pin in the Man of Steel's name. I knew a lot about him. Even where he was really born. And it wasn't Krypton.

After the individual talks, we jumped into an overview of human language and communication. I drew a timeline the length of the white board from 30,000 BCE to the present. First noted were the prehistoric Paleolithic paintings found in the Chauvet Cave in France. Then Egyptian hieroglyphics and Sumerian. I drew the flood linkage from Gilgamesh to Noah. Abraham, Moses, Jesus and Mohammed made appearances. So did the dates of the Torah, Gospel, and Koran. The Rosetta Stone had its own special place. Modern communication was represented by the invention of the printing press and the Gutenberg Bible. The chronology progressed to newspapers, telegraph, radio, TV, mobile phones, cable and satellite TV, 24/7 news, Internet, Google, MySpace, Facebook, and iPhones. The students agreed that life without mobile phones and the Internet would be bad. They had known no world without them.

I asked this question: "If the earth is only about five thousand seven hundred years old, did man walk with the dinosaurs?"

All of the students, all Sunni Muslims, except one, said, "Yes."

Saif Hamood, the leader of the Omanis, had the answer. "Allah made everything."

Only Mohammed Saif, an Emirati sitting in the first row next to Abu Dhabi, said, "No. But I also don't believe in Darwin's Monkey Theory."

That was an eye-opener. The students might have been alarmed, or at least bemused, to learn this belief gave them common ground with evangelical American Christians and Orthodox Jews. The true believers of the three sky religions all valued God's handiwork over science.

CHAPTER 25

Islamic Interest

DINNER WITH THE FALAHIS QUICKLY BECAME A FAVORITE part of my second-semester routine. With Fatima no longer my student, I felt no awkwardness about accepting invitations. I had no reason to question the appropriateness of my being Faraj's "big brother." He had now twice signaled that he hoped to engage me in talking about his children's—his family's—future. We'd not yet gotten to that, but there was a whole spring ahead of us for discussion. I was ready with a response at any time.

Dinner was usually a late-night gathering, with family drifting in and out. The women were always in attendance, Faraj and the sons more intermittently. Hilal was often busy, either at the museum or the racing-camel farm. Sultan, who worked as an EMS supervisor for Al Ain, did overnight shifts. Issa was a guard at the regional prison. Why would a sheikh's son work at a prison? For that matter, what would an Emirati prison be like? I couldn't picture a labyrinth full of shivs and gangs, as on an HBO series. I couldn't in fact picture anything. Unfortunately, Issa spoke no English, so I could not ask him.

Hardy and Hardy usually claimed to be studying, which meant playing video games or stalking Al Ain Mall. Eventually they confided that they regularly went looking for fights with boys from other tribes. Abdulla boasted, "We never lose!" Mohammed explained that they *had* to do this, to maintain their clan's position. My *quid pro quo*, fighting "greasers" on the streets of Cleveland Heights.

Mariam had a job as temporary assistant to the administrator of Al Ain Hospital, and hoped she'd be kept on. Fatima was occupied with her newspaper internship in Abu Dhabi city and graduation in May. That's when Abdulla would graduate from high school. Sarah studied hard and kept up good marks in the sixth grade at a private school. Mohammed was dealing with the rigors of organic chemistry as a UAEU sophomore, and being a gadabout.

The little princess was Mimi, Issa and wife Aisha's two-year-old daughter, and the only grandchild. She would scamper around the *majlis* from one aunt to another and end up on a knee to be bounced and fed. It is custom that the wife lives with the husband's family. They lived in one of the two smaller, modern villas in the family village. Sultan and his wife, Salama, lived in the other villa and were expecting a baby. Everyone prayed, *insha'Allah*, that it would be a boy. I smiled, but refrained from adding my "amen." A name had already been picked out—Zayed bin Sultan al Falahi, in honor of the UAE's patriarch and Faraj's uncle.

But every night after I drove my Yaris back to the apartment, I brooded. Would I be welcome if they knew the truth? I suspected I would. But if that was the case wasn't I some kind of impostor until I came clean? Just upped and told them that Doctor David is a Jew.

That was another kind of bluster. The moment would, *insha'Allah*, present itself. I simply had to wait and be ready. I would look for the right spot and then act. The right time would be coming. That was certain.

My having a rented car didn't cut into time spent with Noor. If anything, we saw one another even more. With Tony now earning extra money by teaching an MBA course two evenings a week in Abu Dhabi city, the second semester gave me more open social hours. I would do the odd meal and Rotana health-club routine with Dan and Carol, but after Brian's death they were less and less. I'd see my Yemini friend Mohamed—and, of course, I was practically on full board at the Falahis. Still, my number-one preferred activity was hanging out with Noor. If I kept teaching, in the UAE or elsewhere, there would always be faculty, expat and not, for company of my own kind. Waziristani taxi-driver philosopher-theologians would not be so easy to come by.

When the new faculty moved into the Falahi Apartments, we had been told it was for the duration, that we'd never get better housing. This pissed off a lot of people, especially faculty with families, trying to live in six-hundred-or-so square feet. It sent Mohamed, my Yemeni colleague, over the moon. But just after winter break that all changed, and my small social circle took a major hit.

Despite the "this is as good as it's gonna get" edict, the university announced it *would* offer new housing to some of us. The relevant *wasta* would be a function of families-with-children and the deliberately vague "rank." Since Carol was a bigwig, she and Dan were the first to relocate. Others would follow and soon we'd be scattered all over the city. Our little academic apartment community, forged at the Intercon and in shared experiences as expat greenhorns, was to go into Diaspora.

So, no more hanging out as if we were in college. Probably just as well.

Tony, Mohamed, and I faced a shared decision—move to a new villa, way out near the Al Ain Airport close to the Abu Dhabi Road, or stay put? Mohamed had decided to resign from UAEU. He'd finish out the year and leave in June. Until then he'd stay put. It turned out he'd actually quit while we were still living in the Intercon because of the broken promise over housing only nobody took him seriously. Since our move to the apartments, Mo had disconnected socially. He would no longer countenance Tony—"He drinks too much!" which I think was really an objection to his drinking at all.

In our way, Mohamed and I remained friends. As at the Intercon, Mohamed would stop over regularly to talk about world affairs or whatever else. Sometimes he popped in to borrow cash to tide him over to the next payday, Islamic interest, of course. Or ask me to accompany him shopping or to Pizza Hut or Chili's. Occasionally, he took me to a Yemeni restaurant for Red Sea fish rubbed with red spice.

"It is even better in Sana'a," he'd say. "You will like it when you visit with me there." I always joked that I looked forward to that day—and to the possibility of being kidnapped, but doubted the time would come. I wrote it off altogether when I learned of his official quitting.

Indeed, UAEU's engineering dean had apparently not believed Mo had resigned over housing. For whatever reason he had been ignoring it, which set Mohamed off even more. Over the winter holiday his former university in Oklahoma had come courting with a raise, full tenure, and a promotion to associate professor. He jumped at the lifeline to return to the U.S.

Thus dies, I thought, my fellow teacher's dream of coming home to help his people. UAEU, and the country's caste culture, looked him in the face and said, "*Your* people? You're not one of us!" More of that Arab solidarity Samah had decried as a thin veneer. The backpedaling promise of better housing only added insult to injury. Mohamed flatly told me he wouldn't return in the fall, under any circumstances. Now I believed him. He was through being a third-class citizen. Or was it fourth class? If that meant moving back to Oklahoma, with its tornadoes and cowboys, so be it.

The news sent me back to the window, with something new to meditate on as the *muezzin* began his final chant. Here in the heartland of the Arab world, a sheikh and his family welcomed an American Jew at their table, but a fellow Arab, because he was Yemeni, was kept down. Of course, the sheikh and his family didn't know their American friend, guest and uncle was a Jew. Or did they suspect but didn't want to openly inquire? February and I was right back where I'd been at the end of the year, stuck between my own personal rock and hard place.

With Dan and Carol living across town, and Tony occupied teaching, Noor became my main man. There were moments he was my sidekick, but generally—and happily—I was his. I was delighted that he made my small apartment his second home often bringing friends and cousins.

Opening the door delighted him. He enjoyed the confused looks of shock and bafflement when his friends came face to face with Zayed gazing at them from the wall. Noor would laugh and tell them the portrait was there to "confuse the Emirati police when they come to arrest David." That made them laugh, too. We guest workers had certain fears in common, the two-a.m. knock being one.

To provide proper hospitality I kept my refrigerator stocked with fresh fruit and Noor's beverage of choice, peach juice. Few of my first-time guests spoke much English, but Noor brought them to meet his American friend nonetheless. I enjoyed the status, among Noor's Pashtun tribe, the Dawar. It's a testament to Noor's human gifts, much more than to any of mine, that I loved thinking of myself as an exhibit at the Museum of Natural History. I don't know whether Noor had told his clansmen that I was *Yehuda*. What I knew was that our respective religions made no difference to either of us.

It struck me one evening when Noor and his cousin, Like, were over: It really was this simple. Noor accepted me, sure. But the point wasn't acceptance. He would cringe at the arrogance of "accepting" another human being God had, in His wisdom, put on earth. The point was merely that he knew. That was, for me, the difference.

Noor's cousin Like (pronounced "like"), who he had brought to Al Ain and whose verb/adjective/noun of a name at first rang strange in my ear, was by now a regular. Noor's elderly Emirati had also agreed to sponsor Like, and the cousins dreamed of going into business together, sharing a vehicle. Of course, the vehicle would have to be registered in the sponsor's name, but the kind, aged Emirati told Noor they would write a contract saying it belonged to Noor. He remembered his own hard days, when he worked as a common laborer, before the oil boom made him wealthy. He told Noor that, when he died, he didn't want his "lazy son" to rip off Noor and steal the vehicle.

Without his taxi Noor bought old cars in Sanaiya, fixed them up, and resold them to other Bahtan. My friends hired him to do odd jobs. For weeks we continued to search the Internet for a used Tata bus. But there were few on the market, none affordable. One night over a dinner of

Famous Chicken, Noor admitted, "Maybe this is not a good time to buy, because work is very slow, even in Al Ain. Maybe it isn't time yet. My God will take care of me. I have faith. Maybe I will look to buy something else."

"Noor, do you truly believe that Allah will take care of you?"

I had a good idea of how he'd answer. He didn't disappoint.

"My God has always taken care of me. When the right opportunity presents itself, Allah will guide me to make the right decision. Buying a Tata bus now would be crazy. Maybe a six-wheeler tipper truck that I can use it to haul sand and stones."

"A dump truck?"

"Yaya, a truck that tips up and dumps its load, a tipper truck."

"How much do they cost?"

"Maybe ninety-thousand dirhams for a used one. Something like that."

He grinned broadly. "Maybe if I need some money you can loan it to me? I just sent my family ten thousand dirhams, and only have twenty-five thousand left. Like's brother-in-law has a good business here and may help. I brought him here many years ago and he is now very successful. Like and I would like to work together. But he also wants to buy maybe a twenty-seat bus. Something like that."

If it came to making a loan, I thought, it would be *insha'Allah*, no problem. At Islamic interest.

CHAPTER 26

"Are you Jewish?"

SAIF HAMOOD'S EYES POPPED OUT OF HIS HEAD, A LA MARTY Feldman as "Eye-Gore" in *Young Frankenstein*. Following class, after nearly all of his colleagues had left the room, the Omani student stood before my desk and asked a simple question: "Doctor, what is your religion?"

Finally, a student with the guts to ask directly. Not quite "Are you Jewish?" but close enough. Hell, I'd dropped enough hints, and at least one student, in addition to Samah, had apparently figured it out. Others probably had, too, but for whatever reason it took an Omani, not an Emirati, to ask.

I asked Saif Hamood to guess but he declined. Spoken words might fade into the din. So I grabbed a green dry-erase pen, turned to the whiteboard and in big block letters wrote: J E W.

He nodded, turned and met two fellow Omanis standing by the doorway. They walked out chattering animatedly in Arabic.

Before leaving the classroom, I erased the three letters. Not a good idea to leave the word J E W floating around out of context on a university whiteboard. I left myself, more than curious as to what the next session of this class might bring.

Two days later on the drive to Falaj Haza, I went back and forth in my thinking. Stick to the syllabus and begin the lesson on nonverbal communication? Nah, that wouldn't work. Thirty minutes of silence as I had done in the fall with the girls didn't seem to be in order, or burping either.

"Excuse me, Doctor," an Omani male student, wearing a bright *kummah*, might ask. "You are acting strangely. Is this normal behavior for a J E W?!"

At the start of the semester I'd instituted a one-dirham fine for tardiness. The kitty would be used for an end-of-term party, of the students' choosing, and I promised to match the "contributions" one for one. Arriving fashionably late was a chronic problem in all classes, but I only nicked the boys. Call it chauvinism, sexism or anything you want. The fund, managed by Funny Man and Handsome Ali, was growing quickly. Collecting a total that day of six dirhams, I noted that the classroom was unusually full. Saif Hamood was seated, as always, on the aisle in the third row. As usual, he wore a *kandura* and *kummah*. He looked moderately uncomfortable and his classmates started to look his way. So I sidled up.

"What did you ask me after the previous class?"

He squirmed and looked around at his countrymen. Then he fixed his large, dark eyes on me. "I asked about your religion." He habitually spoke in a soft voice.

"Just so everyone heard what Saif Hamood asked me," I said, going for broadcast-quality timbre, "he asked me what my religion is. He is, so far, the only person at UAEU who has had the guts."

The Omanis around him exchanged nods. The rest looked in Saif Hamood's direction, puzzled. Apparently, the Omanis had kept the news among themselves.

"What did I answer?"

He took a deep breath. "You're Jewish."

His answer was just loud enough for the class to hear.

Silence. As in pin-drop.

I moved squarely to the middle of the room. Hands planted on my hips, I cocked my head. "Is that an issue for anyone?!"

A Jebel Hafeet beehive could not have topped the buzz in the classroom. I tried to read the room. My heart pounded and I wondered whether the students could hear it. I wanted to mask even the least unease, and here I was all but vibrating. They had known me long enough not to jump, I hoped, to applying a label. Anyway, the deadline for dropping the course had passed.

In that split second while you read the room and divine whether it will eat you alive, some things become abundantly clear. Not an epiphanic moment, exactly, but something like one. It hit me: I didn't care. Whichever way my male students reacted to the news that Dr. David was, in fact, a J E W would be fine. If they chose to see me thereafter only as a label, well, many people do look no further than the brand, and these boys had for the most part been raised to be devout consumers.

I'd come to the UAE to teach, a noble-sounding excuse to get away from my old broken life. But that mission was the last thing keeping me here now. I'd lost my zeal for teaching at UAEU because it was obvious that no one in my position could *teach* there. Sure, I had that three-year contract but that didn't mean much. Look at what *they* did to Dr. Beverly. I'd make it through today's class, but another year, or two? Did I even want to be Dr. David, the J E W, that always being the 800-pound gorilla in the room? At some point, someone wouldn't like the idea—but I'd probably get sick of the idea myself well before getting put on a plane. I was getting ahead of myself. Chosen by fate from among all the Jews in the world, this Clevistani Yid, who'd played the *yarmulke* card only when a friend suggested it, had to explain himself and the "Chosen People" to a room filled with young male Sunni Muslims.

Insha'Allah at play? I racked my brain to recall any references I'd heard to God's will suggesting *He* had a sense of humor. I watched the class, growing strangely calm, merely curious as to what type of storm would kick up.

The answer: none. I could hardly have asked for a better reaction. Questioning looks. Puzzled expressions. Confusion. Not much else. I told myself that I could hold the room for the hour.

It struck me then that I'd have felt more on edge among a gathering of *Haredim* than I did in this room. Among the black-clad black-hatter *Hassids*, I stood out like a *goyim* in a tan two-piece suit—and sometimes felt like a gentile. They knew, I always surmised, that "he's not *really* one of us. He's not a *true* believer!" Jews are harder on each other than outsiders could ever fathom. Just ask Yeshua, better known to gentiles as Jesus Christ, the first Reform rabbi. I pictured how things might be in this room had the students' first Jew been one of those ultra-Orthodox types.

"So, nobody's got any problems with the professor's being Jewish?" I tried to intone it not as a provocation, but more like, "Hey, if anyone does, let's talk about it."

Abu Dhabi spoke first. "You are Jewish? Really?"

The way he said, with a comic's high-pitched dramatic lilt, brought a smattering of laughter. Sometimes I thought he would fit right in with Hardy and Hardy, the Falahi comedy team. All three were the same girth and shared a common wit.

"Yes," I said, with a smile.

"OK with me!" Abu Dhabi yowled.

The class, in its entirety, had the same reaction. What would Bob and my friends back home say now? How would these boys have reacted to a confession that I was Canadian? The married man from Sharjah, who admired Martin Luther King, announced, "You're the first Jew we have ever met."

Heads nodded. No surprise there.

Munther, an Emirati with wire-rim glasses, asked the requisite question, "So you're not Christian?" There was something charming in his question this time.

I laughed, still ruing my non-answer answer to that very question in Samah's class. "No, I am not Christian. Or Bahá'i. Or anything else. I am a Jew. An American Jew from Cleveland, Ohio. We are different from New York Jews and Beverly Hills Jews and from Israeli Jews."

The room buzzed again. Was it the Cleveland part? Was my hometown a punchline here, too?

Mohammed Saif, the brightest and most open-minded of the Emiratis present, asked, "That's why you don't wear the black clothes and big black hat?"

"I'm not that kind of Jew. Only some Jews wear the black hat. My brother did."

Noor Aldeen, one of the Jordanians in the back, cut to heart of the matter. "You are Jewish and still came here?" He paused. "Are you crazy?!"

The room erupted in laughter.

I took a few steps toward Noor Aldeen. A strikingly handsome young man with thick black hair parted down the middle, he had, along with his best friend, Qais, distinguished himself as a thoughtful student with a strong command of English. His question was still the right question. Was I crazy?

The young men in this class had gotten to know me, without the Jew label. That had been my choice; I like to think of it as strategic, not cowardly or crazy. First indications were it had worked. I stood near Noor Aldeen. "I came to see your world so I can go back and describe it first hand."

That's what I had told others, and it startled me to note that it had turned out to be an honest answer. I hoped it rang true for the young men listening. If it sounded phony, I would lose them. I added with a smile, "But, yes, maybe I'm crazy."

Noor Aldeen laughed out loud. "No, professor. You are *really* crazy."

The uproar that followed filled me with warmth. Why had I expected anything different? They had gotten to know me first as the teacher, not the Jew. To them, I was still the teacher. In an ironic sense, their *rabbi.* I remembered the hero Handsome Ali had declared, back at the beginning. I strode to the front of the room and stood before him. "You said that Superman is your hero?"

He nodded.

"Do you know who created the Man of Steel? And where?"

He shook his head.

I had the class's undivided attention. The perfect segue. "Superman was created in the 1930s, in Cleveland, my hometown," I trumpeted. "By two Jewish guys."

Handsome Ali cocked his eyebrow in disbelief. "Superman was created by Jews?!"

"When Hitler was on the rise. He was a fictional Superman created to counter the propaganda about a 'Master Race.'"

Abu Dhabi wondered aloud, "Who created Batman? Jews, too?"

The answer to that, too, was "yes."

Abu Dhabi smacked his palm to his forehead and the class erupted in laughter. From the back of the room, Noor Aldeen hollered, "So, professor, are you saying that Jews control the world's greatest superheroes, along with everything else?!"

"Not Spiderman!?" Abu Dhabi roared.

"Yup, him, too." The class let out a collective hoot. Tears, as I've said, don't come easily, but I could have wept for joy to hear it.

The remainder of the hour felt more like a movie score by John Williams than a planned lesson. One melody flowing into the next sprinkled with moments of tension, and others of clarity and insight. Qais shouted that he had always heard stories about Jews murdering entire villages of Palestinians to steal their land at the time of Israel's creation. That, understandably, did provoke an uproar. Many others nodded in agreement. I thought again about Samah and that helped shape my answer.

"Both sides have killed innocents and it continues." Though, yes, today—the latest Gaza conflict may have recently ended but the wounds ran generations deep. "I believe there should be a Palestinian homeland along with a secure Israel. It's time for that. But how?" I took a deep breath. "Not every American or Israeli Jew agrees with everything the government of Israel does. Does that surprise you?"

"Not all Jews support Israel?" Abu Dhabi asked. "Even *in* Israel?"

What would normally seem like a wisecrack question coming from an American college student sounded entirely sincere coming from Abu Dhabi. How would he know any different unless he had a reason to go beyond his regional media feed? How often had I done that, prior to coming to the UAE? And, no, BBC World hardly counts as "beyond my regional media feed."

"Most American Jews support the state of Israel, but some don't. For many, it's their biblical homeland, but that doesn't mean they support the government in power and its policies. Just like I don't always agree with the American government I also don't always agree with what the government of Israel does, but I don't live and vote there. I support the state of Israel and its right to exist as the only Jewish nation in the world. I do because the Holocaust proved that Jews need a homeland as a last safe haven."

Most of the boys looked skeptical, or at least surprised, at my assertions that not all Jews agree with Israel right down the line. I do support my tribe's claim to a homeland and always have. That's part of what belonging to a tribe means. No one, I was sure, had more capacity to grasp that than these young men. Mohammed Saif pushed the discussion back to Dr. David, the Jew. "What kind of Jew are you?"

Tony's question. The question I had asked myself my whole life now posed by a Muslim student.

"I am a Jew." I shrugged. "A *Jew* is a *Jew*. We don't all dress alike, and we don't all think alike, but we're all Jews, equally." Time for my bottom-line definition of what a Jew is and why. "I believe if you are born a Jew, you are always a Jew. That's the way it is in this world. Hitler reminded us of that. If you have an ounce of Jewish blood in your veins, you may be killed because of it."

The mention of the *fuhrer* created a new stir. Did they know that his attempt to eradicate the Jews of Europe resulted in the creation of Israel and sixty years of conflict? The first big domino? That was news to Noor when I explained it one evening as I played *Hatikva,* Israel's national anthem, on YouTube.

Mohammed Saif took the basic question a step further. "Are you secular?"

I didn't look like a religious Jew and certainly didn't act like one. Would a religious Jew dare stand in front of a university class filled with young Muslim men in country without a minion?

"Some religious Jews would say that I'm secular. I was born to Jewish parents. I'm a Jew. A *Jew* is a *Jew*. Jewish law says if your mother is a Jew then you are a Jew. I belong to an Orthodox synagogue. I was circumcised, like you were. I was bar mitzvahed at age thirteen. I've read the Torah. But I drive on Saturday and eat bacon. I'm an American Jew. A breed apart."

Abu Dhabi perked up at the mention of bacon.

Mohammed Saif pressed on. "Do you believe in God?"

"Do you, Professor!?" Qais and Nour Aldeen shouted in unison from the back.

"Do *you*, Professor!?" Mohammed Saif repeated. "Do you *believe* in God?!"

It was a chance to answer a question with a question. I *believe* and *don't*. I *hope* but *doubt*. But that was not, *insha'Allah,* what I intended to say here.

"Do you?" Looking at the others, I added, "Do all of you believe in Allah?"

Their answers came fast and unanimous.

"Yes," Mohammed Saif said. "In Allah and His Prophet."

"We *all* do!" Noor Aldeen announced, speaking for the others.

In no American college classroom could this hour ever have happened with such a sincere display of blind faith. Everyone saying they believed in God?! Maybe at a Baptist Bible seminary. Naw. Or Jerry Falwell's Liberty University. Not there, either. And certainly not at Ohio State.

"Do you believe in God?" Abu Dhabi asked.

Here's the answer I gave. "I hope there is a God. I hope there is someone who gives us a higher reason for living. I hope that when things can't be explained through science or reason that there is something or someone else."

CHAPTER 27

"We are all cousins"

FARAJ WAS AWAY ON BUSINESS IN ABU DHABI ON THIS MARCH evening. My boys' *Intro* class now knew that their professor, Dr. David, was a Jew and some others still did not. I sat around the table with the Falahi women. The boys were off working or, now that it was getting late, stirring up trouble at Al Ain Mall. Little Mimi bounced on Mariam's knee. Just as well she was happily oblivious, as the conversation took—out of nowhere—a somewhat morbid turn.

"Uncle," Fatima said as Layla cleared the main dishes, "my mother has a question." She cut a piece of homemade double-chocolate cake, put it on a plate and slid it to me. I accepted the serving of dessert and awaited the question. "She wants to know if she can be buried in America, under green grass."

Now that was a curious inquiry. Had I talked with Amna about the visit Noor and I had recently paid to an old Muslim graveyard, reputed to hold the remains of a holy man, a "carrier," near the Al Ain Oasis? That sacred space was a sandpit and functionally a litter box for feral cats. I could understand why Amna wanted to be buried someplace else. But the question concerned being laid to rest under sod, not sand. Much later I learned her father owned the land on which the cemetery was located.

Muslim funeral rites bear similarities to Jewish custom. The body is wrapped in a simple cloth, a *kafan*, and buried without a casket, lying on its right side and facing Mecca; this is to happen within twenty-four hours of death. Cremation is *haram*. The Prophet forbids fire to be used on His creatures. It's believed that the dead, still possessing their souls, can still hear and feel. Immolation would only add to their suffering.

Orthodox Jews also require burial within twenty-four hours, unless the Sabbath interferes. Under strict Jewish law, cremation is also forbidden. That's because when the Messiah comes all of the tribe, including the dead, will be reunited in Jerusalem—except those who've been committed to the elements in the form of ashes. Many fundamentalist Christians, sharing the belief of the "resurrection of the physical body," also prohibit incineration.

Amna sat at the table awaiting a reply. Flanked by her daughters, she gazed at me anxiously.

"I will be glad to tell your mother anything I can about how burial works in my country," I said, spearing a forkful of cake. "But I should start by saying I don't know much about it."

"My mother hates the sand and the desert," Fatima said. "She hates the idea of being wrapped in a shroud and buried under sand. She loves nature and trees and the color green."

Gardening, greenery and animal husbandry were her passions, and she often proudly showed me newborn baby goats or a new Saudi sheep. These were her *jemels*, on a smaller domestic scale. In the UAE women drive vehicles and Amna drove her white Porsche Cayenne all over Al Ain with its many gardens and flowers lining the roadways.

"That's why all my father's buildings are painted green," Fatima added.

"Like an apple," I said. "I knew he painted everything green, and now I know why."

"To honor our mother. Now, Uncle, she hopes she can be buried in a green place in Cleveland. She knows there is no desert there!"

Of course she knew. She'd spent a winter there when Zayed was hospitalized at the Cleveland Clinic and had seen the snow, white, not green, although the city's nickname is the "Forest City." I was sure Fatima had no illusions about my *wasta* among the Clevistanis, but Amna might imagine that it was sufficient that I, on my own, could grant her wish.

"Please tell your mother I am more than confident she can be buried under green grass in a cemetery in Cleveland."

Fatima laughed, then offered up a new gem. "Did you know that my family has a beautiful house in the Al Ain Oasis that we don't live in any more?"

The Oasis had became my retreat from the harsh desert climate and the aridity of UAEU. When I could no longer stand the sand, tedium and the bullshit, I headed there. Alone under the cooling canopy of ancient date palms and enveloped by green vegetation I felt rejuvenated. Inside, there were chickens pecking for food and running water in the *falaj* canals. Outside, the barren landscape was relieved only with concrete roads and blocky buildings baked by the relentless sun. People had sought refuge in this oasis for at least four thousand years. But I hadn't heard of the Falahis' oasis home.

It made perfect sense that the family would have a home in the oasis. Amna's father was Al Ain royalty and Zayed's palace is located on its edge. Inside the Palace Museum, where Hilal presided, Faraj's father was represented by one of the distinguished golden leaves on an exquisite family tree tracing the UAE founder's lineage. Now it sunk in deeper why Hilal had made it a point of showing Max and me his grandfather's prominent gilded leaf upon our December visit.

Fatima smiled broadly. "We lived there for a long time, but we moved out many years ago because the house became overgrown."

"Overgrown?"

She gave her mother a sly smile. "My mother wouldn't allow any of the green plants and trees around the house to be cut, because she could not bear to hurt them. So we moved here and they have now completely taken over the oasis house. We will go there for a visit sometime."

A cynical Westerner would wonder about an Arab tree-hugger, but then what sensitive soul wouldn't prize greenery living in a vast desert? I understood now why there was a national law making it illegal to cut down a desert scrub tree, what they called an "Emirati tree." It would be criminal to destroy a spot of shade in the desert. Anyway, I was no longer that cynical Westerner. Instead, I wondered: Do trees and plants *believe* in Allah?

"Maybe I have seen the house but didn't know it was yours."

Fatima went on a riff about her mother's tribal lineage, the Bani Yas, and the legend of a solid gold elevator in her fraternal grandmother's Abu Dhabi villa. I remembered how Noor had talked about golden elevators behind walls in Al Ain. He was right! I let that question pass and my thoughts stuck on the phrase, "solid gold elevator." The sheer weight of it, let alone how much power would be needed to lift it, made me wonder if such a thing could be real. How many pounds of gold would it take to build it? And how many foot-pounds of force to lift it? Security? It'd be hard to heist such a thing.

"When my grandmother died, the family tried to decide who would get the villa and the golden elevator," Fatima said. "After much debate, my father decided his younger brother could have it. In exchange he got land in Abu Dhabi. He may build a skyscraper there."

However much gold was in that elevator, Faraj got the better end of the deal. Another skyscraper in Abu Dhabi still made sense, although new construction in Dubai had ground to a halt and bankruptcies abounded. These details were new to me. Tonight's theme seemed to be revelation.

"When my parents married, some in both families were not happy. They didn't like that they married outside their clans. My father is *of* Abu Dhabi. My mother is *of* Al Ain. People still grumble. Sometimes we feel like the black sheep, but my mother and father married because they love each other."

I had learned much about the Falahis, but not this. In a culture in which men commonly have several wives, Amna was Faraj's one and only. By everything I witnessed, they were still very much in love. Together they had created a strong family, one notably well grounded amid a churning world. Each had haltingly intimated to me her or his fears for their children's futures. They would bring it up, sigh, and shrug, *insha'Allah*. In some ways I thought they wanted me to solve the dilemma for them, to divine, *insha'Allah*, a plan for each and just present it as *fait accompli*.

Faraj relied on Hilal for the family businesses and wanted Sultan and Issa to find careers they were passionate about, beyond government sinecures and guaranteed incomes. Both he and Amna wanted their daughters to get graduate degrees and know English well. The comedy duo had the talent to be pretty special—Mohammed as a chemical engineer, or as he might prefer a hegemon, and Abdulla in another science. The family had serious money—I never knew how much or cared.

But Faraj and Amna knew there was more to living a fulfilled life. Amna celebrated nature in a dry, dead world. One night in the desert Faraj said to me, "Doctor, here we have money. We have powerful cars. We have everything now." He sighed. Then tapped his heart. "But we are losing our culture and our way. We are losing our young."

Old ways die hard, and the fact that Faraj married outside his kinship group, so closely connected to Al Ain royalty, evidently raised extended family issues. Did that amount to diluting hard-won *wasta*? A dramatic image flashed to mind—Faraj and Amna as a modern Emirati *Romeo and Juliet*. But this one surely had a happy ending; the two had built a strong and caring family.

"My father loves the desert and camels, as you know, Uncle," Fatima was saying. "And my mother doesn't. But they love each other."

It was time to reveal to my Emirati family who Dr. David really was.

"Fatima, there's something I would now like to ask you."

She took the chair next to mine. "What is it, Uncle?"

For a moment, I thought I'd made the dumbest choice. Here we were, in the comfortable family *majlis*. Whatever unease anyone might feel in response to what I was about to say, I'd given them little way to deal with it privately. "You do know that I'm Jewish, don't you?"

She chuckled. "I thought you were because of things you said in class, but I didn't want to ask."

"You didn't hear about it from other students? Samah didn't tell you? Mohammed hadn't heard from other students at the boys' campus?"

"No, Uncle, he's at the other boys' campus. But from the way you speak about things I knew you were different and thought you could be Jewish."

All the others were looking at us. Those who understood English better with knowing eyes, those who didn't as well with rising curiosity.

"Yet you still didn't ask."

"I knew that if you thought it was important you would tell me, and you are."

I began to ask Fatima something else, but she raised a hand so she could translate for her mother. I was grateful, as I was—unintentionally—being rude.

Amna's face broke out into a big smile. "Cousins!" she exclaimed. "Muslims. Jews. Cousins."

Fatima looked back to me. Mariam got Fatima's attention. "Uncle just said he is Jewish?"

"Am I the first Jew you have ever met?"

The sisters looked surprised, even incredulous. "Yes, Uncle. Of course," Mariam answered.

Abdulla waddled in. Hardy and Hardy had just returned. Yes, from Al Ain Mall. I saw no bruises. The cake distracted his focus. "What's going on?"

Sultan broke the news. "Uncle said he is Jewish." Abdulla nodded. Sarah approached and stood at my side, with her winning smile. "I still love you!" I watched Mimi bounce on her grandmother's knee. Sarah cuddled up to her mother. It seemed every night I was there the Falahi women came together with a warm and sincere family bond, at least one of a kind I had rarely witnessed in my life—an unconditional flow of love, affection and respect.

Amna fixed her eyes on me and adjusted her *sheyla*. "Good, Doctor, very good."

Why had I doubted this would be simple? Fatima cut a much bigger slice of the cake and plunked it on a plate for Abdulla. "My mother also thought you might be."

"What about your father?"

"He doesn't know."

How would the news sit with Faraj? Would he think I had deceived him by keeping this information from him? For that matter, did I think that myself? Mohammed, who'd been busy parking his Cayenne, joined us. "What's going on?" he asked, repeating verbatim the other Hardy's question.

Abdulla, around a bite of cake, answered matter-of-factly, "Uncle is Jewish."

His brother turned to me, stunned. "You are Jewish?!"

I gave him a fierce look, as I always relished yanking his chain. "Shall I quote Wittgenstein? Do you have any issues?!"

He doubled over, laughing. "*Insha'Allah,* no problem, Uncle. So Max is Jewish also?"

I nodded. "By his heritage, yes, but I believe by his choice as well."

Mohammed suddenly appeared troubled. "Uncle, may I speak to you privately for a moment?"

I followed him across the *majlis* to a quiet corner. "Uncle, do you remember your promise not to tell my father what Max and I did at the *shisha* cafe?"

The young man had on several occasions stopped in at my apartment and spent time with me, talking and arguing on a variety of topics, even confiding in me. We had discussed his future and I urged him to go to college in the U.S., mentioning Case Western Reserve University in Cleveland.

"I do."

He looked anxious. "You will keep your promise? If he knows, he will kill me."

I smirked like a Cheshire cat and slapped him on the shoulder. "*Insha'Allah,* no problem. I always keep my promises and protect my sources, especially people I like! So just don't piss me off." I slapped him hard on the back and walked away.

The next evening Fatima called. Her father was back from Abu Dhabi, and the family expected me for dinner, at nine.

As soon as I entered the family *majlis*, Faraj rose from his seat at the table. He called for Layla. When the family's Ethiopian maid appeared, her employer pointed, discreetly, at the small gold cross resting in the nape of her neck.

He smiled, looking at me. "Christian."

He brought his hand to his heart. "Muslim."

Then he tapped mine. "Jewish."

"We are all cousins." Then he pointed up to the sky. "All the same God."

That was all my friend, brother and—as his wife noted—cousin ever said on the subject.

CHAPTER 28

Into Yemen

"THIS IS FRESH. I CAME DIRECTLY FROM THE QAT MARKET.
Next time maybe you'll go with me?"

"When in Yemen," I answered, accepting a long blue bag "Of course."

Who wouldn't love to drop in at a folkloric bazaar, as I imagined, dedicated to a single product. But to a drug? Weed, coca leaves or, as in this case, qat, Yemen's national drug.

Observing all the ceremony with which I had taken delivery, way back in 1970, of my first lid of Acapulco Gold—retail price $15—I accepted the package of qat offered by Mohamed's brother, Abdul Ghani. Wrapped in blue plastic, maybe eighteen inches in length, the sheaf of leafy twigs surely surpassed the densest Thai sticks I'd ever handled. So, how would the qat high measure up?

A few days earlier, a trip to Sana'a, Yemen's ancient capital, had been among the farthest things from my mind. Yet already, my first big score on my first day. But is legal procurement a *score*, exactly? It's not nearly as much fun as the illegal kind. No matter, now I was prepared for the evening's event, the every-Thursday qat and *kibitz* party convened by leading lights of the nation's medical profession. Hosting this gathering was an esteemed thoracic surgeon, who in fact ran his own hospital. Mohamed had told me many times how he blamed the sorry state of affairs in Yemen equally on the country's entrenched dictatorship and its qat addiction. As with many of Mo's rants, I listened while sprinkling on a measure of salt. Even the physicians were hooked, along with the rank-and-file?

I'd flown in with Mo expecting something like a tribal Arab version of the crowd at a Grateful Dead show. So far, the reality had defied my expectations at just about every level.

The trip had begun in Dubai, early that morning, midnight, precisely. By 1:30 we were still stuck at the departure gate. At last, one of the flight attendants—speaking confidentially, not over the PA system—let a few of us in on the joke. "They forgot to load the luggage."

Mo turned to me. "That's Yemenia Airlines for you. Never on time. Always something idiotic."

I had a hunch my colleague was speaking literally: *never* on time, as in not once in the company's history. Anyway, our whole venture was fly-by-night so maybe it was time I learned one of the subtle regional meanings of *insha'Allah*. In the comparable modernity of the UAE, "God willing" translated to "maybe, maybe not!" A fifty-fifty thing. And at times you got a nice warm feeling that the speaker, while accepting no responsibility, had his or her fingers crossed. From what Mo had told me I suspected I was headed to a land in which the phrase translated more accurately as, "Fat chance, dude."

We'd get to Yemen in due course, or we would not. If we did, I would have roughly a hundred hours to get a sense of the place, about the most dysfunctional polity I'd ever been. The recovering journalist found himself easing back into reporter/editor think. But having found, finally, the occasion on which to make a full confession to the Falahis, I felt I was ready to do what I'd come, unwittingly, to the Mideast to do. Namely, to get in touch with some of the things my tribal membership meant to me, or might. How many Clevistani Jews ever had a chance like this to visit Yemen with a native son?

The following Tuesday I had to be back at UAEU to make up for the class I'd canceled. Sunday, the university had declared, would be an unscheduled holiday—to honor the eve of *Mawlid an-Nabi*, the Prophet's birthday. The actual birthday, however, would be business as usual. Mohamed fumed that it was like celebrating Christmas on December twenty-fourth. Out of the blue, a four-day weekend. Anticipating that few of my students would attend class on the Prophet's birthday, I was making it five. When Mo renewed his invitation to visit his country's capital, I agreed quickly.

Only later—on the plane, waiting for the luggage to be loaded, did I stop long enough to weigh the pros and cons. On the negative side: endless State Department warnings about events in the ancient realm of Sheba, the Arab world's poorest country, including deadly Al Qaeda attacks on the American embassy, the USS Cole bombing and kidnappings of tourists. On the plus side there was Mohamed and his intriguing Yemeni family and country and the remnant of its once illustrious Jewish population. In particular, there was Yemen's last rabbi, counted by Mohamed's family among its acquaintances. Hands-down verdict: Hell yes! *Insha'Allah*, no problem, I'll go. Having lectured others on *critical reasoning*, I duly enumerated my contrived rationales.

One: Putting some distance between Al Ain and myself would be a good way to consider the question glaring at me from the background of my medium-term future, whether to keep teaching here. It was growing more evident that I would never be UAEU's "journalism expert." The latest department meeting left no doubt that the following academic year I'd be stuck teaching rudimentary courses, trapped in a prescribed curriculum, PowerPoint obligatory, a prospect about as appealing as gefilte fish with marmalade. Could I really continue to wear the smiling mask of fake journalism professor? Sure I could, but could I stand myself if I did? And really, had I no other options? Was I stranded on the Gilligan's Island of this institution of so-called higher learning, like so many of my colleagues, on a three-year tour?

Two: No, I wasn't stranded. Faraj, following the success of my "come to Jesus" moment with the Falahis, had tossed out remarks about our doing a business together. Or I could take shifts driving Noor's tipper truck. I didn't need UAEU to keep up and strengthen the local ties that mattered to me. My commitments in the Emirates were to people, not to the job that had brought me here. A trip to Yemen was a new way, a radically different way, to dig into the heart of the Arab world: a strategic retreat of a new kind for Old-Testament soul-searching in an ancient land. But there was a journalistic strain to the trip, too—Mohamed's mentions of his family's acquaintance with Yemen's last rabbi. While I doubted I'd write it up for any media outlet, I had a strong curiosity about this man and his culture—a curiosity that felt personal, connected to my own strange, stranded presence in the UAE.

To reinforce this intuition, the morning before our departure Mohamed confided the news that the rabbi's cousin and the family's driver, Da'ood, had suddenly vanished from Sana'a. I tried delicately, even as I shuddered, to ask what the young man's disappearance might mean.

The bearer of the news shook his head, echoing Noor's phrase: "Not good."

The newsman side of my nature got the jump on my humanity. I *was* alarmed, and concerned about Da'ood's fate. But the reporter inside me heard the far-off sound of possibility, which added up to rationale number three: There was a *story* out there, unfolding in real time.

Someone at Yemenia eventually remembered the luggage, so we got off the ground and disembarked in Sana'a at five a.m. The one thing I'd permitted myself to learn by googling: the capital's airport, tagged by IATA as SUH, sits at an elevation of 7,216 feet. There were mountains, I knew, in this part of the Arabian Peninsula, but that conjured up visions of the Andes.

Stepping through the plane's door, braced for rarified high-altitude air, I was greeted by a most-foul stench rolling across the tarmac. The capital's obsolete waste-treatment plant, Mohamed cheerfully explained, sits adjacent to the runway of the capital's international airport.

"Yemen is beautiful, Dave," he laughed. "But a lot depends on which way the wind is blowing."

Passport control exacted 11,000 *rials* (US$55) for what was termed an emergency tourist visa. As we sauntered through customs without a glance from anyone, Mohamed and I speculated as to what "emergency tourism" could entail.

His brother, Abdul Ghani, waited outside SUH's perimeter under yellow fluorescents in the family's beaten-up white Land Cruiser. The off-road vehicle looked like it could school all the UAE's Cayennes and Range Rovers about what "off road" means. Yemen, so far, was everything I'd hoped it would be, from the stench onward. Dressed in a crumpled white stained gown, the native *thobe*, Abdul Ghani welcomed me to Sana'a. His cheek bulged. Mohamed embraced his brother, and before he'd even let go, jumped in with an anxious question. "Have you heard anything more about Da'ood?" There was nothing to report. Mo sat shotgun and Abdul Ghani maneuvered out to the main road.

Dawn broke soon, and the morning was devoted to a nap, the afternoon to all the meet-and-greet forms of arrival among a friend's people in his land starting with a wonderful meal of hot Yemeni flatbread and a delicious Red Sea fish crusted with red spice. The company at that meal of Abdul Ghani's wife, Aisha, and five-year-old son, Yusef, made the experience about perfect. Next, a trip to the meat market for the purpose of acquiring a fresh sheep's liver. On our exit from the family's high-walled villa, Mo observed that the daughter of Yemen's president lived in the gated compound next door. At the butcher's shop, a sheep carcass hung from a hook, slit open—I believe to Mo's order, entrails spilling onto the floor like a slimy pink Slinky. The man who did this work, in a blue rubber suit covered in blood, was eager to have his picture, *sura,* taken. The men attending the customers and minding the cash box, were eager, too.

Beyond the meat market, a tiny motorbike carrying three boys zigzagged past us and we bypassed a truck laden with watermelons and another piled with cut branches. Ah, yes, the famous qat, Yemen's addiction. Microbuses, *dababs*, more jammed with passengers than the most crowded clown car in the Shriner's circus—most of those passengers, and the driver, rhythmically chewing away on qat—careened everywhere. At a traffic signal, a girl no more than ten, wearing a brown-and-white headscarf that contrasted beautifully with her black skin, approached the Land

Cruiser. Without a word, she pushed her up-turned hand through the open driver's window, almost into Mohamed's face.

"This girl is here every day, all day," Mohamed lamented, handing her ten *rials*. "This is her corner. She fights others for this spot. It is like this now on every street corner. At some spots women offer themselves for sex. This is what Yemen has come to. It is a big shame."

Mohamed had not brought me to Sana'a to present the sanitized version. He pointed to a group of workers holding painter's poles who were in no way engaged in anything resembling work. "These men chew qat all day. If you need work done, you drive here, negotiate a price, and they work very cheap."

I noted that they looked moderately out of it, but hardly like dopers one would see around the grimmer parts of an American city. Mohamed made clear to me he was not the person to ask about the finer points of qat's effects.

Last stop of the preliminary tour was the neighborhood of the World Bank's Yemeni branch. Concrete traffic barriers placed to block vehicular bombings turned the district into a maze. At a security outpost, Mo stopped the Land Cruiser. Three armed police advanced, proudly displaying their AK-47s. A fourth simply raised the barrier. As we crossed through, however, an officer, four gold bars on the dark-blue epaulettes of his light-blue shirt, shouted for Mohamed to pull over. He pointed past Mohamed at me, and said, "*Sura!*"

"*Sura?*" I asked the officer, uncertain.

"*Sura!*" he responded, pointing at my camera and motioning for the others to join him. The three abandoned their posts and joined their commander on the stone sidewalk. They wore yellow-and-black camo-uniforms, black boots and helmets, and carried their assault weapons slung over their shoulders.

"*Sura!*" the officer said, as they snapped to attention. I clicked off a few pictures. The soldiers gathered around the camera to see their digital images flash across the display. They were all smiles.

Mohamed shook his head as we drove on. "I don't know what it is about Yemenis and cameras."

At the next checkpoint an AK-47-laden policeman simply lifted the metal gate as we approached. I looked across at Mohamed. "They know the car. My ex-father-in-law lives in this district."

The father of Mo's former wife was the prominent surgeon we were soon to visit. The street was crowded with parked vehicles, and we found a spot near the walled compound. Abdul Ghani clutched long blue bags and stood outside the gate talking animatedly with a small elderly man, his cheek bulging, in a crisp white *thobe* and a *jambiyas,* the Yemeni ceremonial dagger, centered in its hilt in an embroidered gold belt that would make a WWE champion envious. The older man—Mo's ex-father-in-law's constant gardener—opened the gate onto beautiful, illuminated grounds and we ascended the villa's exterior staircase.

"Every Thursday night, my children's grandfather and his colleagues gather to chew qat. As my guest, you've been invited," Mo said.

Abdul Ghani, Mo and I stood in the hall serving as foyer to the upper-story receiving room. We removed our sandals and stepped across the threshold. Through panoramic windows, the setting sun glistened off the neighborhood's white rooftops, framed by mountain peaks and wisps of grey clouds against a backdrop of blue mountain air. Within the *mafraj,* two-dozen middle-aged men occupied thick cushions pushed back against its walls. Some sported the traditional *thobe* and *jambiyas,* others Western clothing. Distributed randomly among those gathered were bottles of water, Pepsi and bags stuffed with twigs. I took a look into the blue plastic bag Abdul Ghani had procured for me. The leaves could have been bay laurel, ready to go into a spaghetti sauce, but fresh and a darker green.

A man in the group rose and came to meet us. With a firm grip on my hand, he addressed me in English. "Welcome to my home. Please, sit here next to me."

He was Dr. Mohammed, grandfather of Sabah and Akiel, Mohamed's teenage daughter and twelve-year-old son, who lived there with their mother. I took the place of honor offered, a cushion separated from Dr. Mohammed's by a padded armrest. Mo planted himself between me and a young man wearing a *thobe* and *jambiyas,* with whom he exchanged warm greetings. Abdul Ghani handed me a bottle of water and moved across the room. Was the protocol BYOB—bring your own bag? Unsure, I set my private stash at my feet.

Mohamed indicated the man next to him. "This is my cousin, Dave. His name is also Mohammed and he works with my ex-father-in-law running the hospital. He manages the business."

His cousin laughed, noting that nearly everyone in the room was an accomplished medical practitioner. "If someone threw a bomb into this *mafraj*, medical care in Sana'a would come to a halt." In the exchange that ensued, I learned that he'd taken his degree in my neighborhood, at Northern Kentucky University, and that—like his cousin—he refrained from chewing the leaves of the tree that had brought us all together that evening.

Dr. Mohammed tapped my shoulder. "Here, take this." He handed me a small baggie of green sprigs. "These are the tips. They are better."

"Take it, Dave," Mo suggested. "It's the finest quality and superior to what my brother gave you. The leaves at the tip are considered the best."

With that endorsement from an avowed non-user, I disdainfully pushed aside the bag at my feet, and plucked a few tender shoots from my new baggie. While most of the foliage arrayed around me did look like bay leaves, undried, this could have been that perfect sprig in a mint julep. My first hesitant taste of Yemen's fabled intoxicant put an end to such delicate thinking. More like hedge trimmings—which I have nibbled while pruning and know to be bitter. The two cousins watched, bemused.

My silent reaction: *Yech! Yuck! Ick!* But I managed to keep my lips from curling, and tried for a poker face. When in Yemen.

Soon I had the beginning of a chaw tucked into my own cheek, and was surveying the gathering. Dr. Mohammed pointed out various figures in attendance. "That one's an orthopedic surgeon. He's a vascular. Behind him is an orthopedist..." I got it, everyone was a prominent doctor and they were all chewing away. Were any "on call" for emergencies?

Despite the bitterness pervading my mouth, I shoved in more leaves, working to build the bulge in my cheek up to the girth of theirs. Surely the celebrated high would be worth it. It had to be. Why else would anyone indulge in a drug that makes you look like a cow working her cud? Mohamed's cousin Mohammed picked up the exposition. "Every Thursday, many of the most prominent professionals in Yemen come here. They chew qat and tackle the world's problems. They even overthrow the government. Then they go home, go to sleep, and nothing changes."

Dr. Mohammed raised his hand, and the *mafraj* fell silent. "This is Mohamed's friend from America, Dr. David. He teaches journalism at the Emirate's university." He looked at me. "Welcome."

I was dutifully asked the questions about my impressions of Yemen and was lucky to have been in country so short a time as to be able to beg off—offering any opinion after just a few hours would be premature, but I was very happy to be here. Next, naturally, I was expected to weigh in on Obama, in office all of a few months. There, too, I had the easy way out: too soon to tell. I did get a chance to clarify that I was not a medical doctor, and for that matter no kind of doctor at all.

We all got along famously, and after several hours nothing in Yemen, or the world, had changed. Not even my state of consciousness. All the work to masticate hedge trimmings, and the indignity that came with it, for what? I thought of that first time I'd smoked hashish. It took me and my friends a while to figure out whether we were stoned. Maybe this was the same way? No, I was grasping at straws. I didn't have the least buzz on. Not even the effect of a cold Lone Star on a hot Texas day.

Could qat be a huge letdown?

No matter. Yemen had other excitements to entice the unwary tourist. Two doctors held up their hands for quiet. "If you wish," one announced, smiling, "we can arrange your kidnapping." The other piped in, "We come from the area where many take place." The first doctor added, "They treat you well. Feed you. You just can't leave. In the last two years, only two have been killed because they didn't behave right. Usually you're held for a month, a ransom is paid and you're let go."

Mohamed leaned over and said softly, "Seriously, Dave, they could arrange it." In a softer whisper, "Let's not tell them you're Jewish." It hit me only then what I'd done. Having finally gotten to the J word in the UAE, I'd decamped immediately deeper into the heart of a world in which I had to keep that aspect of my identity secret. Mo added, "My father said I was crazy for bringing a Jewish here. It can only cause trouble." He paused then added, "He's sorry to miss you. He's in Germany for medical care."

As the pros and cons of my own disappearance got chewed over, I shoved in more qat, expanding my cheek like a ball player in the dugout. The leaves' juice isn't to be spat out like tobacco slosh, but swallowed. That's what delivers the high. I soldiered on, it tasted vile, but I got it down.

I was asked by someone to weigh in on the question of whether Obama would be any better than Bush. So maybe it was a good thing my high was slow in coming.

Dr. Mohammed touched my arm gently. "If you will permit me, Professor." He turned to face his guests. "Everyone here tonight hopes that Obama is successful because the world—and the Arab world—needs him to be. If Obama can finally resolve the Israel-Palestine problem, then the twenty-three Arab nations, who love America, would embrace your country." He then turned back to me. "And you couldn't have any better friends in the world."

Mohamed was nodding as his former father-in-law spoke, but was not at all deferential in his commentary. "We can't keep looking to America, or Obama, to solve the problems of the Arab world. Or Yemen's. We have to do these things for ourselves. If we want democracy, we have to do that for ourselves, too. We can't have America do it for us."

Our host, now moderator, turned to me. "Professor?"

I took another swig from my water bottle. Nodded to Mo. "Mohamed makes a good point. Whatever the reasons for America's invasion of Iraq, seven years of occupation have shown that democracy cannot be imposed. It has to be chosen. If it isn't, it is undemocratic from the start." I gestured toward Mohamed. "I tell him he should return to Yemen and run for president. He tells me I am crazy."

The *mafraj* broke into cheers and there were several cries of "Yes, Mohamed for president!"

Yemen's future president took center stage. "Obama has been president for fifty days. He can't fix everything at once. Many people are hoping Obama can get America back on the right path again, but he is not a miracle worker. You all know that I am an American citizen. I never thought America would elect a black man president. But he can't fix *our* country. We must do it for ourselves."

His last line was met with vigorous nods. How much influence was gathered in this room? These men congregated to debate issues on which they took no action? Maybe qat was, as Mohamed had insisted, undermining Yemen's national will, breeding an *insha'Allah, bukra* nation.

A bit later, on our way to the front gate, I gagged as I spat wads of masticated green qat into colorful flowerbeds, hoping the old gardener had gone to bed.

Mohamed watched me retch. "You didn't like it?"

I took a big gulp from my water bottle, rinsed, spat, quaffed again, spat again, and kept at it. "No, but I couldn't spit it out inside." I picked a green speck off my black shirt.

"But tell me, Dave," Mohamed asked. "Did it affect your mind?"

"No!"

"No?"

"No!!"

"Maybe it only affects Yemenis," Mohamed offered. "Maybe it only makes us crazy."

Yemenis didn't strike me as crazy. They lived in a country beset with problems. Most nations, facing half so much trouble, would be hooked on something a lot stronger than these leaves.

At midday on Day 2, as we pulled off the crumbling highway onto the dirt road, a dozen men scurried quickly along the edge to escape a torrent of traffic. They were holding a yellow-and-green wooden litter, a body wrapped in a white shroud rocking perilously on top.

"A funeral procession," Mohamed noted, somewhat unnecessarily. He sped up to get ahead of a truck stacked with yellow plastic chicken coops filled with white clacking fowl. A few kilometers down the dirt road, about thirty kilometers outside Sana'a, past fields planted with green trees I now recognized, ruefully, as qat, Mohamed turned off into an empty parking lot. We strolled to the edge of a cliff. The precipice looked out over a vast valley stretching far into the distance. Mohamed gestured across the vista. "This is Wadi Dahr. The Grand Canyon of Yemen."

Flowing as far as the eye could see, bounded by weathered rock cliffs, was a panorama from biblical times. Clusters of stone-and-mud homes pocked the land, amid geometric stonewalls enclosing orchards and fields. All this, I imagined, had surely been there since the reign of Sheba.

"Over there!" Mohamed pointed across the wadi to a tall rock chimney with a magnificent structure perched on top. "That's *Dar Al-Hajr*, the Rock Palace, built by Imam Yahya. It is the national symbol of Yemen. That is where we are going."

Another thirty minutes over rugged dirt roads and through several crumbling stone-and-mud villages that looked like they hadn't changed in a thousand years, we approached the Rock Palace. It loomed above us, looking impregnable. This natural redoubt has been inhabited since prehistoric times and used for defensive purposes since the start of the first millennium—BCE. Majestically shading the Rock Palace's entrance stands a gnarled tree that appears in legends going back seven centuries.

Rising as high as eight stories, at angles something like a pueblo, though far more vertical, the majestic structure stands on a monolith nearly of the same height. Inside that rock are burial caves dating to the Iron Age. There's a spot that offers a view down into the deep, dark recesses of its natural stone cistern. That's what made the place a one-of-a-kind location, an ideal spot for holing up against a siege. During our self-guided tour— few tourists were visiting—I marveled at the hydro engineering deployed to collect rainwater. Shallow catch basins placed at different levels on the Rock Palace's many roofs captured precipitation, then conducted down to fill the deep underground reservoir. The water system enabled the fortress to hold out virtually indefinitely.

Mohamed had promised "signs of the Jewish" at the Rock Palace. Inside the thirty-five-room citadel were scores of ornate stained-glass windows, many crafted by Jewish artisans, and featuring the six-pointed Star of David formed by two superimposed triangles. Other levels revealed more wonders—royal sleeping chambers, meeting rooms, sitting rooms, baths, and a carefully preserved kitchen. The commanding views of the wadi and the village from various points in the Palace offered glimpses back in time. The vistas, as I'd begun thinking earlier, had no doubt changed little over the centuries—at least not once you squinted to filter out the broken-down cars and trucks littering the road.

Outside we strolled to a royal guesthouse that featured a courtyard with spring-fed fountains. It was a ready-made set for an Arabian Nights movie.

"I told you." Mohamed beamed.

"This is an extraordinary place."

He grew serious. "You saw what the Jewish did here? It is beautiful. The Jewish were the artists, the craftsmen, the silversmiths. Now they are gone and it has hurt Yemen terribly. There is nobody that can replace them and what they meant to us."

At the fortress's edge Mo pointed out Bayt Bas, an old Jewish village, empty of Jews.

I tried to picture their exodus.

"Wadi Dahr is as far outside Sana'a as I will take you," he cautioned. "Things are not secure outside the capital. They're really not that secure here."

Saturday was devoted to less remote touristic highlights. Mohamed seemed to alternate the grand and picturesque with his own version of gritty realism. The capital's traffic, a kind of rolling chaos, was a free-for-all. After the parades of luxury cars on the UAE's superhighways, it was a nice change. In Yemen, if it had wheels and a motor it was on the road. A motorbike meant for two riders would carry at least three, two sitting and one squatting on the luggage rack over the back wheel. Parking was wherever a car was left, traffic rules and signs just more clutter to ignore, and one-way streets anything but. If "saloons" and mobile-phone stores were the main retail businesses in Al Ain, honey shops were tops in Sana'a selling regional Yemeni honey.

By afternoon, scores of men carrying plastic bags poured out of neighborhood qat markets, retail locations to which the cuttings were trucked in fresh daily. We fell in with the flow of traffic, and it took us past the six-minaret Al-Saleh Grand Mosque. Named by Yemen's long-serving chief of state in honor of himself, the $250-million house of worship is another magnificent monument to Allah's majesty, but clearly intended to glorify its sponsor. Mohamed grumbled, "President Saleh said he used his own money to build the mosque for the people. The problem is that he thinks the country's money is his."

A stop at The National Military Museum turned out to be a kitschy treasure trove-cum-time warp. It housed battlefield relics—armored vehicles, field cannon, swords, battleaxes, flintlocks, mortars, a Soviet MIG—all set in a context of heroic, quasi-Soviet murals. Passing into the room dedicated to Yasser Arafat felt like walking through a Stargate into a parallel reality. The Arafat memorabilia commemorated his leadership in the struggle for Palestinian rights and his friendship to Yemen. I stared, thinking of all the damage Arafat had caused, let alone all the lives his leadership had cost, the billions he stole. Mohamed summed up the exhibit. "He is loved here. We always honor the wrong men."

As we drove away from the museum, the summation of the day: of all the signage I saw during my stay, the acronym spotted that evening stands out—SNACC. It dominated the façade of the nation's Supreme National Authority for Combating Corruption.

At the villa later that night we found Abdul Ghani sprawled on a sofa in the *mafraj*, chewing qat, drinking Coke, surfing the net, and watching Yusef watch cartoons. Asked for the latest news on Da'ood, he relayed there was none. *Insha'Allah*, the brothers agreed, he was unharmed. Still a missing Jew. Kidnapped? Murdered? Where is he? How much should I care?

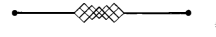

The Christian Sabbath saw my return to Jewish Yemen. On Sana'a's outskirts, as we bounced over rock-strewn roads, there loomed an ancient stone fortress perched on the edge of a cliff. Mohamed was taking his children and me to an abandoned Jewish village that he described as "mostly forgotten." We parked in an empty lot and descended a steep path toward a gigantic fig tree. The ground was littered with copper-laced rocks and trash. Dung pies drying in the sun ringed the edge of a cistern filled with lime-colored water. "The Jewish lived there for as long as anybody remembers," Mohamed said. "I wanted my children to see it with you. It was famous for its silversmiths and has been long deserted."

Beneath the shade of the mammoth fig tree, two boys, ten to twelve at most, spotted us and came running. "Hire me," one exhorted us in rudimentary English. "You see this tree? It is more than four hundred years old. It is where the Jewish came to settle disputes."

Hired, the boys led us up a rocky path, steep but wide enough for a donkey cart. We entered the ancient ghost town through a narrower rock archway. I looked at the fortifications, simple but effective. Men with spears could readily mount a defense, if there had been any men. Passing through that old stone gateway took us back in time. Our young guides scurried about leading us down even narrower stone-paved streets. We slipped in and out of stone structures, some three-stories high. This was not an archeological dig to unearth an ancient past, but a living museum, in ruins. It had been inhabited in my lifetime, or close to, before most of Yemen's Jews fled to the new state of Israel. Now its only denizens were a few squatters hiding in the shadows, living a hand-to-mouth scavenger existence that filled ancient rooms and courtyards with rubbish.

As I wandered the warren of constricted streets, I found myself in strange company. The place was filled with Jewish spirits, and I pictured busloads of *landsmen* stopping here to connect to our people's rich history. Their guides would take them to the Rock Palace and more of Yemen's lost Jewish heritage. With the exception of Israel, Jewish roots reached deeper here than anyplace else on earth.

At caves outside the fortress our young guides introduced us to their siblings. They lived beyond the dung-pie lined cistern, behind filthy blankets in a grotto dug into the cliff's side. Small heads peaked out from behind the heavy wool. "My brother and I live here," the eldest said. His brother darted inside and three younger dirty children, two girls and a boy, dressed in rags, followed him back out.

"You see them?" Mohamed said to his children. "This is what Yemen has come to. These people have no home, so they live here. Their only fuel is the dung pies. It is a shame."

Our urchin band took us to what they said was an ancient Jewish synagogue. It was a mess of tumbled stone, half-collapsed walls, over-grown with weeds. It could have been anything, but in my Jewish-heritage theme park of the future, it could be a synagogue. But when this village was restored, *insha'Allah*, as a *living* Jewish heritage museum, where would the squatters, our eager guides, go?

The question clung to me as we walked back to the Land Cruiser. Mohamed and I passed out *rials* to our guides that, he said, "will feed their family for weeks."

At sunset Mo and I stood atop a forty-foot battlement near *Bab al-Yaman,* the Yemen Gate, a thousand-year-old portal framed by two Arabesque turrets set in thick clay walls, the iconic entrance to the Old City. Outside its massive wooden doors throngs of men wearing *thobes* adorned with *jambiyas,* some sporting blazers with *kufiya* hanging over their shoulders, milled around. A ragged collection of peddlers hawked sunglasses, athletic shoes, clothing, spices and food. All the while a steady stream of people passed in and out through the gigantic opened gateway.

Mohamed swept his hand across the vista. "Tradition says Sana'a was founded by Noah's son, Shem. It's one of the oldest continuously inhabited cities in the world. Many thousands of Jewish used to live here and there were many synagogues."

Inside the Old City we wandered narrow streets flanked by tower houses—most about five stories, some up to nine. Visible influences dating from Persian and Byzantine times melded with Islamic geometries and design. Each grand house, built of stone and clay, covered with gypsum plaster, was an historical entity unto itself, not yielding a square inch on the ground or vertically. Here, the din of car horns and tang of car exhaust abated, but the sounds and smells of an historic urban center filled in.

"About 50,000 people live here," Mohamed said. "Some families from before The Prophet."

From a perch on a worn stone step, a very old man trying to sell a single *jambiyas* watched the street. Across the way an adolescent boy showed off a selection of the daggers at a tiny stall. All along the narrow streets micro-shops offered textiles, sunglasses, fruit, lingerie, brassieres, polished stones, pottery, silver, hot bread, copperware, large sacks of green henna—and, of course, *jambiyas.*

Two teenage boys, who had to be brothers, decked out in jeans and MTV t-shirts, approached us. "Let us show you the Old City," said the older brother in serviceable English. "We know all the special places," the younger brother chimed in—and they did.

In a basement room they showed us a camel tethered to a millstone, now resting and chewing a mouthful of grass. The stone floor had a deep round groove made by camel hoofs walking over the same path, probably for centuries. From a rooftop we looked down on a residential balcony where a horned brown goat stood tied to a stake and chomped on a pile of fodder. Beyond sat a large flat roof surrounding a central courtyard, a golden glow spilling out.

"What's that?" I asked.

"The Grand Mosque," the older brother said. "We will go there?"

Of course, but first I wanted to buy a few pieces of "Jewish silver." In a busy plaza in the heart of the Old City, where peddlers sold hot bread and purple-red prickly pears, our guides steered us toward a particular dealer. The cluttered shop's display cases overflowed with bracelets, earrings, amber beads, necklaces, rings, and of course daggers with ornately crafted handles and scabbards. Antiques—swords, *jambiyas*, and Bedouin rifles—hung on the walls; whether for sale or simple décor I couldn't tell. Behind the locked cases stood two salesmen and I asked to see Jewish silver.

I pointed through the glass to several intricately crafted silver cylinders. The elder salesman, maybe thirty, laid them out on a black felt pad. "These are Jewish made and were used to carry Koran passages." I indicated a dagger with a silver hilt and worn leather scabbard inset with a shield of silver filigree. "This piece is also Jewish." The man pointed out where someone had long ago scratched a Star of David on the silver dagger's handle. "It is at least one hundred years old, maybe older, we don't know. All Jewish silver is at least that old. Some much older. That is all we know."

Mohamed negotiated and I walked out with two silver cylinders, one stamped with the symbol of Bayt Baws, the old Jewish town near the Rock Palace, and the dagger. Final cost: 20,000 *rials*, the equivalent of two hundred American dollars. I hoped the brothers got a commission for leading me there.

The Old City's al-Qa' quarter had once been home to more than eight thousand Jews. At the time of my visit, that number had been reduced significantly. It stood at zero, unless I counted myself as one, and looked unlikely to rebound any time soon. The brothers escorted Mo and me down empty, dark residential streets past several *hammams*, traditional bathhouses. There were buildings here that likely predated European civilization, and had been continuously inhabited since its dawn. My mind wandered to a time back in those olden urban streets, lasting more than a thousand years, when the Jews alone among the city's residents believed in one God, as the first practitioners of the first "sky" religion. Even then, they would have recited the *Shema*.

The older brother pointed up. "See! Jewish!" Yes, there it was, inset in the ornate brickwork of a tall square residence in a stately neighborhood: the Star of David. Down the street, at the upper level of another magnificent brick villa, were stained glass windows featuring the six-pointed stars.

I saw with my own eyes the external differences between the Old City's Jewish and Islamic houses. I learned afterward that Jewish homes had rooftop courtyards as focus points, from which all the main rooms opened and descended. It was a Jewish peculiarity to arrange rooms so that two seldom sat on the same level—the principal entertaining room being highest, next the *diwan* or sitting room, downward to the kitchen, and at the lowest level the lavatory—not of course that these houses had what could be called indoor plumbing back in the day, but as gravity is a constant, many things roll downhill.

"Once there were many synagogues, a dozen or more, in the Old City," the younger brother said. "There are one hundred mosques now, including the Great Mosque, but no synagogues."

"It's prayer time," the older brother said. "We can look, but cannot go inside."

Mo and I were fine with that. From an entrance, we watched worshippers kneel on carpets and touch their foreheads to the floor under a soft buttery light. The Great Mosque of Sana'a, one of the oldest in the world, is linked to The Prophet. After he had slipped out of Mecca in 622, the story goes, driven away by rumors of assassination, Mohammed commissioned the mosque in the nascent days of Islam—not to glorify rich sheikhs, but Allah. It post-dates by a few hundred years the original basilica of St. Peter in Rome and Hagia Sophia in Constantinople. Today it houses the oldest extant copy of the Koran. The *Oldest*! An *Original*? A simple building hemmed into an urban square, for glitz and grandeur it could not compare to Zayed or Saleh's mega-mosques. For its feeling of a humble spirituality, however, and ability to inspire awe there was no comparison.

"Things have been this way here since the beginning of Islam," Mohamed said. "Islam and the Jewish lived together in peace for a very long time. It is the shame of Yemen what it has done to its Jewish. There is no replacement."

I nodded, avoiding his gaze, not wanting to betray my feelings. Hell, I asked myself, have there ever been a people who could duplicate the achievements of the Jews? The presence of so many ghosts was reinforced by such palpable memory of their contributions to the local culture. Three artifacts of which I'd acquired to take out of the country, to rescue.

Beyond the Yemen Gate, the plaza was nearly empty. Only a few pedestrians moved in and out of the Old City. The surrounding city, beyond, was hardly quiet. The yellow streetlights gave off an eerie glare, and the traffic's cacophony filled the air with horn blasts to punctuate the rattle and roar of engines. The prospect of leaving this haven and its tranquility put me off.

I had once walked the streets of Jerusalem's Old City, which comprises barely a third of a square mile. The City of David, since the time its namesake conquered it in the 11th century BCE, has been heavily fortified with strong walls that had been breached in holy wars. Jerusalem was already a city at least a thousand years old before Sana'a existed, even if legend had it founded by Noah's son.

All the same, this place on this spring evening awakened something in me, an ancestral memory. Many kingdoms had laid claim to Sana'a. Persians, then Jews, then Christians inhabited the Old City's most venerable quarter, al-Qati, even before Islam took root. When the Prophet ordered the building of the Grand Mosque, he decreed that it be erected in the garden of the Persian governor. A band of Hebrews had settled here seven hundred years before Christ. My tribe was not the only one with a vast heritage concealed in, under and around these stone streets.

Beneath my awe and admiration lurked dismay. No, that was too mild a term. I had passed through the Yemen Gate despondent. Another nation emptied of Jews. An epic history reduced to trinkets, like those I carried in my neatly tied parcel. This was the 21st century CE. What had changed?

And, yes, when we met Abdul Ghani in the *mafraj*, Da'ood remained missing. I thought of Chevy Chase's old joke about General Franco, from *Weekend Update.* Now as then, it didn't make me laugh.

At last, on Monday afternoon, word of Da'ood had arrived and, in a way, it was as much an anticlimax as a relief. A jubilant Abdul Ghani rushed into the *mafraj*, found his brother and me drinking coffee, and delivered the news that Da'ood was safe. He clasped my shoulder. "I just talked to Suliman, Da'ood's father, and he said he'll bring his nephew, the rabbi, to our home after it's dark to meet you, if they can get a permit to leave Tourist City, near the American embassy."

Mohamed moaned. He would be unable to join us as he was spending the final evening with his children. Abdul Ghani burst out with, "I told Suliman that I'd have qat for them." He locked eyes with me. "We need to go the market!"

"The rabbi chews qat?" I couldn't picture it.

Abdul Ghani chuckled. "Everybody in Yemen does. Just not my brother."

Off we went to make a score, five-year-old kid in tow. Abdul Ghani parked the Land Cruiser haphazardly and clambered out. He scooped up Yusef and carried him across the busy thoroughfare to a teeming neighborhood market. Peddling the leaf from rickety stalls were scores of dealers, the retail sector of Yemen's biggest industry, employing 3.5 million people. This industry is the principal reason Yemen is running out of water; qat cultivation puts the country further into hydro-deficit each year.

Hundreds of buyers scurried around handing over wads of *rials* for clear bags of leaves or long branches in blue plastic wrap. I had my trusty digital camera.

"*Sura, sura*," said two young men in *thobes*, bags of qat hanging from the hilts of their *jambiyas.*

"*Sura, sura*," said the young dealer wearing a Zidane soccer jersey.

I clicked off a few shots and showed the men their images. "A lot of Americans would love to have pot markets like this," I told Abdul Ghani. "But people wouldn't want you to take their pictures."

He laughed, squeezed his son's hand, and set him down on his feet. "It's like this everyday here. Yemen is the poorest of all the Arab countries, but many of us would rather chew qat than eat." He patted his stomach. "I do both."

"*Sura, sura,*" followed us through the market, our progress slow because I always obliged the request. But soon enough, three large bunches of fresh stalks under his arm, the best earmarked for the rabbi and Suliman, Abdul Ghani led us back to the Land Cruiser. Driving home, he said, "Suliman said the rabbi wants to meet the American Jew who teaches journalism with Mohamed in the Emirates. He wants you to write what is happening to the Jews of Yemen."

My stories were both still incomplete, but they'd just converged. I thought it advisable to lay off the qat for the evening. Once was more than enough.

In 2009, the Prophet's birthday fell on the thirteenth of Adar, *Erev Purim*. Meeting Yemen's last rabbi on this night was ironic. Purim, the "Hebrew Halloween," celebrates deliverance from annihilation at the hand of Haman, an early Persian prototype of Hitler. The holiday's spirit is joyous, in mockery of the man who sought to engineer the Jews' extinction in Babylon. Had Haman succeeded there would thereafter have been no Jews. Ergo: no Jesus, no Prophet Mohammed. No sky religions.

At half-past nine on the eve of Purim, in a Yemenite Muslim family's *mafraj*, the nation's last rabbi shoved a few qat leaves into his mouth, feeding the already good-sized bulge in his cheek. Still, I was happy I'd abstained. Yahya Yousef Mousa took a sip of Coke and leaned to his right, reclining on the pillow armrest separating us. On my right, his uncle, Suliman, sat cross-legged on the sofa cushion, also chewing qat. He offered me a branch. "*La la,*" I said, adding a "no, thank you" in English.

Abdul Ghani chortled. "I never thought to ask if you speak Hebrew!"

I told him I only knew prayer book Hebrew and was informed that Yahya and Suliman only spoke Arabic and Hebrew. With Mohamed away visiting his children, Abdul Ghani offered to act as interpreter. My first question was whether I had the rabbi's permission to record our discussion. I did.

A slight man with long, braided *peyos*, sidelocks, Yahya had classic, even stereotypical Jewish features—deep-set brown eyes, a protruding hooked nose, wispy moustache and scraggly chin whiskers. Just as I would picture a Canaanite, who historians think made up the original Hebrews. He wore a dark blazer over a white *thobe* with an embroidered tan *sumata*, a large shawl, draped over his shoulders. He had an embroidered *yarmulke* on his head. A lapel button bore the image of President Saleh.

Suliman's full head of hair was bound in a turban. Curled *peyos* dangled over his long salt-and-pepper beard, the whole accentuating a prominent hooked nose. He wore a white *thobe* under a blue blazer. Briefly studying the men, I couldn't discern their ages, but I gathered Suliman was younger than me, and that his nephew, the rabbi, was in his early thirties. Our vintages notwithstanding, it felt very much as if these men were my elders. By at least a millennium.

Courtesy of CNN International, the Stars and Stripes billowed on the muted TV in the corner. My next question was what they had learned about Da'ood. Suliman and Yahya told the young man's tale, punctuated with many "*insha'Allahs*"—an odd phrase to hear, I thought, spoken by Jews. Of course, I used it all the time, and I was a greenhorn.

Da'ood had gone missing two weeks before. Days before Da'ood disappeared, the woman he was to marry had cancelled the engagement. After that disappointment, without telling his father or cousin, Da'ood vanished from Sana'a. Because of the "troubles," his family and community feared the worst. An Air Force officer had murdered a Jewish schoolteacher because the teacher wouldn't convert to Islam on the spot. Connected to influential people, the pilot was able pay bribes and got off with only a hefty fine. The teacher's family was offered "blood money," but refused it. The Jewish community had all known the martyred man, and was put on edge by the crime. But Da'ood was safe.

It took me a moment to put things together from there. Da'ood had been spirited out of Yemen? A Jew being smuggled out of a hostile land?

This *was* a story. Da'ood had contacted them just today from Israel. He had already met a woman there, another Yemeni Jew. He and his father, however, might never see one another again in this life. Da'ood, like all Jews who have left Yemen, despite their having been citizens, is barred from returning. Were Suliman to visit his son in Israel he could not return. Any reunion would have to take place in Israel.

No doubt an effective mechanism for driving out an unwelcome population—without, technically, expelling them. Less hew and cry that way from the international community. After Israel was founded in 1948, and after violent attacks against Yemen's Jews, nearly 60,000 were relocated to the Holy Land by the Israeli government in a massive airlift, Operation Magic Carpet. Today, only a few hundred remain, most living under government protection and restriction, in Tourist City near the heavily guarded U.S. Embassy, which is where the rabbi, his uncle and their families lived in isolation.

Now there was one fewer.

It hit me how poignant, for Mohamed, Da'ood's story would be. It was a shame he was missing this. He'd made an extraordinary journey of his own—from scholarship student in the U.S., fearing Jewish professors, to professor himself in a foreign land and befriending me. He had potential to be one of Yemen's future leaders. Now he might be one of Oklahoma's future leaders. Mohamed, too, saw his country as offering him, and his children, no future. He was determined to move them to America.

Over the next few hours the rabbi and Suliman told me that less than four hundred Jews remain in Yemen, few hundred in Raidah, a village seventy kilometers north, and those in the capital. Two years earlier the al-Houthi, a radical Shia group backed by Iran with a stronghold in northern Yemen, had attacked and looted their village, Ghareer, in the northern province of Sa'ada. The al-Houthi warned the Jews that if they stayed they would be killed. Their family along with others, numbering three score, had fled the homes where they had lived for generations. They abandoned their houses, furnished and decorated with treasures and heirlooms handed down since the days of remote ancestors leaving with no more than they could carry. A Muslim tribal leader had given them protection and safe passage to Sana'a.

They had lived since in Tourist City under the nominal protection of President Saleh, but conditions were growing desperate. The government prohibited them from working, citing security concerns. All their silver-smithing tools had been left behind in Ghareer. The food rations they were promised hadn't materialized nor had the three hundred square meters of free land to build a house that the president promised. To live they had been forced to sell their personal silver jewelry and exhaust their savings. In a deadly terrorist attack on the U.S. Embassy, they had been caught in the crossfire.

In Ghareer, priceless religious artifacts and texts had been burned, destroyed or stolen by the al-Houthi. A few years before Ghareer's Jews had been turned into refugees, a rich American Jew had come to the village and offered Yahya's father one hundred thousand dollars for a religious book hundreds of years old. The book, which his father had declined to sell, was destroyed by the al-Houthi.

As wards of the Yemeni government, the rabbi's family received 55,000 rials (US$275) a month and had the use of a two-bedroom apartment. The family numbers eleven, and includes the rabbi's father, also a rabbi, paralyzed and therefore retired after a stroke. Drugs to ease his condition cost twenty thousand rials a month, and he cannot get the medical attention he needs.

As I listened to the back and forth among Abdul Ghani and our guests, I learned that Rabbi Yahya studied in Brooklyn at a Satmar *yeshiva* and that one of his classmates was the murdered teacher. To many Zionists, the *Satmar* are an irritating and persistent bur denying Israel as a Jewish state.

I noticed Abdul Ghani shake his head. "The rabbi said that Jews here are slandered in the market, but that is no big deal—it is a constant. When something happens in Gaza or Israel, however, it gets more aggressive." I asked what it was like for them during the recent Gaza War. As the question was conveyed, I stole a glance at my digital recorder. The red light was still on.

My interpreter resumed. "The rabbi told the media that Israel was wrong. He rejected the killing of innocent human beings as being against all religion, all faith, and all humanity. Many Yemenis were very surprised to hear his condemnation of Israel. He thinks his statement relieved the pressure. Others told him that they expected him to side with his friends, even if they are wrong. They expected him to support Israel, and when he didn't they thought it exceptional."

Exceptional indeed. But Satmar were like that, deeply religious Jews who in Israel, Brooklyn, and elsewhere were devoutly anti-Zionist, which enraged other Jews. In Yemen, however, that position was practical and shrewd. The rabbi was using the lesson of Purim: Do what you can to live and pray another day. His statement wouldn't fly in the U.S., where the Jewish establishment would denounce his view as a sell-out. "He's a *Satmar*," they'd say. Easy to say as long as you're not the last rabbi of Yemen! Abdul Ghani inquired for me how the rabbi would respond to diehard American supporters of Israeli.

"The rabbi said that you have to be just in your view. You have to be right without any fear of how people condemn you or judge you." I studied Yahya and Suliman, chewing qat, doing a Q&A with a defrocked American journalist. Their faces, their *peyos*, their beards, their head coverings, the qat in their cheeks, the way they sat cross-legged on the cushions—all just shouted, "These men, these Jews, are authentic. They are the real thing!" Living anachronisms, yes, but surviving anachronisms.

How about me? Descendant of European Jews, with a driver's license issued by the State of Ohio, and a National ID issued by the UAE? A few months earlier, I'd romanticized myself as a "stateless person" because my U.S. passport was tied up in bureaucratic foolishness.

Still, we were connected, by a very old commonality. Yes, we originated from the same afflicted ancient tribe, of which in a very real sense all Jews everywhere are the remnant. But the connection was more specific— we had all held-on and held-out against a long history of those who would extirpate us, and often did. We remained a people, albeit one scattered in bits and pieces around the globe, and some of us, no doubt, "more Jewish" than others. To this day, "who's a real Jew" is a flashpoint among my tribe.

Today, Suliman had received the bittersweet news that his son was safe, in exile, in his people's ancestral home. But Yemen was his family's home. Their roots ran deep here. Whereon an inventive, skilled and thriving people had been reduced to living in cramped government-handout apartments behind the barricades of a militarized zone. After a 2,700-year run, since before Nebuchadnezzar's destruction of the First Temple in 586

BCE, Jews had lived in Sheba's kingdom. Now the curtain was brushing the stage floor. *Judenrein* in Yemen. Would the al-Houthi rid Yemen of all Jews?

I had not yet posed a new question, but the rabbi was speaking once again at some length. The lulls brought by the process of translation were something of a blessing, as they gave me time to think.

Abdul Ghani interrupted my thoughts. "The rabbi wants me to tell you this word for word." He looked at me, to be sure I was listening, and looked at the voice recorder. "The rabbi said, 'We believe in God's will. Whatever happens in God's will *will* happen. God will never leave us. People who worship God appropriately and follow their religion, God will never leave them. If they are following His teaching, they will not be alone. When you are born and live in a country, it is very difficult to leave. We will die and live in this country. We will stay here even if it means marching to the sea."

As the rabbi's words hung in the air there was a commotion outside the *mafraj*. The clock above the TV with its still-flowing U.S. red-white-and-blue registered almost midnight. Hearing Mohamed's voice, I went to investigate. He had returned from the evening with his children and was escorting an elderly woman into the house. She wore a headscarf and *abaya*. Very small in stature, the way she was stooped over made her seem even smaller. I thought of my *bubbe*.

Mohamed introduced her as the rabbi's mother, the sister of the man accompanying him. "She was waiting outside in a car." He shook his head. "She didn't want to come inside and bother anyone."

Jewish mothers the world over! "Don't mind me; I'll read in the dark." I wanted to embrace her.

Abdul Ghani returned from the kitchen with a glass of water. As he offered it to the rabbi's mother and she drank it gratefully, Mohamed pulled me aside. He suggested we should give the rabbi donations. In Hebrew, *tzedakah*, charity. A true *mitzvah*. We pooled a good wad of Benjamins. I was light on cash, so Mohamed advanced me some. At Islamic interest. A real *mensch*.

The rabbi accepted the money quietly. He left with funds to cover his father's medicine for a while and enough remaining to tide the family over through several months.

By the next evening, Mohamed and I were back in Al Ain. I had enough material for several stories. I listened to the recording hearing the rabbi's voice so many times I felt I understood his words, even in Arabic, without Abdul Ghani's translation. As I began to work on an article, unsure where I would place it, another memory from the trip to Yemen kept coming back: the abandoned village.

The crooked streets and jumbled rock walls still spoke to me. But as they did, I heard Mohamed speak to Sabah and Akiel, showing them the poverty of the squatters. *Look what is becoming of our people.* His anguish, even desperation, echoed in the place's silence.

So did my own thought in response. *Look what has become of mine.*

CHAPTER 29

Jinn or Gin

"YOU WERE IN YEMEN?" FARAJ ASKED, A TWINKLE IN HIS EYE.

The evening after our second Yemenia flight—amazingly close to on time—touched down in Dubai, my Emirati family had requested that I attend dinner. Fatima voiced concern when I answered my Nokia that she hadn't heard from me in a week, and that I hadn't been answering my phone. True, I hadn't. It had been left behind in my apartment because it wouldn't work in Yemen.

I had just handed Faraj a bottle of the finest Yemeni honey I could find, but nothing close to 3,000 dirhams a liter. The family, sitting around the dining room table, gave a collective "Ooh." Amna and Layla had prepared a feast and I was hungry.

"Yes, over The Prophet's birthday. I went with my colleague, Mohamed."

He asked what I did and I told him. The whole *megillah*. The poverty, the crazy clown buses, the Old City, abandoned Jewish village, Wadi Dahr, Rock Palace, the Al Saleh Mosque, SNAAC, and the honey stores. He'd never been there. I finished by describing the qat market and the party at Dr. Mohammed's villa, but left out the part about my sampling of the country's fabled drug.

Faraj had asked me once whether I drank or smoked, and I had responded in the negative, which was largely true then, but not now. Here I was at his house after having consumed a tall tumbler of vodka and watermelon juice before I had arrived. I was a bit tipsy, but he didn't notice.

Faraj's eyes lit up. "Did you try it?!"

We both knew I knew what "it" was. He and the family had accepted me as a Jew. Would they accept me as a qathead?

"Yes."

"You did?!"

"I did."

Faraj cocked his head and a smile spread across his face. The family watched him look at me and smiles spread across their faces, too. And then he let out a big belly laugh.

"I am angry with you, brother!" he bellowed.

My heart sank.

"You went to Yemen and tried qat!" He paused for effect. "And you didn't take me!"

And my heart bounced back into place.

I felt a tad guilty because I'd never mentioned that I was going to Yemen. But it was not my nature to report my activities or whereabouts, even to my family in Clevistan. Fewer questions that way. Since my return I was in some odd kind of decompression mode, or recompression mode, whatever scuba divers do to avoid getting the bends. My plan that evening was to stay home and catch up on American TV via the Slingbox. I'd finished listening to the recording of Rabbi Yahya and had done up a first draft of an article. I wanted to fiddle around with it, but I kept coming back to that troubling inner voice: *Look what has become of mine.*

No, rather, look at what has become of *me* and *mine*. I was drinking too much, and …

The rabbi's last statement: *"We will die and live in this country. We will stay here even if it means marching to the sea."* He was speaking of Yemen, of course, but he could also be speaking for all of the Jews in Israel and around the world. Many still spoke about driving Israel's Jews *into* the sea. And here I lived comfortably in an oil-rich Arab country whose maps show a blank spot where the state of Israel exists. If there are only four hundred Jews in Yemen how many could there be in the UAE? Me and who else? Was there even a secret *minion*? Not that I would join it, but it would be comforting to know.

My words were not going to save Yemen's Jews, but I'd finished the story focusing on my conversation with the rabbi and his account of their plight, rather than on the disappearance and reappearance of Da'ood. I had written the piece to sort out my own thoughts. They were coming into focus as I considered whether I could stomach teaching at UAEU for another year, trying something else in the UAE, or return to my family in Ohio. There are about 60,000 Jews in Clevistan, about the same number that had once lived in Yemen before Israel's independence. The Diaspora had taken many of my tribe from The Pale and dropped them in Northeast Ohio. Where would they be in 2,700 years?

Having told the rabbi I would do my best to fulfill his request, I was honor bound to seek out a place to publish the story. My gut told me that if the last descendants of those wandering Canaanites left Yemen, something would be lost forever. For the world, sure, but I was thinking more personally.

In the morning I re-read the story and asked, "What would I say to the Girls in Black if this were a piece by one of them? What would they say to me?" I know: It's too long and the lede is wordy. Before I left for school, I had the article cut back. I was proud of the piece, and back on the horse. Not back in the game—my newsman days were behind me, but something was ahead. And I owed my next shot at reinvention—in a circuitous, beautifully *insha'Allah* way—to Mohamed of Sana'a.

I'd gone to Yemen with serious doubts about my near-term future and returned with none. For our mutual good, UAEU and I had to part company. With only so many of my three-score-and-ten left, I wasn't about to waste two more years battling school bureaucracy or pretending that computer-assisted reporting could be taught without databases, much less that a women's toilet could double as a classroom. The question remained open, though, as to how many of those years might be spent in the UAE.

While I pondered various next phases for a soon-to-be-58-year-old self, I immersed my still-57-year-old self in teaching. Detached, in my mind, from the institution, I focused on my students. No matter my internal questioning I maintained my zeal to try to open as many minds as I could. One memorable session of *Intro* with the boys began with a haul of six tardiness fines, putting our party fund over 100 dirhams, and a pointedly off-topic question from me.

"How many of you believe in *jinn*?" The digital recorder sat on the desk.

Jinn, as I understood them, are entities of divine mythology, magical, made by Allah from "smokeless fire." They enjoy free will and are otherwise similar to humans, with one major difference—*jinn* are ordinarily invisible. And can travel long distances in a flash. (I had encountered nothing in the tradition, written or oral, to the effect that *jinn* can leap tall buildings in a single bound.) Quasi-malevolent, *jinn* like to possess and harass humans, their motives to do so ranging from infatuation to revenge. The human and *jinn* worlds are supposedly separate, but we share the same earth and on Judgment Day both will be dispatched, according to our/their deeds, to Heaven or Hell. I learned from one writing that *jinn* served King Solomon—another exciting fact suppressed by my Hebrew School.

Of my thirty-six students, just one refrained from raising a hand: Mohammed Saif. Not so gullible as to buy into Darwin's "Monkey Theory" in a previous class, he wasn't going to be a pushover, either, for creatures made from fire—even if the Koran said they existed.

Seated in back, with the rest of the gang of five Jordanians, Nour Aldeen spoke. "We all believe! Jinn are in the Koran. God created jinn."

Though *jinn* were my point of entry, my aim was not to challenge superstition, but to get a sense of its place in my students' thinking. How did knowledge by faith relate to knowledge by empirical methods and critical reasoning? The ensuing discussion wound up going beyond those questions, to question the existence of God.

In my test-drive of the lesson plan with Tony, he had advised, "Faith rules. While truth itself is a valueless commodity, the *illusion* of truth is omnipotent." His ability to cook up such Churchillian pronouncements amused and bemused me, which is a requirement of a good foxhole buddy. I faced the class and silently intoned, "*The illusion of truth is omnipotent.*" Whatever the hell that means. We were already forging ahead. "So," I asked out loud, "who's had experience with *jinn*?"

That time, the homonym brought a roll of laughs.

"We do not drink," Handsome Ali said, with a nod and grin.

"Not the kind that gives some of Englishmen red noses."

More laughs.

"Who has seen a *jinn*?"

Maroof, our lone Nigerian, spoke up in his lilting English. "You can't see *jinn*. With my cousin once, a *jinn* entered his body and make him do unnormal, strange actions and say strange words. We tried to get it out of him, but it take a long time."

Precisely the sort of testimony I'd asked for. Eyewitness. "A *jinn* took over his body and possessed him?" That drew a nod. "How long did it take to get the *jinn* out?"

"Two years. It was in his body for two years."

This elicited a comment from Mohammed Saif, who voiced his doubt diplomatically. "Some people say *jinn* do not enter your body. They say that this is a psychological problem."

The debate underway, my gaze ping-ponged from one speaker to another. After letting it rage awhile, I raised my hand. "So we have a divergence of views." Ping to Mohammed Saif: "You say a *jinn* is a psychological problem." Pong to Maroof: "You say that *jinn* are living and possess people's bodies."

Both signaled their affirmations, many others nodding with them. I checked the recorder to make sure it was doing its job. I might need a record of this, not to avoid being put on a plane, but to get myself out of jail so I could be put on a plane. "How many of you believe in jinn? *Absolutely* believe?"

Again, all raised their hands except Mohammed Saif.

"So, what's the proof that jinn exist?"

Abu Dhabi replied. "When you go into some places in the desert, you see some footprints in the sand and you think they are animals, but they are *jinn*."

"So *jinn* leave footprints. And that proves they exist?"

Funny Man jumped in. "A *jinn* does not leave footprints."

"Maybe they were animals," Abu Dhabi recanted, with a laugh. "Maybe I was wrong."

Again Noor Aldeen's voice rang out. "I believe because it's written in the Holy Koran."

"So, you do not need proof because you believe?"

Many nodded. Yet Mohammed Saif looked torn.

I pressed on. "Who has had a *personal* experience with a *jinn*?"

The *jinn* phase of today's discussion would, left on its own, go in circles. A motorcade of *jinn* driving their SUVs manically through Al Ain's Pizza Hut roundabout. I wasn't quite ready to turn off, though. "I understand that *jinn* are in the Koran and some of you deem that to be proof. For the moment, the question is, 'How many of you have had a personal, direct experience with a *jinn*?'"

That tickled Funny Man. "Personal? Me? Myself?"

"Yes, you yourself. With your eyes, ears and other senses."

He pondered theatrically, and shrugged. "No, not personally."

Maroof cut in. "My cousin! The *jinn* entered his blood and it made my cousin do strange things."

Enter Abdullah, an Emirati in a middle row, speaking up for the first time all semester. "Someone videoed a man with a *jinn* inside him and a holy man reads the Holy Koran and you see the *jinn*…" Then he clapped his hands loudly… "and the *jinn* leaves him."

The classroom responded with "oohs" and "ahhs," whether in approval or skepticism, however, I could not tell. An important sheikh's son turned the tables on me. "Professor, do *you* see *jinn*?"

"I have no experience with them. In my world, *jinn* do not exist. In America, however, many people believe in ghosts, or at least like believing that they believe. But the thing I want to focus on is this: There's no *proof* that ghosts are real."

"Do Christians believe in ghosts?" Funny Man asked.

"Christians are not supposed to believe in ghosts, but many do."

I marched to the front of the room. "The Koran says *jinn* exist, but we've arrived at no proof, in the form of things we can observe, that they do. The evidence cited is that the Koran says so."

God, the believers believe, handed down this form of proof, *Himself.* The conversation in progress might never take place in an American college classroom, except possibly at an evangelical Christian institution. That exchange would be decidedly different and *jinn*-unfriendly. Maybe at a *yeshiva.* The most-orthodox Orthodox Jews, not the so-called Modern Orthodox, also profess to believe everything in the Hebrew Bible as literally true although different sects argue about the exact meaning of certain words and phrases. Did man and dinosaurs walk together? Of course they did. The world had its grand opening only 5769 years ago.

I was trying—and I saw my effort was doomed to failure, if not quixotic—to preach to the converted, only its opposite. My point was that *jinn* are part of a belief system, not part of rational, empirical knowledge. For the students before me that premise was a non-starter. And while they were pretty easygoing, we all knew it was more; it was heresy. The Koran defines all understanding, rational or otherwise. Period. End of story. Momentarily, I enjoyed the irony I was trying to get away with. UAEU had hired me to teach Muslims, but no *yeshiva* on earth would let "Dr. David" in its doors to teach Jews.

I strode behind the desk. "We're done with *jinn.* Now we'll move on to a bigger discussion."

My opening gambit would eat up the hour without getting us to critical reasoning and empirical thinking and all the other things that underpin the Western journalist's hope for something that passes as objectivity. So, it was time to drop the big question: "Who believes there is no God?"

Saif Hamood, the Omani who'd asked about my religion, silent until now, asked, "No God!?"

"No God. Have you ever been asked that question in school?"

"There is no need to ask that question," Saif Hamood replied. "We all believe."

I wondered whether this new provocation, which really was going too far, would be reported to the administration. What, I wondered, would happen if I posed the same question in the Kingdom of Saudi Arabia? Beheading? And *then* put on a plane? In two boxes, one large and one small?

"You all *believe* this in the same way?"

"Yes, Doctor," many voices called out.

"So all Muslims believe that God exists *in the same way*?"

Amid the "Yes! Yes! Yes! Yes! Yes!" a single off-key "NO!" from Mohammed Saif.

"That's a lot of yesses. All of you must be Jewish to believe in God all alike."

Abu Dhabi let out a roar. "No! We are all Muslim."

"So Sunnis believe exactly as Shia believe?"

The all-Sunni chorus sang out, "No."

"Similar," Mohammed Saif said. "But different."

The chorus shot back. "Yes! Yes!"

Maybe this angle would get me somewhere after all. The same God but different ways of fulfilling one's duties to the deity. Maybe I could take a little poll on henotheism, the view that one's god is best, but that other people's gods may exist, too. I knew plenty of Jews and Christians who accepted such thinking—though it always sounded more like liberal politics than theology.

"Many in the West think all Muslims are the same," I said. "Just as many of you thought all Jews were the same until you met me. But Muslims are different just as Jews are different. The Sunni and Shia do many things differently. Regardless of the differences, however, all believe God exists. Correct?"

That met an affirmative response.

"So what's the *proof* that God exists?"

Nour Aldeen jumped to his feet. "Everything! You! Me!"

"Us? We ourselves constitute proof that God exists?"

"Yes!" Nour Aldeen exclaimed. "Us!" The class waited for his next words. "I have never been to a doctor, but I know I have a heart."

"How do you know?"

"I know because of *Who* makes you."

"Who makes you? God? Allah?"

"Yes, Who makes *you*?!"

"Ah, Who *does* make *us*?" I took an agonizingly long pause. "A question we are *not* going to answer today." I looked up at the imaginary eye-in-the-sky. "We are not going to answer *Who* created man. La, la, la. No, no, no."

The class erupted in laughter. We did get to some wonderful topics. God and prayer give our existence its purpose. Miracles, which happen all the time, constitute proof of God's existence. (When I asked for an example of a miracle, I got the fact that Funny Man was getting married, Handsome Ali was his "best man," and even more surprising, I was invited.) The boys' belief, and their certainty *that* they believed, was affirmed at every turn.

Finally I asked, "Do monkeys believe?"

Maroof responded immediately. "Yes. Yes. Of course."

"It's written in the Koran," Funny Man responded.

I shot him a look. "Monkeys believe in God? Does a monkey read the Koran?"

"It's written in the Koran," Funny Man said.

Mohammed Saif stated the rational alternative. "We do not know."

Just as it took only one of the Girls in Black to give me hope, one voice saying—to start—that not all Jews are evil, Mohammed Saif's response was enough. It wouldn't happen that day, and probably not in that course, and maybe not while I was still breathing God's good air, but the possibility of critical reasoning was there. Not a denial of faith, a renewal of something the Prophet himself had exhorted the faithful to pursue. Maybe I'd switched my goal in order to reach it, but that felt like a small victory. The point was the spark was there, and I *hadn't* ignited it. I'd tried. But Mohammed Saif grasped all along, before I asked about *jinn*, the depth of what he'd just said. *We do not know.*

That no one but me paid any attention hardly mattered.

Back at the desk, I clicked off the recorder, and tossed it into my faded black canvas briefcase. Funny Man and Handsome Ali waited outside the door in the central courtyard. I was due at my next class in fifteen minutes. I had to drive to Maqam and scarf down my turkey sandwich on the way.

"Walk with me," I said, and they followed.

"This was the best class, professor," Handsome Ali announced, passing through the archway to the car park. "We've always wanted to talk about these things, but never have."

"Now we are graduating and we are finally learning something," Funny Man offered, with sincerity. "We have never had a class like this at UAEU."

I waited for the punch line. None came.

Next to my Yaris, Handsome Ali smiled. "*Insha'Allah*, Doctor, I'll see you at the next class."

I*nsha'Allah*, indeed. It was in His hands. People have been put on planes for lesser sins.

If I had been deported the next day because I had questioned the very existence of God in a UAEU classroom, it would have been OK. Young Muslim Arab men and I had engaged in conversation about faith and God and the world had not come to an end. How I could top that class, no matter how many years I would teach, was beyond me. There's a song in the Passover *Haggadah*, "*Dayenu*." The word means "enough." It's used to thank God for every little thing He had done to help the Hebrews escape bondage in Egypt. I knew there was no way on God's brown sandy desert, unless He willed it, that I could ever teach a class like that again. I would not ask. He'd done enough. *Dayenu*.

A week after Purim, in which no one had escorted me to Dubai airport to put me on a plane, my article about Rabbi Yahya and the plight of the Jews of Sana'a was picked up by the Jewish Telegraphic Agency (JTA), which claims the title "global news service of the Jewish people." The article focused on their living situation and broken promises, not the disappearance of Da'ood.

As Mohamed was my host and guide in Yemen I wanted to share the story I'd written. I was confident that this was what the rabbi wanted told. I thought Mo would appreciate reading it so I invited him over and as I recited it aloud I watched him go cold. What had happened? It was a good story, if a little wordy. When I finished reading he glared at me with daggers in his eyes and left without speaking. I sent it anyway. Jews and non-Jews around the world read this via the JTA website:

Yemen government breaks promises to relocated Jews

SANA'A, Yemen – The religious leader of Yemeni Jews relocated by the government to the capital city from the northern province of Sa'ada to protect them from a radical Shia group says that promises to take care of them have been broken.

In a three-hour meeting on the day before Purim, Rabbi Yahya Yousef Mousa said pledges of providing money, food and land to build new homes in Sana'a have not been fulfilled.

Although he said the government is once again paying a monthly stipend of 5,000 rials ($25) per month per person to the 12 families, and 65 Jews, now living near the American Embassy here since being forced to leave Ghareer more than two years ago, the town where they lived for at least 1,000 years, he said conditions are now getting desperate.

Not allowed to work because of security concerns, Mousa said families are resorting to selling jewelry and other possessions they were able to take with them when they were forced to flee under threat of the al-Houthi, a radical Shia group that has a strong foothold in northern Yemen.

The article closely mirrored our conversation and concluded as it had:

"We believe in God's will. Whatever happens in God's will *will* happen. God will never leave us. People who worship God appropriately and follow their religion, God will never leave them. If they are following His teaching, they will not be alone. When you are born and live in a country, it is very difficult to leave. We will die and live in this country. We will stay here even if it means marching to the sea."

CHAPTER 30

The Richest Horse Race in the World

ON THE WAY TO THE RICHEST HORSE RACE IN THE WORLD, Tony's Porsche Carrera 996 Turbo's speedometer tipped past 250 kmph. The car snugly hugged the even pavement on E-66 taking us from Al Ain to Dubai on the last Saturday in March.

What was taking us there was the Dubai World Cup, which boasted more than US$21 million of prize money. This would be the last time that event would be held at Naq Al Sheba—that horse track was slated to be replaced the following year by the new billion-dollar Meydan racing complex being built next door, the biggest and most-expensive in the world. Natch. I felt like the old sports editor again going to find an end-of-an-era story at a singular event. I might not have made it to a camel race yet (getting up at five a.m. didn't appeal to me), but there was no way I was going to miss this extravaganza.

The marine blue Porsche purred along E-66 passing six-wheel Mitsubishi trucks hauling camels, luxury cars, and South Asian men hitchhiking. Tony and I had been trying since the fall to gauge the depth of the world's economic crash. The only way was to piecemeal the story reading between the lines in the Emirates' English-language press, keeping an ear to the Pashtun grapevine, picking up anecdotes and observations. The *Khaleej Times* had slipped into a recent story about *new* work visas the fact that the government had cancelled 400,000 foreign worker permits—essentially exiling about 10 percent of the expat workforce. We'd heard reliable accounts about expats dumping luxury cars at Dubai's airport as they fled the country. Tony stole this car, the 2003 Dubai Porsche Show Car of the year, for a song from a man who was fleeing.

A line I'd not thought of in a good four decades since English Lit slithered into my head: *I am Ozymandias, King of Kings! Look on my works, ye mighty, and despair!*

OK, what the hell. I added the tag this time. "Round the decay of that colossal wreck, boundless and bare, the lone and level sands stretch far away."

"Just as you say," Tony answered. He glanced across at me, apparently impressed a Clevistani Jew had heard of Shelley. *"Castles in the sand."*

"Blowing in the wind."

Our plan was to be at Naq Al Sheba by 5 p.m. We had started planning our day at the races two weeks earlier. I'd investigated VVVIP packages but we decided against paying from 1,500-to-more-than-3,000 dirhams to sit in the assorted grandstand venues drinking with expat dandies. Instead we'd attend for free with the general public. Rub elbows with the "P's."

Despite a perpetually blue sky that rarely offered a cloud for shade, Nad Al Sheba sat bathed in a gray atmospheric haze and steady drizzle. We parked in a remote lot. That venue offered a clear view of Dubai's skyline, punctuated by the needlepoint top of the Burj Dubai. Rising adjacent to Nad Al Sheba were dozens of yellow construction cranes, engaged in building its replacement, Meydan. Next year, the new hippodrome would host its first Dubai World Cup. A project to be completed at all costs.

A free shuttle bus deposited us near Gate 2 into a teaming mass of the "common people." Disembarking into the light rain, we were greeted by an Emirati policeman hollering *"Khallas! Khallas!"* He wasn't singling us out, but directing the order at the wet throng pushing, shoving, line jumping, and queuing up within a maze of steel barricades, all bottlenecking at the lone metal detector at Gate 2—the only point of "free" entry.

"*Khallas!*" the officer spit out, sounding like he was clearing his throat. "Enough!"

Busloads of Western expats drove by in luxury coaches to special entrances. At Gate 2, however, nobody had been let through in fifteen minutes. A rumor swept through the crowd that the metal detector had broken. When a nearby gate mysteriously opened, a swarm broke out of captivity and ran in its direction. Tony and I joined this rogue human wave stampeding along a high barbed-wire fence.

A phalanx of police stood in the way, bellowing *"Khallas! Khallas!"*

The crowd zoomed past and we joined the flow through the free entry onto an expansive green lawn inside Nad Al Sheba. "This way," Tony directed. We darted among even commoner-looking people who loitered on the grass in front of half-empty free metal bleachers. We were at the far end of the track, beyond the finish line, but at least we were in.

We zipped down to the inside rail, running along the dirt track, and followed the hedges toward the finish line. A Sudanese family picnicking on a carpet blocked our path; we swung around them and past Egyptian men sitting in lawn chairs drinking tea. Next we skirted the climate-controlled Al Dhana Marquee, a dining pavilion offering food, drink and a poor view of the track—at 2,400 dirhams a head.

In front of the Maktoum Grandstand and Terrace—sold out at 1,400 dirhams for a sheltered seat and food—we wedged into a spot along the shoulder-high hedges lining the rail and staked our turf.

On the dirt infield sat a huge video screen. The infield grass, planted with thousands of white orbs, resembled an alien melon crop. I puzzled on that only briefly. I was focused on carving out my square foot by the rail. Next to me a woman in a matching yellow print sari and headscarf sat on a damp carpet, cradling a wrapped infant.

Tony pointed down the track. "There's the finish line. I'd say we've found a pretty good spot, and it didn't cost a dirham!"

I scanned the first row of the Maktoum Grandstand and fixated on two blondes and a brunette, all spilling ample cleavage. Among them they had nine empty wine glasses lined up on the railing. The brunette puffed on a long, thin cigarette, and the platinum-er of the blondes sported a Roaring '20s flapper-style hairdo. This was festooned with a big yellow flower on her bonnet. The natural-er blonde was showing off an oversized, floppy straw hat that would be much envied at the Kentucky Derby. Not that this was Ascot, but the Dubai World Cup featured bonnet and costume competitions.

"Look," I said to Tony, pointing up. "There… and there… and there." I waited for him to see what I had. "We could have been sitting with them up there and out of the rain."

"Dream on, young David," Tony said, with a laugh. "I'm just where I want to be."

In close proximity to us, two more women, one wearing a black *neqab* and the other a matching pink-and-black polka dot sari and headscarf, sat cross-legged on a folded green blanket. The space the blanket defined as theirs was littered with plastic food bags, amid which crawled two moist toddlers.

"You don't see *that* at a Clevistan racetrack," Tony chortled. He was right, of course.

The two women looked harried and bored by the prospect of a horserace. Neither could claim the beauty of those sitting above. But they reaffirmed my sense that my place was, yes, here on the ground.

It was time for the races. The first was the one I wanted to see most. It pitted the world's best Arabian Purebreds against one another on a short track. The horses' mythic origin story and place in human history had always held fascination. They kept company with Allah, Abraham, Solomon and Sheba, Mohammed, and T.E. Lawrence. Of course there was Napoleon's Marengo. The movies had given me "The Black Stallion."

The steady sprinkle went on as the bell clanged and the Arabians exploded out of the gate. As they did, a wave of *hoi polloi* swept toward the track. Tony and I were crushed like sardines into the prickly hedges.

"I can't move," I hollered to him over the roar of the crowd. "And I have a dozen tiny Bangladeshis crawling up my ass."

On the mammoth TV screen across from us the horses charged ahead, rounding the clubhouse turn, flying past the Irish Village, Bubble Lounge, and the Clubhouse itself. Under the bright lights and escalating excitement they pounded toward the finish line.

"Look," Tony said, holding high the video cam he had retrieved from his vest pocket. "Here they come!" As the Arabians galloped past the finish line—and us—the crush of bodies abated. "Thrilling!"

I grabbed the back of my shorts and yanked down. "My ass will never be the same!"

All the same, I'll say there is nothing more thrilling than a stampede of Arabians. The winner of the $250,000 purse, by three and a half lengths, was Fryvolous, a six-year-old French-bred gelding owned by His Highness Sheikh Khalifa bin Zayed al Nahyan, ruler of Abu Dhabi and president of the UAE.

One thing I'd learned as a sports editor: Far too often the hype is bigger than the event. Case in point, most Super Bowls.

One championship that lived up to its buildup was the 1982 NCAA Final Four held in New Orleans's Superdome between Patrick Ewing's Georgetown Hoyas and James Worthy's North Carolina Tar Heels with a freshman named "Mike" Jordan in support. I covered that game for *The Minneapolis Star*. Sitting courtside with colleague Paul Levy, I witnessed close-up as "Mike" sank the winning shot with time running out handing chain-smoking Dean Smith his first national title. That's the day that jumpstarted the Jordan Legend as "Michael, not Mike" emerged. After the smoke cleared, the other scribes rushed off to meet deadlines and I, writing on a late deadline for a dying afternoon paper, eyed the now-alone freshman in the nearly empty locker room. I approached, we shared a few words, and I filed my column. Reflecting on that moment what had stuck in my memory these many years was more the look in Jordan's eyes than the electrifying game. Did he know what was before him? Was it God's will? My story about that game would run in *The Star's* penultimate edition before it ceased publication.

Who won the races that evening fade into background. What remains is the color of the evening. What was taking place around me not on the sand and turf. I could always see fast thoroughbreds run but never again in an environment like this. This was the curtain.

Just before the million-dollar Etisalat Godolphin Mile, an impromptu *Maghrib* prayer service convened in front of the white-picket fence at the base of the Maktoum Grandstand. A diverse group of South Asian, Omani, and Sudanese men threw down a peculiar collection of prayer rugs and got down on their knees facing Mecca in the drizzle. Dozens more worshippers joined in, alternately standing, kneeling, and lying prostrate.

"I bet you've never seen that before at a racetrack in the U.S.," Tony said, pointing in their direction. "Doubt Jews would ever do that."

I let out a belly laugh. "Never would. Jews don't pray on their knees."

Before the third race the rain stopped and dusk set in. Under this rare cloud canopy the early evening air was soft and cool. The $2-million UAE Derby was won by 16-to-1 long-shot Regal Ransom, a dark bay three-year-old colt. But it was what happened after the race directly in front of me that captured my attention. A tall Sudanese man under a white turban lifted a small boy from his shoulders and planted him softly on the tarmac. Then I watched him crumple a betting slip and toss it at my feet. As there was no legal betting in the UAE, I was intrigued. "You lose this race?" I asked, looking up at him.

He shook his head in disgust. "I picked the first two winners. Not the third. Now I have no more reason to stay." He grabbed the little boy's hand and walked toward an exit.

A Florida colt won the last race of the undercard. Big City Man collected a purse of $2 million. That year's Kentucky Derby winner, Mine That Trail, would earn just $1.2 million.

The reason for the alien melon field came into sudden focus. The racetrack lights dimmed and the orbs glowed white and then blue, green and purple. More long strings of the glowing melons rose into the sky in a bright rainbow of primary colors. Music blared and tracers burst high above the racetrack, exploding in arcs of hot white light. Another huge column of colored orbs rose up, suggesting a Wobbling Tower of Pisa. Fireworks shot into the sky and exploded in new bursts of color. The crowd of 25,000 roared. We commoners, I believe, outshouted the stands. After the last explosion, many families around us packed up and departed. They had come to see the fireworks, not the ponies.

When the smoke cleared it was time for the three big races. Total purse: $16 million.

As often happens, the biggest race turned out to be a dud. The title race, the $6-million Dubai World Cup, with the single biggest winning purse—$5 million—was won by Well Armed, a six-year-old Kentucky-bred bay gelding. A horse with no balls thumped the field winning by fourteen lengths. Dubai's Maktoum and his family won most of the races. But not the biggest. I'd heard they created the Dubai's World Cup so they could show off and win some of the millions of the billion they'd invested in thoroughbreds.

As if by *insha'Allah*, the instant Well Armed crossed the finish line the sky opened like a spigot. We common people took off running toward Gate 2—smack into a bottleneck set up by Emirati police.

"*Khallas, Khallas!*" several screamed.

"*Khallas!*" the crowd shouted back.

"*Dayenu!*" I added for emphasis.

The rain fell in buckets. Bolts of light flashed across the horizon, striking the world's tallest lightning rod—the Burj Dubai—and exploding in crazy arcs of electricity grander than any man-made fireworks spectacle ever contrived.

"Did you see that?" Tony marveled. "Now *that* is spectacular."

"*Khallas!*" police shouted.

A Sudanese man beside me shouted. "We are not even goats to these Emiratis!"

"*Ma'hatha, ma'hatha,*" Tony yelled.

"*Khallas! Khallas!*" an Emirati officer screamed. "*Khallas!*"

"Ma'hatha, ma'hatha," Tony yelled again.

Angry men in the crowd raised their fists shouting at the police. We pushed through the gate.

BOOM!… another bolt exploded at the top of the Burj, spitting out bright photon capillaries.

"What are you saying?" I asked Tony, rain cascading off the brim of my CBS News cap.

Tony let out a howl. "It's basic Arabic. It means, 'What is this?' But nobody knows it!"

"Look around," I hollered. "There are few Arabs here. Mostly Bahtan and Africans."

A figurative light bulb lit up over Tony's head. "Wait, you're right! Most of these people speak Urdu. They don't know what *ma'hatha* means."

"Neither do I," I laughed. "But you taught me that *dicki* is the Arabic for chicken. And that's what I'm feeling like right now. A Kentucky Fried *dicki*! This crowd is getting mad and it worries me."

"Not only that, but the sky is falling."

More busloads of VVVIPs drove past in a slow procession, blocking the way to the shuttles. Police continued to yell *"Khallas!"* Bahtan screamed back at them. The Sudanese man hollered, "They treat the horses better than they treat us! We are not even people to them. We are less than animals."

Tony leaned over to me. "Hell, we're not even P's to them. He's right."

BOOM!… BOOM! Lightning exploded off the top of the Burj. BOOM!

"Khallas!" Emirati security officers shouted. *"Khallas!"*

I bellowed at Tony as the rain pelted us. "We could have been VVVIPs or even just VIPs for fifteen hundred dirhams. We could have been fed, drunk and dry, but you had to be a man of the people!"

Tony turned nose to nose. "Young David, I wouldn't have missed this for the world!"

CHAPTER 31

Beginning of the End

NOOR'S USED SIX-WHEEL MERCEDES DUMP TRUCK, BOUGHT
with financing from Like's brother-in-law, had arrived from Germany by
freighter in late March. From Abu Dhabi it went to Sanaiya for a general
overhaul, including a new paint job and prep for carting loads of sand
and stone. Noor took me to see his truck and it was in pieces. He hoped,
insha'Allah, it would be ready by my birthday in early May. Noor hadn't
taken me up on my offer of a loan, and I hated thinking that had delayed
the purchase. There was a lot of work to do, and Noor had little or no savings left to tide him over.

I had a future to think about, too, and in some ways I was on an even
tighter timetable. After the visit to the truckyard, we went to a Punjabi
eatery around the corner.

I spent the second part of dinner describing my latest tussle with
the university. Noor had heard many of my UAEU tales, beginning the
first day with that class at the women's toilet. He knew all about Beverly's
situation and about how I'd been intentionally left out of faculty meetings.
He had heard Tony and me, among others, bemoan the "new *new* direction" UAEU was taking under its latest provost, to attain its pipe dream
of becoming an internationally recognized research institution within

five years. Nobody was happy, especially the Arab faculty. My position, along with others, was uncertain even if we did have contracts. They could be nullified at any time. There was talk of a 10 percent faculty reduction. Apparently Sheikh Nahyan bin Zayed al Nahyan's *wasta* didn't protect UAEU from budget woes.

We were wrapping up a meal of *rogan josh*, extra hot, and a double order of tender lamb ribs. Sweat poured from my face as the remnants of our meal littered the table. A stack of tiny rib bones had piled up on a metal tray. This macabre work of sculpture centerpieced a mess that included scraps of onion *naan*, clumps of rice, and paper napkins. I used a few more of those, fresh ones, to mop my brow.

Noor had listened politely as I recapped my petty concerns. For weeks I had regaled him with the play-by-play of a skirmish with the department secretary, Mariam, over handing in all of my students' tests and written assignments. It was policy, she said, to collect materials so they could be secured and not used for cheating. So I took a page from the Emirati playbook, and responded with the equivalent of *insha'Allah, bukra*. When I questioned Dr. Ali from Erie, Pee-ay about the alleged policy, he professed ignorance. But of course he wouldn't know; he didn't run things. Rule Number One: there were no policies until it became necessary to invent one. Now, I related to Noor, I had received an email demanding compliance. I couldn't obey for two reasons: One, it was a fundamental encroachment on academic freedom. He looked at me as if I must be kidding. Academic freedom was not a value held in high esteem—or any esteem—at UAEU. OK, I conceded. I was kidding. Two, a bit less lofty: I'd returned all the papers to the students and had nothing.

"So what will you do?" Noor asked.

"Nothing. *Insha'Allah, bukra*."

"Won't you get in trouble?"

I chuckled. "I've learned that when you begin worrying you're in trouble you already are."

Noor took a deep breath. "Mohamed has quit." He let the air out slowly. "Are you quitting?"

"Mohamed has quit," I said, with a laugh, "but nobody at the university has acknowledged his quitting yet. He's never received a response and it's been months."

"But he's going back to America."

"That's what he thinks, but now that he's not talking to me I know nothing. The deadline for officially resigning is tomorrow."

"Are you sending an email?"

I'd tried to sidestep the question, but he didn't buy it. I'd already made up my mind.

"I don't plan to," I said, and launched into an explanation of my thinking.

The reasons boiled down, again, to two: flexibility and money. First, while I planned on not teaching at UAEU next year, I didn't want to officially quit in order to keep my options open. It was common knowledge that some expat professors never returned after their summer holiday back home. Instead of officially resigning they just stayed away. Before they left, they sold off cars and what furniture they could, and—like the mythical Arabs in an old saying—folded their tents and silently slipped away. Annually, UAEU lost more than half of its first-year expat faculty.

My plan was still vague. Return to Ohio, finalize my divorce, and play it by ear. Maybe just not return next school year. No need to send an email now. Second, I had done the math and realized it would cost me thousands of dollars to resign through official channels. To begin with I would have to pay back at least 20,000 dirhams of my housing allowance. It just made sense to follow Rule Number One: Ignore their rules. What's more, the Dow Jones had just sunk into 6,5000 territory, less than half of what it was when I left Ohio in August. Like many others who put their faith in capitalism, I was screwed.

Noor took it all in. When I finished, he cocked his head and grinned.

"You cannot do it that way, my friend." He paused. "I understand why you might not want to teach at the university next year but you cannot break their rules."

That took me by surprise. "Why not?"

"Because if you don't follow the rules and don't come back to teach, they might not let you back into the country." He paused. "And then you won't be able to see the Falahis and Tony and me!"

It hadn't occurred to me that UAEU could certainly have me barred from returning to the UAE. I had ignored Noor's advice before and never to good result.

"I think you should send an email," he continued. "Maybe they will make things better for you so you stay. If not you can come back and do another business. Maybe, *insha'Allah*, with the Falahis."

That night I sent an email to Dr. Ali tendering my resignation, effective at the end of the spring semester. The next day I told Fatima what I'd done and she laughed. "I am not surprised. They don't treat you right. But you can get another job here. My father trusts you." Then she asked me to promise not to leave before her twenty-second birthday in mid-June. Instantly I responded, "No way I would miss it."

When I arrived for dinner the following night Faraj was waiting. "Doctor, Fatima tells me you are leaving the university. She told me why. I understand." He took off his glasses and looked me in the eye. "If you want I can call Nahyan for you." I shook my head. Then he pointed to his heart. "If you need money, I will give you money. If you want a business, we will do a business. We'll talk more later."

For him, as for his daughter, any trouble between UAEU and me was a minor matter—*wasta* trumps everything but *insha'Allah*, and Faraj and his family's *wasta* was my *wasta*.

A future in the UAE, free and clear of UAEU, was open. Few moments in my life—and it's been an often-careening roller coaster so far—have let me feel as free. Free to follow my own will, or that of *insha'Allah*. Best of all, I had a feeling that we were in sync.

The few weeks that followed gave me ample time to consider the decision, indecision, or non-decision I faced. That thing I do called Strategic Procrastination. The time also gave me a few object lessons to reinforce or undermine the various ways I was thinking. The trip to Yemen had reignited my desire to return to America. I had chosen to run away and ended up here. As Tony had pointed out, I could have gone anywhere. But UAE, and even UAEU, had added up to the right place and time; going to Yemen was a part of the mystical, restorative journey. I had a renewed sense of where I belonged.

Noor, while I doubt it was his intention, provided me a clear, stark picture of life for those who come to work in the UAE and have no *wasta* umbrella to shade them. As to *wasta*, I had it here via my relationship with Faraj, but I bristled at the very notion of ever using it. That was just not my style.

One hot Friday April afternoon, Noor drove us toward Oman, past the falconry center, as Faraj always did on our way to the racing-camel farm. We wended our way past Zayed, the Second Military College, St. George's Syrian Orthodox Jacobite Church, and the camel market. As we approached the far fringes of the city, Noor gave me a briefing. We were headed to a private labor camp owned by an Emirati construction company with a reputation for treating its workers well. "I have friends there. They are all Sikhs, but they have cut their hair and their beards. Today is their day off."

I had indeed expressed an interest in visiting such a place. Sikhs don't cut their hair or beards for religious reasons. Did they do so here because of the heat? Or had they stopped believing?

Soon, in a location that can only be called desolate, he pulled to a stop. Before us stood a whitewashed high wall of concrete block. Saving the blue metal door planted squarely in the middle, the pale wall radiated the intense sun. In response to Noor's solid knock, two tall, thin men, both with short-cropped dark hair, one cleanly shaven, the other sporting a thick mustache, welcomed us. As they led us inside, I noted that both were barefoot.

Noor and these two men exchanged warm greetings in Urdu. The man with the mustache turned to me and spoke in English. "You are Noor's friend and you are welcome here."

"See, they wear the Sikhs' pajamas," Noor whispered as we followed them farther inside. "But no turbans or long beards."

The two men led us to a brick-paved courtyard. Two rows of single-story buildings, also of concrete block painted white, created a tunnel effect. Several gigantic satellite dishes sat on the roofs and in the center of the pathway, out of two tiny patches of earth, bloomed flowers and small trees. An alcove running into the building to one side held a four-shelf metal rack, filled with sandals and tennis shoes.

An open door led into a common kitchen space, large but sparse, with a floor of brown-and-tan tiles. Stone countertops ran along three walls. Atop these sat five heavy-duty double-burner gas cooktops, hooked up via rubber hoses to propane tanks on the floor. There was a big metal sink as well, an air conditioner hanging above it. Between the burners, and sitting on top of a few, was a collection of clean metal pots, ceramic bowls, plastic containers, and a variety of coffee mugs. The whole place struck me as notably tidy for a kitchen serving a group of hardworking manual laborers. I remarked on that to Noor.

"This is a good place." He grinned, but added gravely. "Not like others."

"How many live here?"

"Let me ask." He put the question to the clean-shaven man. "He said maybe thirty-five or thirty-six, something like that. Some come, some go. These have been here for several years. They have good jobs and send money back to their families in India."

Approaching a dormitory, we stepped through a portal left open by a green metal door that hung ajar. Inside, another clean-shaven Sikh sat cross-legged on a pillow, watching TV. "Welcome," he said, and went back to his Urdu-language satellite program.

The walls here were sky blue. Three pairs of white steel bunk beds lined the room's longer walls. Thin mattresses rested on plywood, stacked with neatly folded blankets and pillows. The lone air conditioner stuck in the wall above one of the sets of bunks. A fan lazily rotated in the center of the ceiling. Scattered around were small metal lockers, also painted sky blue. Under the lower bunks lay piles of clothes, gym bags and personal belongings. On the walls beside several lower bunks were personal shrines devoted to gurus. The only other adornments were colorful pictures, of other gurus, near the door.

"This is how they live," Noor said. "In this room there are fourteen. Most are married and see their families maybe once every year." He added off-handedly, "I lived like this once."

Noor's mustached friend spoke to him in Urdu. I half-listened and looked around, trying to imagine what it would be like to live in a room with thirteen men, never see my family, and thus never be with a woman, while working far from home to support the family I so seldom see. This is how hundreds of thousands of workers live in the UAE. I also lived in this modern state that runs on something barely better than chattel slavery and severely restricts workers' rights—particularly those of South Asian laborers. Even college professors, if they had a conscience, chafed at being shackled by restrictive academic chains. Anxiety not to sell out was epidemic among the faculty.

This labor camp, as Noor had pointed out, was one of the best. He interrupted my thoughts. "The one watching TV is going home next week. My friend hopes to leave for good next month."

"I'm sure he can't wait." I engaged the man's eyes and nodded. He seemed to know why and smiled back. "He's told me that before," Noor continued. "They all dream of being back in India, to stay."

Noor chatted a moment more with his friend, and said, "Now it's time to leave. Let me take you to another camp. The one run by the Al Ain municipality. I lived there."

After a short drive we reached another walled compound. A sign, in all-caps that I gathered mirrored what it said in Arabic: "STRICTLY PROHIBITED TO ENTER EXCEPT FOR STAFF."

Noor ignored it and drove in. This desert courtyard, the size of a football field, was deserted but for an intimidating, ten-wheel tipper truck. Dwarfed by it, a few men stood in the sand. "Not many are here today," Noor observed.

"Odd that there's no security."

Noor let out a big laugh. "They think a sign is enough. Usually it is, but not for us."

He guided me to the residential compound. We entered an enclosed quadrant, through an open doorway. Inside, a smaller courtyard of sand was planted with a dozen big satellite dishes—and a lone tree. Clotheslines tied to poles were so thickly hung with garments that they obscured the view. Not that there was a view. At a plastic table with a red-and-white-checked cloth in one corner a few men, Bangladeshis, sat drinking tea. They looked up briefly at us and went about their business.

Surrounding the courtyard, beyond brick-paved walkways, were single-story block dormitories. These, too, were filled with bunk beds. Inside, in dirty, cluttered rooms, a few men sat and watched TV. The kitchen was similar to the one at the Sikh camp, with several two-burner cook tops connected by hoses to blue propane tanks. Instead of a metal sink there were three water faucets jutting out from the tiled wall, and a large tiled sink rising from the floor. Flies swarmed the counters.

"How many people live here?"

"Maybe a few hundred."

Noor was already leading me out, back to the car. "And the toilets? Like everywhere else?"

"Yaya, holes in the ground."

CHAPTER 32

To See for Myself

IT TOOK SEVERAL WEEKS FOLLOWING MY EMAIL AND PUNJABI dinner with Noor before anyone at the university responded to my by-the-book resignation email. Actually, the reply came in reaction to my *second* email, asking whether they had received the first. So far, this was going just as expected.

The respondent was Dr. Ali, who expressed regret and asked me to reconsider. It was a pleasant enough discussion. He wanted to know what it would take to keep me. I told him I'd like to know what I would be teaching next year—and would I be the "journalism expert"? That he couldn't say. Again, no earth-shattering revelation or any grave disappointment. *Insha'Allah, bukra.*

He said he'd pass my resignation, along with my concerns, up the food chain. That's where it languished. Nobody, including the dean, appeared to know quite what was happening with the budget cuts and big changes to take place in the fall. In the meantime, my in-class evaluation had been scheduled. I had watched other first-year faculty scramble and then panic, preparing for an observation. Like Tony, they had few options outside UAEU. The university, probably by accident rather than strategy, had its teachers locked into a desperate game of musical chairs. As part of that strategy, they fostered a palpable tension between the Arabic and Western faculty. Like my colleagues, I would face a three-person panel "of my peers," appointed to pass judgment on my teaching. This despite the fact I had resigned.

All of my peer-inquisitors were Arabs. Two turned out to be the Emirati and Egyptian professors from Mass Com. In advance of the evaluation, tiny Mariam ordered that I provide copies of tests, student papers, PowerPoints, and examples of classroom technology employed. There was a little problem with that—I had none of those things, and she knew that. Additionally, she requested I deliver a PowerPoint for each class in which I'd be observed. By then they all knew I never used that dubious medium. Jumping through hoops into fire for this gang? That held no appeal. Unlike everyone else, I didn't have to. I sent yet another email. This one to the Potemkin panel, declining the opportunity to be evaluated. The reason cited: my impending departure from the faculty.

Pyrrhic victories can be satisfying, but the satisfaction doesn't last. Letting go of UAEU, I felt liberated but unmoored. The Falahi's offers and assurances were sincere. They could come to something in the UAE; they rang true even in my self-doubting mind. Noor would stay in the UAE, trust in his God, and make it. His fate and his life gave him no choice, and his faith insured that he would succeed. Our relationship transcended my job. Tony would be around for a few more years before calling it a career and settling in the south of France. I could stay if I really cared to do so. *If it really felt right.*

Earlier self-reinventions had been forced more than willed. I could step back into my world in Ohio, *insha'Allah*. Even if things didn't seem so keen in the U.S. at least now I had a better idea of how to apply Rule Number One, and a perspective on how to re-approach life. That felt *right-er.*

I had come to the UAE to "see for myself," and I had seen plenty and heard plenty more. Now my choice was to return home. I had a story to continue and maybe to tell. One odd Jewish life, among so many in the Diaspora, had followed a path to the heartland of the Jews' sworn enemies. The UAE had shown me how that path led back to my own country and people.

I would return the middle-aged American Jew who taught at the national university of a conservative princedom in the midst of the oil-rich Arab world. Who found out that being open about his "Jewishness" didn't necessarily mean donning a Technicolor *yarmulke* and an in-their-face approach. That other paths to disclosure, maybe less direct and immediate, could construct bonds rather than barricades. I would leave as a teacher whose revelations and provocations may have sown or nurtured seeds in the minds of several outstanding young people. Their fierce allegiances to their tribes gave this outsider new ways of feeling about his ties to his own.

I am an American. I am a Jew. I am not a Jewish-American. No hyphen for me. The first covers my relationship to my country, the land that took in my grandparents and is the home of my family. The other asserts a religious, and some would say an ethnic identity and heritage. I am an American, who is Jewish, from Clevistan, a struggling village on a big lake across from Canada.

We Clevistani Jews are different from New York Jews or Chicago Jews, let alone *sabras* and Yemeni *Yehudas*. My particular little lost tribe settled in the Diaspora's Rust Belt ninety years ago. The Jews are my people, but America, not Israel, is my nation-state; I have a vote here not there. For Mohammed Falahi, as for Samah, it's the identity with one's people— the Bedouin, the Falahi/Nahyan, the Palestinians—that comes first. The Emiratis, like the Kuwaitis and Iraqis, live in made-up nation-states and to a great extent are invented peoples. The Jews are not an invented people. Today, against all historical and contemporary odds, they have fashioned a modern nation in their ancient homeland.

What would come next, *insha'Allah*, I had little idea, but I was ready for it. I would, *insha'Allah,* in a matter of weeks return to Ohio. To that the small corner of the world where my ancestors' wanderings put my clan, Cuyahoga County, which every four years, the pundits say, decides for Ohio and therefore for the United States of America, who will be the next President.

Back in Northeast Ohio we are not facing, *al ham do lielah*, pogroms, cold-eyed inspectors at Ellis Island, or the al-Houthi. We're up against mundanities, aggravations, defeats and pains, both psychic and psychical, like everyone else. On top of that layer a financial system that's called our bluff and come crashing down on our heads. I managed to get away, to flee, and take this break.

But now I'm saying "thank you" and passing them up. In declining my friends' pledges of wherewithal and support, I'm accepting their friendship. So what is essential now? That I communicate the decision in ways that say: *Your friendship has been, and will be, far more than enough. I love having found a place in your lives, but I'm ready to go back to mine.*

One evening in early May, in a memory I know to be fact rather than nostalgia, I looked down from that same window into the parking lot of the Falahi Apartments. Sabah and Akiel were clambering into a familiar Toyota Prado, their father watching as he conversed with Abu Ahmed.

I bounded down the stairs, bolted out the front door, and strode to the SUV. Mohamed coolly watched me greet his children. Did they know about his alienation from his Ohio buddy, their recent traveling companion in their family's ancestral homeland? Since storming out of my apartment after I had read my article on the last rabbi of Yemen, Mo had avoided me.

He spoke parting words to the Egyptian watchman and came over to the open car door. Akiel pulled it shut, but cracked the window in the heat. I looked Mohamed squarely in the eye, but kept my voice low. "What's wrong? I miss you."

We stepped away from the vehicle.

"Dave," he said, "you betrayed me." He sucked in a breath. "You wrote a story about the rabbi."

That much I had figured out. I told him it was my understanding, following my article's appearance, that others had been written highlighting the plight of Rabbi Yahya and his family. Had there been ugly repercussions from my article I'd not heard about? What had gone down in Yemen? I braced myself as I spoke. "Did something happen to the rabbi and his family?"

"Nothing bad has happened," Mohamed responded. "But you betrayed him by writing the story!"

A crucial piece of something had been lost in translation. At the time it took place, yes, the meeting had been clandestine. It was the rabbi who asked me to tell his story.

I took a deep breath, letting it out slowly. Here was the cultural difference I just couldn't quite get squared to. We Jews are faulted for many things, but being insufficiently blunt is seldom on the list of indictments. My friends' and hosts' indirectness drove me nuts. This moment, however, was not the one in which to voice my frustration. Mohamed had not asked me about this betrayal for the same reasons, I surmised, that no one but Saif Hamood had asked, or could feel right asking, "What's your religion?"

"Mohamed, I wrote the story because the rabbi asked me to."

He shook his head. "He asked you to do it?"

Many times in my life I had done things without thinking through the potential repercussions and often for no good reason at all. This was not one of them. "Yes, both directly and through Abdul Ghani." I laughed. "I guess you don't know me as well as I thought. I'm lazy! The reason I wrote the article was that I had given the rabbi my word I would try to get his story out someplace outsiders might see it." I chuckled. "Since the request first came to me via your brother, I figured you knew."

Mohamed shook his head vigorously and I sensed mutual relief. "I feel like an idiot."

And just like that, friends again.

A few hours after Fatima's graduation in mid-May, that male parents were not allowed to attend but male faculty bedecked in cap and gown were, I stopped at the villa. Against university regulations I had snapped off several *sura* of the graduate crossing the stage to receive her diploma and I showed them to Faraj. With Fatima still in her black graduation *abaya,* richly embroidered with golden thread and pearls, and a matching *sheyla* with a black mortarboard perched on top, I suggested that I take a picture of father and daughter.

Faraj liked the idea, left the *majlis,* and returned a few minutes later dressed like the prominent sheikh he is. In front of Door #1, he stood next to Fatima, the second of his daughters to graduate from UAEU. I clicked off several frames. He wanted pictures of the three of us and told Mohammed to take my camera. We flanked Fatima and her brother snapped a few photos.

Next I proposed a picture of Faraj kissing Fatima on the cheek. He leaned over and kissed Fatima, both daughter and father beaming, on her right cheek. Mohammed got the shot. Then a smiling Faraj looked at me. "Now you," he said, touching Fatima's cheek. "You kiss Fatima *here*. You are her uncle *and* professor." His gesture took me off guard. I had been vigilant in maintaining the appropriate social distance from Muslim women and had been surprised on my first visit when Amna extended her hand. But never had I kissed any of the women—although I had kissed the men on both cheeks and touched noses.

Fatima read my hesitation. "You are my uncle," she smiled. "It is permitted."

I kissed Fatima on her left cheek. I was *Doctor Uncle David Al Falahi*.

CHAPTER 33

The Pashtun Feast

THE ARRIVAL OF DARKNESS AT THE GREEN MUBAZZARAH was timed to coincide with my own. A neon glow illuminated the mountain park's perimeter and fluorescents lit up the picnic area and ring road.

Noor and Like weren't yet due. I parked the Yaris, walked to the picnic area, and watched families arriving, growing animated after the heat of the day. In the cooler months, from November through March, the park at the base of Jebel Hafeet had been a wonderful greenspace, but by June it had turned spotty brown. Still it had its palms, but the flowing stream was not even a trickle.

In the middle of the sculpted grounds rose a man-made mini-mountain, and I climbed the steep stone steps to its summit. From that vantage I could survey all beneath, like Moses on Sinai. Below, a child rode a pony, led by the animal's South Asian owner, as other children and their mothers followed. Families were spreading blankets on the scorched ground, setting up on picnic tables and lighting fires in metal grills. Several luxury vehicles cruised the perimeter road filled with young Emirati men inside barking their admiration at clusters of giggling young women in traditional black garb.

For weeks Noor had been planning a Pashtun farewell feast. Earlier in the day, Like and he had gone to the goat-and-sheep market, selected a young ram, had it slaughtered according to *halal* law, skinned, cleaned, and butchered. He told me that every Dawar tribesman in Al Ain was coming to my last supper, as were a few cousins from Abu Dhabi.

The goodbye to Noor would be the hardest. Fatima's birthday tomorrow was fixed by the calendar, so here I was saying farewell to my friend on my penultimate night in the UAE.

To help me arrange my departure, Noor had negotiated with a Pashtun friend running an airfreight service to ship my possessions to Cleveland at the Pashtun price, ten dirhams per kilo. Two days earlier, he, Like, and other friends, had arrived with a flatbed truck to move me out of the apartment. They transported my furniture to Tony's flat, where I was spending the next few nights, and delivered other items purchased by faculty around town. When I offered to pay, Noor refused. Had anybody told me that a chance meeting the first day of Ramadan with a Bahtan taxi driver on an Al Ain street would evolve into this kind of kinship, I would have scoffed. How could a Pashtun Muslim from North Waziristan and a middle-aged Jew from Clevistan forge such a golden bond? I didn't even know, then, what a golden bond was. Yet the differences between us never got in the way. Not the religious, cultural, age, geographic, economic and educational ones. In many ways, they brought us closer; though we had been driven to this hot, strange land by different realities we were both strangers, outsiders in a society gorging on *nouveau* oil riches and losing itself in the process.

Noor's life was different from anything even remotely in my experience. He had lost two children in childbirth and lived separated from his family for years at a time. The Taliban forced him to leave his job as a school administrator and he'd migrated to the Emirates to make a living. He'd lived in labor camps, worked as a municipal laborer, arranged visas for other Pashtun and driven a taxi. When his livelihood as a taxi driver was taken away, he went on resolutely believing that his God would intervene and sustain him and his distant family. And *He* did. Or at least Noor saw that *He* did. *He* made Noor the driver-owner of a tipper truck. Nothing fate could deal was capable of reducing this man's stature.

Noor opened for me portals into a world my kind—Westerners, let alone Jews—are seldom permitted to glimpse, let alone enter. He allowed me to know him as a proud Pashtun and devout Muslim, and not only acted as my guide, interpreter, negotiator, and protector in navigating life in the Emirates, but also made me family. I was a generation older and he thought of me as his elder, but above all as a friend. His trustworthy character and drive to provide for the family he rarely saw, and his faith that *his* God would provide for them, were for me both endearing and frighteningly naive. I might not have Noor's faith in God, but my faith in Noor was strong. To say I had been humbled by our friendship is inadequate. Knowing Noor had led me to a question I might never have reached on my own: What did *my* God want for me?

A superficial answer was easy. Nothing. I knew in my heart as well as my mind that *He* had no divine plan for my life. If *He* had one, which I doubted, *He* hadn't seen fit to reveal it—and I wasn't holding my breath. No Job was I. I had never, not even briefly, believed the God of Moses gave a damn about what happened to me. I couldn't tell Noor that.

I had once told Noor that God's "chosen people" were selected not because they were anything special back in biblical times, but simply because *He* decided to choose someone and it happened to be *us*. That made *us Jews* either the luckiest people in human history or painted our backs with the biggest target ever. Whichever, *He'd* sent *us* out into the world on a destiny that was unique.

As a Jew, even in my most agnostic moments, getting little inspiration or solace from ritual and belief, I had never doubted my place within my ancient scattered tribe. Atop my artificial Sinai at the foot of Jebel Hafeet, I wondered in how many ways Noor had changed me. It was he, more than all the other benevolent influences my time in the Emirates had brought to bear, who showed me where my place with my tribe should put me—with my family in Clevistan. Separated from his own by eleven hundred miles, he was never more than a prayer away from them. I was seven thousand miles away from mine.

Surveying the Green Mubazzarah, I caught sight of the white Corolla. It pulled into the parking lot, followed by Like's white van, in turn followed by several other vehicles. Men piled out, each carrying something, including four big aluminum cook pots. Altogether, I counted a group of twenty, already setting up for the feast.

Descending from the mountaintop, I watched several of the men spread a vast red carpet on the ground near a picnic table, and others cover it with a plastic sheet. The four pots were placed on the rug's four corners, amid stacked covered serving dishes.

I called out and waved to get Noor's attention. He was directing some men in placement of liter bottles of Al Ain water and Pepsi. Others distributed plastic cups, rolls of paper towel, loaves of Pashtun bread and platters of vegetables—an assortment of tomatoes, cucumbers, mint, herbs and lettuce—on the carpet. He turned and rushed over.

"My friend!" he exclaimed with a big smile, reaching out to seize my hand. "We are almost ready for your farewell feast. But if you have changed your mind about leaving we will still have the feast in honor of you staying."

I put my arm around his shoulder and pulled him close. "Noor," I said, wistfully, "I am leaving."

"Tony says there are no jobs in America," he said. "You are a respected professor here. And the Falahi want to give you a business. You should stay."

"Noor, I am returning to Clevistan."

He sighed. "I thought I would try one last time."

I had to focus on the activity and the food, or I would break down. Amid his precarious life, fearing daily for the lives of his wife and children, he was worried about what would become of me.

At each corner of the carpet, men were dipping into the pots and filling the serving dishes with portions of ram and heaping piles of white biryani rice. Noor had told me earlier in the day that he would prepare the ram three ways: roasted, boiled, and stewed with tomatoes, onions and spices. Several Famous Chickens, plopped on platters, sat at intervals on the plastic.

Noor directed me to sit at the top of the carpet, nearest the picnic table. I knelt on the edge. The others crowded around the rug, and

I recognized several Noor had brought to my apartment for visits. Like directed the distribution of food, filled a plate with portions of the three preparations of meat and rice, and handed it to Noor. "This is for you," Noor said, placing the plate on the plastic before me.

He reached across me and grabbed a platter with a whole chicken and placed that in front of me, too. "This Famous Chicken is for you, too. It's your last in Al Ain, for now."

Tearing off a piece of warm Pashtun bread from the pile, I used it to pick up a chunk of stewed mutton and tomato. The meat was tender and spicy and I used the bread to mop the plate. Noor watched me closely. I nodded and he fixed a plate for himself. All around the carpet, the other Dawar ate, laughed, and talked in Pashto. I was going to miss the sound of that language, the one King David spoke.

"Thank you, Noor, for having this feast tonight for me," I said, picking up a slice of cucumber. "I couldn't think of a better send-off."

"You can still change your mind," he said, smiling mischievously.

"You know how much trouble I had making up my mind. And for once, my mind is made up. Max is meeting me in Rome on the way home."

Like placed a platter of vegetables within our reach, and sat down cross-legged next to Noor. He whispered in his cousin's ear, and Noor turned to me.

"Like tells me that every Dawar in Al Ain who isn't working is here, and that our elder, Ibrahim—" he pointed toward a man with a long, henna red beard "—has driven in from Abu Dhabi with his son to meet you. You are well known among the Dawar."

"I hope that's a good thing." I laughed.

"Yaya, it's good. I have made you very famous—like the chicken."

"So does that mean I can visit you in North Waziristan?"

"Oh, no," Noor chuckled. "You would get killed also like the chicken."

He took several pieces from the platter, added vegetables, and turned back to me. "When will I see you again? Your leaving is not good for Noor."

"Tony will still be here."

"Tony is a good man, but he is not you."

"Tony is your friend," I tried to reassure him.

"*Insha'allah,* we shall see."

"Sometimes, Noor, people come into other people's lives for a short time, but stay in their hearts and minds forever."

"I like to talk to you face to face."

"You can always talk to me in your head and we will talk on the phone."

"But where will you live when you divorce?" he asked, looking concerned.

"I'm not sure. An old friend, Jack, whose wife died from cancer, said I could stay at his house."

"That is not good for you."

"It is what it is. I'll find a place to stay and a bed, *insha'Allah*, until I figure things out."

"A bed is not enough. What will you do for work?"

"I'm not sure," I said, shrugging. "Every college I applied to turned me down. There are no university jobs in America, and no media jobs. But I'll find something to do."

"You still can have a job here," Noor responded. "The Falahis want to give you a business. The university asked you to stay. You can have a nice villa, like Tony."

"Yes I could," I sighed, placing my hand on his shoulder. "But I'm going and, *insha'Allah*, everything will work out with me just as it did with Allah's help in guiding you to your tipper truck."

"My God directs us even in the smallest things because only He knows His plan for us. But when will you come back to visit me?"

"Noor, you once told me that God directs every sperm, so it is up to Him to direct my return. I will come back, *insha'Allah*, when it is my time."

"You do not have as much energy as a sperm, my friend," he said with a big laugh.

"No, but I make up for it by being stubborn. And I have a longer shelf life."

Behind Noor, Like waited while his cousin and I laughed. Beside him stood Ibrahim.

I stood up, Noor rose beside me, and I placed both hands on his shoulders. "You know I will miss you the most of anyone here."

A smile expanded slowly across his face, and his eyes grew winsome. "More than Tony and the Falahis?"

"I will miss them, but in a very different way. You have been my closest friend here, and in many ways I feel like you are both my little brother and teacher. I will see you again, *insha'Allah*. I promise."

"When I saw you and Mohamed for the first time on Ramadan," he said, reflectively, "I asked myself whether I should stop and how much should I charge you. I said to myself, 'Maybe this is what my God wants me to do.' So I did and charged you very little. I know, *insha'Allah*, that my God will bring us back together again."

We turned to Like and Ibrahim. "This man with my cousin is the elder I told you about," Noor said. "He is eager to talk with you and so are others. We will have more time together later."

Ibrahim offered his hand and I took it. "Let's walk up the mountain and talk," he suggested, pointing to the mini-summit on which I'd stood not that long before. Hand in hand, we ascended. Half way to the top I turned and looked back. Noor waved and I felt a hole open in my stomach.

CHAPTER 34

Fatima's Birthday

I'D SPENT MY EVENING WITH TWENTY-ONE PASHTUN MEN, all of whom lived lives that were models of necessity and courage. I slept fitfully on my own bed, for the last time, now located in Tony's guest room. We'd stayed up to all hours in the "foxhole" talking and toasting before my deployment home. Tony had become that foxhole buddy I had divined he could be on that first morning in the Jebel Hafeet room, and our high-speed adventures in his famous marine blue Porsche Carrera 996 Turbo, the 2003 Dubai Porsche Show Car of the Year, were the stuff of middle-aged male legend and tomfoolery.

This, my final day in Al Ain, was Fatima's birthday. I'd spend it with her, and my Emirati family. Giving up the apartment, having sold and given away a good deal of my stuff, I dropped off my bags at the Intercontinental and turned in the Yaris at EuropCar. The Falahis' Egyptian driver picked me up around noon and transported me to their home. The family wished for me to stay with them my last night, but I'd made other plans. For my final night in Al Ain, I'd booked the same room I'd lived in during the first two months. It would be easier for the university's driver, per rules, to collect me there, at dawn.

Since my announcement that I was leaving, Faraj had kept peppering me with questions and speculations as to what he could do to convince me to stay. We had virtually the same exchange every time: "If you want money, I will give you money. If you want a business, we will make a business. Tell me." To which I replied, "I have to go home, but when I return we can talk about business."

But how sincere was he really? For that matter, how sincere was I? I didn't *have* to go home. I *wanted* to go home. I *chose* to go home. Yes, I chose to leave the UAE. But I was, thanks to what my friends and students here had given me, going *to* much more than I was going *from*. But that didn't mean I didn't want to come back. Because I had followed Noor's advice, repaid thousands of dollars, and jumped through all of the departure hoops, I would, *insha'Allah*, have no problem gaining reentry. The dean even left the door open for me rejoining the faculty. That would not happen, but I thanked him.

There was opportunity here—much more than in Ohio. Maybe after I got my life in order, I'd consider returning to explore doing some kind of business with Faraj. If I deserved to be included as trusted family, a separation shouldn't mean anything. Maybe I could straddle two worlds and make a go of it, both in the USA and the UAE. It wasn't such an out-of-this-world thought. An American Jew and an Emirati Muslim—partners. Of course, I'd have to find a place for Noor.

For the week before Fatima's birthday, Faraj had been in Abu Dhabi. Fatima assured me that her father would be home in time to say goodbye to "his big brother." She added, with her serene confidence, "He will be here for my party."

The Egyptian, *insha'Allah*, was only a half hour late picking me up at EuropCar in Sanaiya. Sarah and Mariam greeted me at the door and took me into the family *majlis*, where I joined Amna at the table. The "boys" were not there. Hilal was at the Palace Museum, Issa was at his job at the nearby prison, and Sultan was asleep after his all-nighter at Al Ain's EMS center. As usual, Mohammed and Abdulla were still dozing.

"We have been cooking all morning," Fatima said, carrying a tray. Layla, following, held another. They unloaded the platters, filled with eggs and tomatoes, eggs and spinach, several kinds of *hummus*, and two covered serving vessels. One contained *luquiamt*, deep-fried dough balls rolled in sesame seeds and drizzled in date syrup, and the other *billaleet*, sweet vermicelli noodles topped with an omelette.

"My mother hopes that you are very hungry," Mariam said. "We've prepared a special meal."

Fatima shuffled dishes around the table. "How was Noor's feast? He must be very sad you are leaving, like we are."

They had made this banquet especially for me, and my gut was not cooperative. "I think the Pashtun stewed ram upset my stomach," I answered, playfully clutching my midsection and feigning pain. The fact was I had little appetite. Whether that was because my insides needed recovery, or an expression of something more emotional, mattered little. It ran smack up against the feast spread out before me. I was expected to eat. I would eat. Amna had gone all out, as she had for the Christmas Eve dinner. Arrayed on the table was a breakfast fit for Bedouin royalty.

Fatima sensed my distress. "You will feel better after this," she said, motioning to Layla.

The servant handed Fatima a tureen. She removed the top and a rich, savory aroma wafted up tantalizing my nostrils. "This will make you feel better." She ladled soup into a bowl. "It's vegetable broth, secret spices, organic spinach from our garden, and fresh shrimp from the Arabian Sea."

I laughed. "I'll have two, if it cures me like the Jebel Hafeet honey fixed my cough."

"Then I think you will have three," Fatima replied.

A self-anointed soup maven, I had never seen such a broth loaded with tender clumps of greens and such large succulent shrimp. An Emirati version of a Vietnamese *pho*? The Falahi women watched me closely as Sarah nuzzled close to my side and I slurped down two quick spoonfuls. I smacked my lips in delight. "Ummm-mm," I moaned. "This soup is absolutely the best I have ever tasted."

"This is my father's favorite," Mariam related. "You'll get strength for your trip."

"Uncle," Sarah cut in, "you have some spinach stuck on your beard."

I wiped my mouth with a facial tissue. "Did I get it all?"

"Yes, Uncle," she beamed.

I turned to Fatima. "I will want at least one more bowl. I feel that my appetite has improved." Then I spooned another mouthful. "So tell me, what's the plan for today?"

Amna filled a large plate with portions of egg dishes and *billaleet*. On a small dish she added *hummus* with pine nuts and *baba ganoush*. She put them before me.

"After we eat, you will go to Zayed's Palace to be with Hilal and Hamood," Fatima said. "Then you will come back and rest until my party. Now, Uncle, you will have some more soup and eat."

After sunset, Fatima came to retrieve me from the overstuffed blue chair in an empty bedroom where I had been trying, with no luck, to nap since I'd returned from the Palace.

"Did I wake you, Uncle?" Fatima asked. "It is time for my party."

"No, I was just resting my eyes. Is your father here yet?"

"My parents just arrived. They were visiting baby Zayed at the hospital."

Six weeks before, Sultana had given birth to a premature son. He was still in neo-natal intensive care at Johns Hopkins-Tawam Hospital, but was out of danger. During the first days after the birth of Zayed bin Sultan Al Falahi, proudly named after Faraj's uncle, the family shuttled back and forth to the hospital and kept a constant vigil.

"My father will talk with you later," Fatima continued. "I've told you that you are the first person in many years he trusts." She took a deep breath. "Uncle, my father said he'd buy you a newspaper."

"Fatima, I don't think that would be a smart business move."

"That's what I told him."

Over that point of agreement, the two of us had a good laugh.

Fatima sighed. "He is very sad that you are leaving."

While the comment registered, I took it at what I thought was face value. "I am sad, too, Fatima, but I have to go home." I reached into my backpack and pulled out a small box. "Here is your birthday present." I handed her a gift-wrapped jewelry box with a pink bow. Inside was a unicorn necklace, in sterling silver, I'd purchased at the Al Ain Mall.

"Thank you, Uncle," she said, kissing me on top of my head. "I will open it after you leave tonight. Now it's time to join the family."

Dozens of helium balloons with smiley faces and "Happy Birthday" filled the formal dining room. A three-tiered Barbie cake with a big 22 candle on top and *Happy Birthday Fatima* in red icing sat in the middle of a small table with only four chairs. On the main table, where I had dined with the nephew of Sultan Qaboos, Oman's ruler, and his retinue a month earlier, was the evening feast.

Fatima directed me to the side table where Faraj and Amna greeted me. "Doctor, you sit here," Faraj said, directing me to the only chair with balloons tied to it. "This is the seat of honor."

Mohammed and Abdulla entered, walked directly to their father, and kissed him on top of his head. The family was now altogether. There was nobody else at the party.

"Fatima, when do the other guests arrive?"

"Everyone I want is here," she said, sitting in the chair between her father and me. "There are no other guests. This is my family."

"What about your cousins and friends?"

"No, tonight is only for close family—and for my special present."

"What's that?"

She smiled. "You are my special present. You stayed for my birthday."

After dinner, Hilal tapped me on the shoulder. "Uncle, my father wants to talk to you."

I had just cut into my second piece of Barbie birthday cake. "Right now?"

"Uncle, go with Hilal," Fatima said. "My father wants to talk to his big brother alone."

It had been more than a week since Faraj and I had spoken. The last time he had reiterated his offer to give me money or a business. Again I'd thanked him and said I needed to go home. His offer intrigued me, though, and at another time I might have taken him up on it. But this wasn't that time.

Hilal took me out the back. "I will be driving you later to the Intercontinental with Sultan. He pointed across the courtyard, "My father is waiting for you there." Faraj stood at the end of the carport, between the two villas where Sultan, Issa and their wives lived, and where Hilal had his own apartment. "Walk with me, Doctor," he said, extending his right hand. We strolled hand in hand past Amna's vegetable garden and a pen where she kept several Saudi sheep. Faraj gestured to a new foundation and courtyard where wooden stakes were planted among new brick pavers. "I am making everything bigger," he said, with a sweep of his hand. "Sultan has a new baby and needs more space. Issa needs more."

I surveyed the site. "I didn't have much money when I was young so I worked as a laborer digging foundations and carrying bricks to pay for college. I worked like the Bahtan do here."

He nodded. "But you have a good mind. We have many hard workers, but we need more good minds. I fear for my children's future. I am worried about what they will do. It is so different today than when I was young. I want you to help me make a plan for them even after you are back in America."

That last statement hit home. In fact, I had spoken frequently with Fatima, Mariam, Sultan, Hilal, and the comedy duo about their futures. I had brainstormed many ideas. Faraj wanted his daughters to get graduate degrees. He often said that Fatima had a good head for business and for sizing up people. Hilal, too, had voiced the elegiac sense that his country's Bedouin culture was being supplanted—by things he did not even name.

"You know that Sultan is interested in importing classic American cars," I said. "After I return to America, we can see whether he really wants to do that." Faraj nodded and I continued. "I've told Mohammed. and Abdulla that they should come to America for college, so they can get a better education. Both are very intelligent and speak good English."

"They have told me. Now, *insha'Allah*, they have to decide what to do. But that is what worries me. Will they make the right decisions? Make any decision?"

I had a ready answer. "We all make wrong decisions in our lives. God knows, I have made many of my own. When I first arrived in your country, I thought that coming here was a mistake. I was wrong. Living in Al Ain has been very good for me. I have come to know your family. But when you or I make errors, it's what we do after the mistake that's important."

He laughed. "We both have made mistakes, but we make fewer than others." He tapped his head. "Because we are smarter. Now walk with me to the front."

We strolled across the paved courtyard between the villas, past the open front gate, and stopped in front of the tall front masonry wall. "It is hot tonight, but Abu Dhabi is worse," Faraj *kvetched.* "I cannot breath the air there—it is too thick. Al Ain is better."

He was right—Al Ain's dry desert climate was the best in the Emirates. "I agree!"

He put his hand on my shoulder. "Then you should stay! Come back after you go to Ohio. I will call Nahyan if you want. He will make you a professor again. He is my cousin."

It was nice to know that I could change my mind, that the freedom I had felt soon after returning from Yemen, carrying all the anguish I had accumulated there, was real. After all, I now had my little corner of Falahi *wasta,* but I had dropped out of my other life long enough and it was time to go back.

"Faraj, I like the weather in Cleveland more than in Al Ain," I said, with a grin, "although people in America would think that's crazy. When I return, *insha'Allah,* we can talk business."

We stood a moment in silence. He reached out and clasped my hand. "Doctor, you are my brother and do not speak left or right. You are of the Falahi and I trust that you will help my children."

His words left me virtually speechless, but I managed a response. "We speak the same language. I will keep my word."

Then he pointed to an empty patch of land near the front entrance. "There I will build homes for Mariam and Fatima. I will begin with two rooms and baths for each, so they will always have their own home with their family. What do you think, Doctor?"

On the eve of my departure, Faraj was reaching out to me and seeking my approval of his plans for the family's future, as he might consult a true brother. This was something I had once dismissed as a sincere but nonetheless ritualized social courtesy, the celebrated Bedouin hospitality, no more. The proclamation Faraj had made on that first night driving to the racing-camel farm had blossomed into something rare indeed. An American Jew and a member of Emirati royalty had forged a bond of trust and faith. It was as crazy and unlikely as a friendship between that Clevistani Jew and a Pashtun taxi driver.

"I think it is a good thing," I replied, placing my left hand on his shoulder and squaring up to face him. "It is very good!"

"Then I am happy you agree with your little brother." He smiled. "Now it is time for you to go back to Fatima's party. I will say goodbye now."

He leaned forward, we closed our eyes, and touched noses. Together we had power. Pulling away our eyes locked and we gave each other a knowing nod. Faraj stood there and I turned toward Door #1. I thought about how far we'd come since the night Mahasba kissed me under the desert moon.

Hilal parked the white Land Cruiser near the back porch. I heard a loud commotion behind me, by the door. In the dining room, I had said my farewells just a moment before to Fatima, Amna, Mariam, Sarah and Hardy & Hardy. The women followed me out.

My mind flashed through an unedited mental montage of UAE memories as I stood there listening to the Falahi women arguing passionately in Arabic, picking up a tone of great concern and angst. As I struggled to pick out a few words, to understand their distress, I felt that my standing here at this exact moment was a matter of *insha'Allah*—God's genuine will or in my Jewish world a true *Shehecheyanu* moment. I had a hard time following what was upsetting *my* Emirati family, but I was where I was meant to be. Perhaps everything that had happened to me in the last few years—hell, in my entire life—I'd never had under my control.

Does *He*, as Noor believes, micromanage everything?

Or was that only Noor's God, not mine?

Faraj said they were the same.

Of course, the underlying question was the strongest: Could I ever *really* believe? Maybe, but never as my friends did. Nor should I. The faith they had permitted me to witness was theirs. It was up to me to find my own. Some might need an ashram, a chapel, or a bejeweled zillion-dirham mosque. For me, Clevistan, Ohio, was as good a place as any.

Sultan edged up quietly, holding my backpack. "I will put it in the car, but I think you should talk to my mother and sisters before we leave. My mother is worried."

I turned around and caught Fatima's eye.

"Uncle, my mother needs you to come see my father now. She is concerned about him."

I took a step toward her. "What is it?"

"Our father is..." Mariam said, haltingly. "Uncle, we have never seen him like this."

"My mother wants you to go back and see him now," Fatima pleaded. Amna looked on anxiously as Sarah clung to her mother's arm.

"She wants you to go in alone," Mariam added. "He cannot know that we asked you to go back."

In my time with the family, I had never seen the look of concern on the women's faces as I did at that moment. Not even when Baby Zayed was born—because they believed and accepted to their very cores that what happened to the newborn would be God's will. But what had happened to Faraj since we said goodbye? Why couldn't he know they asked me to return? Why did I have to go in alone?

"What's wrong?"

"He is weeping," Fatima sighed. "He says he has lost his brother."

"He cannot stop crying," Mariam added. "He's alone in the *majlis*."

I nodded and walked quickly into the villa. Faraj was sitting in his white leather recliner holding his eyeglasses in one hand, and crying uncontrollably like I did at my brother's funeral. I hadn't shed a single tear after I learned my brother died, not until I stood graveside. Then a tiny white butterfly landed on top of his casket, stayed a moment and flitted away, as it was being lowered into the ground. The dam in my eyes burst. Buried on my birthday, and every birthday since then I see that butterfly.

Faraj wiped his eyes and waved me away. "Doctor, go! I do not want you to see me."

I stood in front of him. "Faraj, my brother, I wanted to come back and tell you…"

"Go now!" he implored. "You have to get up early to go to Dubai."

I put both hands on his shoulders. "I have time to say goodbye one more time to my brother. I came back because I wanted to tell you that I am happy and honored that you made me a part of your family. I promise that I will help your children, but now I must go back to America to be part of my family. I will be back, *insha'Allah,* to see my Emirati family. You have my word."

With nothing left to say, I did what I had seen Faraj's children do, in an expression of their love and respect. I bent down and kissed him on the top of his head.

At dawn the university's South Asian driver collected me at the Intercon. We drove in silence.

Except for that ping-ping as he sped up E-66 to Dubai.

He caught my eyes in the rearview mirror. "We do not want to be late at the airport," he implored.

I was in plenty of time for my flight.

"*Insha'Allah,* no problem," I relented. The sound was oddly soothing now.

Ping-ping.

We pulled to a stop at a bustling Terminal 3. He retrieved my small black roll-on suitcase from the trunk and I slipped on the backpack. My HR briefer had explained that UAEU regulations said that the driver would escort me to Immigration and facilitate my departure. There, my three-year visa would be canceled and he would take confirmation back to university.

"Where to now?" I asked.

He pointed ahead. "You go there. No problem, *insha'Allah.*"

Of course. I'd been fooled right up to the last minute. "Ah. You are not taking me to Immigration? I just go over there?"

"No problem, *insha'Allah.*" He pointed to the busy entrance. "Go there."

From there I could play out the scene. "So I just go over *there*?" I pointed to the entry to Terminal 3. "Go through that door and leave the country!?"

He nodded.

"So you don't need to get a paper to take back to the university?"

He shook his head and laughed. Nonverbal communication. "You are leaving. No problem, *Insha'Allah.* I don't need. They don't care. You can just go, *insha'Allah.* You'll see."

Indeed I had. I came and *saw for myself.* The only response that made any sense popped out of my mouth. "So what you're saying is, 'Good luck and good riddance.' *Insha'Allah,* no problem."

He grinned and nodded. "No problem, *insha'Allah.*"

But he had it wrong. I had learned the proper order.

It is, "*insha'Allah,* no problem" *not* "no problem, *insha'Allah.*"

It is "*God willing,* no problem" *not* 'no problem, *God* willing."

I finally understood the nuance. You ask God first.

Noor knew that intrinsically.

I let out a small laugh. "So I just follow Rule Number One!"

Tony would like that. I'd been a good pupil.

The driver nodded and pointed toward Terminal 3.

I turned and took the first step back into my new old life.

Insha'Allah, no problem.

EPILOGUE

Tony's emailed directions had been simple enough: *Tell the taxi driver to drop you in front of the Dunes Hotel on Oud Mehta Road. Remember, still no street addresses in UAE.*

This time, however, there was no wheelchair-bound boy modeling a Superman leotard to seize my gaze as the taxi pulled out of Terminal 3. I felt a mild nostalgia, as the handicapped Superboy had passed in and out of my mind from my arrival a bit more than four years earlier. None of my reflections had given me much sense of what the image was supposed to mean. Some things remain beyond understanding. Lost forever in translation.

Dubai was rebounding, or so the media said, from the financial crisis. Judging by my taxi, a latest-model Camry, I was willing to believe it. At home, Obama had recently been sworn in for a second term and the stock markets were higher than before The Great Recession. But my thoughts focused on people. Specifically one Pashtun, one Emirati family, and a certain graduate student.

Noor, as I had departed Clevistan some days before for Istanbul, had been at the top of my mind. I'd lost touch with him for more than a year. Emails went unacknowledged. When I called his mobile, someone else answered. Repeated attempts, in the days leading up to my departure, equally unavailing, made me fear I might have lost touch with him forever. Tony acknowledged that he had rarely seen or spoken to Noor since moving to Dubai two years back. That made my mind up and I carved a month out of my winter schedule and booked a ticket. My apprehensions about Noor ran the gamut: Had he been "put on a plane"? Or, worse, had he finally written me off as, in Tony's inimitable phrase, "another Western arsehole?" Was the bond I felt with him just some Kiplingesque delusion?

Fatima confirmed quickly that she and the family would all be in residence in Al Ain. I would see them as soon as I got to their emirate. Samah, like Noor, was incommunicado. The "Girl in Pink" had kept me apprised for a while regarding life milestones. She'd married, had a son, and was a PhD candidate at UAEU. Then things went dark. The email I sent, to tell her I was UAE bound, bounced back. Mysteriously, not two hours later, via Linkedin:

> Hey, remember me? Quick reminder: UAEU about five years ago,
> writing for the media course. Pain in the neck student. — Samah

My eyes popped out of their sockets. Coincidence? Kismet? *Beshert?* An act of *insha'Allah?* I accepted the "connect request." Samah, in her next note, confirmed that she'd lost track of me, and found me by chance. So my email had indeed ricocheted without reaching her. Her old email account having been hacked, she'd lost all her contacts, and created a new electronic address. Linkedin, which she'd just joined, listed me as a connection of a UAEU professor. Her direct email read:

> I've thought about you quite often in the last year or so, wondering
> how you were. The only thing I could remember was the title of
> your book, which I googled a number of times btw. I've been anx-
> ious to read that book for over five years now, throw me a bone
> here will ya! Good luck with everything. Keep in touch. — Sam

I was in Istanbul when Tony emailed that he had located Noor. Everything and everyone was falling into place. In the taxi on my way to Tony's, I checked my iPhone for messages. One leaped out:

> Hi how r u my friend? Tony told me you are coming.
> Good to see u in Al Ain after long time.
> Noor with u.

Next, I checked in with Fatima. I confirmed that I would get to Al Ain on Saturday. That was answered with my instructions: come that night to the Falahis' for dinner.

Tony spotted me standing curbside in the yellow cone cast by a street lamp. "Young David! You've made it!" He sported the same cocky, reassuring grin I'd noted in the Jebel Hafeet Room. Baggy shorts, wrinkled blue t-shirt, and a little more gray in his mop of brown hair, clean-shaven. In a scene corny enough for a *Bucket List* sequel, the two old dogs strode toward each other and engaged in a man hug. Maintenance by internet of friendship was no substitute for that temporal and intrinsically physical thing called male bonding. Rare, it hit me, among men growing long in tooth.

I slid wearily into his and Rozz's tenth-floor flat, which soon enveloped me as snugly as our old Al Ain foxhole. More comfortable, though. By the time I'd deposited my bag in the guest suite, Tony had a scotch on ice ready. The sitting room had a spectacular view of the Sphinx and the largest pyramids outside Egypt (and Vegas), rising up from the Wafi City Mall.

"If I recall," Tony said, handing me a glass with a wink, "you're not fond of gin."

Rozz stepped in with a brace of gin-and-tonics, handed one to her significant other and took a seat on the sectional. We had met in Al Ain when she visited from Australia to apply for work. She soon came to live in Dubai, to teach in Sharjah, to the north, and Tony stayed in Al Ain. They maintained a commuting relationship for two more years. Mid-way through my absence, Tony landed a spot at Dubai-based Zayed University and came to live with Rozz. His most recent employer had been the American University of the Emirates.

Tony, with another wink, punched a number into his smartphone. "Hold on," he said and, with a mischievous sparkle in his eyes, handed it to me.

"Hello?"

"Hello, my friend! Welcome back to Dubai. *Insha'Allah*, I will see you soon!"

Soon, Noor elaborated, would be Friday. He had many tipper truck jobs over the next two days, *insha'allah*, and would come up, *insha'allah*, on his Sabbath. He planned to stop first Friday morning, *insha'allah*, at the Zayed Mosque in Abu Dhabi to hear a renowned imam. Afterward he'd drive, *insha'Allah*, to Dubai. Hearing four *insha'Allahs* in one utterance brought a big smile to my face.

I could answer just one way. "*Insha'Allah*, but where have you been?"

He laughed. "I lost my phone. And I am too busy to check my email."

Good enough. Instant relief. Hell, I have friends back home I don't speak to for more than a year and we stay friends. But they can't be kicked out of the country and sent to the wilds of North Waziristan. We can always find each other when we need or want. How would I ever have found Noor in "Osamaland"? An interesting question, maybe, but a moot point. He was safe, enthusiastic and we'd see each other, God willing, Friday.

Signing off, I recalled how uneasy I once felt about how fully Noor placed his life in God's hands. I'd been living that way, in some sense, since the return to Ohio. Not to nearly the extent Noor did, of course, but to a degree that surprised me. It was in that suspended period, or holding pattern, I started to write a story about Noor and the other people I had met in the UAE. The one Samah waited to read.

So all my worry about Noor for nothing? No, not for nothing. I'd see him Friday, *insha'Allah*. Tony and Rozz came up with the idea of a picnic lunch at the verdant Dubai Creek Park and an evening at the Global Village, midway between Dubai and Al Ain. My reunion with the two Australian expats wound up two hours beyond midnight, with video of their retirement sanctuary in the south of France, and an invitation to visit the following summer, and to bring along the new woman in my life.

At 1:30 on Friday Noor burst through Tony and Rozz's doorway carrying a fruit basket and wearing an electric smile. Lying in wait I clicked off a few shots on the Sony Digital. Noor's black hair and beard now sported streaks of gray, but his dark brown eyes had lost none of their spark. Tony accepted the fruit basket as my Pashtun friend reached out to embrace me. Asking how I was, he placed a well-manicured hand on my shoulder and took a half step back for an appraisal.

Assuring him I was fine, and confirming that he was as well, I added, "You are showing gray."

He laughed. "My wife tells me I do not have to color my hair anymore. I am forty-four now."

"That young!" I laughed.

Before Tony, Noor and I could launch into a chain of reminiscences, Rozz directed us to the balcony. The Pyramid our backdrop, we settled into chairs around a small table with a teapot, cups and a few biscuits on a plate. Tony asked Noor about his family. "Good, *al ham doo lielah*. I have moved them out of crazy North Waziristan. My children and their mother now live in Bantu, a famous ancient Pashtun city. I can afford to send them to good boarding schools, not government schools, that are respected."

Tony and Rozz offered their congratulations.

"Yaya, my son is at the famous university school. Third in his class. He is nineteen and wants to be a doctor. My daughters also are in boarding school. My fourteen-year-old is first in her class." It would not have seemed his smile could grow any bigger, but it did.

Tony cocked one eyebrow. "So you are rich now?"

Noor laughed. "Tony, you see that I still drive the old taxi that I bought when David was here. It still works, *insha'Allah*. I've moved my family out of Waziristan. They are safer, *insha'Allah*." He picked up the teapot and poured into three cups. The first two years after I left, Noor explained, he had struggled to find steady tipper-truck business. Times were lean, and he had to learn the ins-and-outs of hauling in a who-you-know economy depressed by The Crisis. Some months he had no money to send home, but he had repaid to Like's brother-in-law the loan with which he had bought his truck. Business conditions had improved and he had branched out adding "trucking contractor" to his list of services. Because of his good language skills, he could book jobs not only for himself but also for other Pashtun truckers, and take a commission. "My visa might say that I'm a laborer, but I am a businessman who also does labor. Before, as a taxi driver I made, *insha'Allah*, two hundred dirham a day. Now I make, *insha'Allah*, one thousand on a good day, five hundred on a bad day."

This had allowed him to move his wife and five children out of the tribal lands beset with problems. "There is no law in Waziristan. Every day, two or three people show up dead on the street. Some hanging from a wire. It is crazy. People can't live like that." He was supporting not only his wife and five children, but also his parents and several cousins still in North Waziristan. "My father is almost eighty and goes on working as a teacher. I send him money so he can retire. And sometimes he uses the money to hire another teacher to take his place. But he does not retire. He will, *insha'Allah*, soon."

I asked Noor about Like, his cousin, who was one of the few people Noor trusted with the knowledge that I was *Yehuda*. Like had sold his twenty-seat bus and returned to Waziristan. "He had no choice. His brother-in-law went back for a funeral and when he stepped off the bus an old enemy of his family stabbed him to death, in broad daylight. A vengeance killing." Noor shook his head. "Everybody knows who did it, but nothing has happened to him. Now Like has to keep watch over his brother-in-law's family, his sister and their children, and our family."

Tony and I gawked, speechless.

"Without law," Noor went on, "there is nothing. Without good education there is nothing. My wife used to ask me to come home, but now she urges me to stay here. It is the only solution to get the money to buy land and build a house. For now we are renting."

Tony asked, "At what age were you betrothed to your wife?"

"She was fourteen, the same age as my daughter now. I was eighteen." Noor refilled my teacup. "We married when I was twenty-one and my wife, my cousin, was seventeen. My daughter recently asked me, 'Father, will you decide who I marry? I am of the age for marriage,' I said, 'No. It will not be like that for you. It is important that you get an education first. I will not decide who you marry. It is you who will decide who you marry later, after you finish school.'" He laughed again. "Of course, I am her father and will make sure it is a good, educated man."

"Well, Noor, that hardly sounds tribal," Tony offered. "Sounds downright modern."

"No, not tribal. The world is too crazy. The old ways do not work today. But the tribe is still important. I am Pashtun and Dawar."

"Noor," I said. "You sound just like my Jewish mother. Except for the Pashtun-Dawar part."

Noor's face broke out into another big grin, but I heard a question behind what he said. "David, Tony tells me you call me your *rabbi*." He paused. "Now I am your Jewish mother, too?!"

At Dubai Creek Park, on an open patch of green by a spit of salt water lapping the shore, the four of us spread out our picnic lunch. The *dhow* wharf loomed across the inlet, the official "Dubai Creek." This being Friday, the local sabbath, families crowded the vast park along with groups of South Asian laborers and Filipina clerks enjoying their day off. A smattering of Emiratis frolicked in Children's City, but the crowd was predominately foreign, though not Western. It was midday and on our way in we had stopped at a prayer hall so Noor could pray the *Dhuhr.*

The picnic was delicious. Tony and Rozz picked up and announced that they had decided to walk back to the apartment, and would meet us later at the Global Village. A few pieces of fruit and juice cans remained. In that first clumsy moment alone with a friend after a long absence, Noor and I sat in silence. Till then reclining on a thick cushion, I shifted up to my knees. As he had done so often in my old Al Ain apartment, Noor grabbed a piece a guava and a paring knife. He cut two slices of the fruit extending the larger toward me. I took a bite of the slippery wedge, juice running down my chin.

"Tony has told me that you changed your book's title, again."

"That's correct. I now call it *My Pashtun Rabbi.*"

He cocked one eyebrow.

"A rabbi, like an imam, is a teacher, but so far my book has had four titles. I like this title best because you have become the star of the book. It will likely change again by the time it gets published, if it ever gets published."

Noor let out a long laugh. "*Insha'Allah!*"

He had given me my opening. "Tony told me that you are concerned that things in this book I can't seem to finish could get you into trouble?"

He nodded. "This is a crazy place. I worry that something will get someone mad at me and they will make me leave." He paused. "I am the only support for my wife and children. Without the money I earn here, I don't know what they would do."

I told him the measures I'd taken. He asked about a picture and I assured him there was none. Soon, I was telling him the core story beginning at the Women's Toilet, our meeting on the first evening of Ramadan, the drive to the top of Jebel Hafeet, Brian's death, our trips to Sanaiya, the tipper truck, my trip to Yemen, the Falahis, Samah, and my "All Jews Are Evil" students. A life made possible by the things *he* had taught me. None of it even remotely possible without his influence.

"Noor, you have given me your Golden Word. Now I give you mine. I will never let this book harm you, or your family. God willing, it will be a good thing."

"*Insha'Allah*," he replied, and cut a chunk of guava. "You know, I told my friends you were coming to visit me. They didn't believe. You had been away so long. My friends say to me, 'If you and David are such good friends, why don't you have him take you to America? Why don't you have him give you money?" He paused and we locked eyes. "I tell them that they don't understand. That David and I have a *spiritual* friendship. That it is very special. I told them, *insha'Allah*, that if something happens it is fine and if not it is also fine. But that I do not want anything from you and you don't want anything from me. We talk about many things and respect each other. We are *spiritual* friends."

We had to get to our rendezvous with Rozz and Tony at Global Village. I rode shotgun in Noor's taxi, we paid our entry fee and found them at the Ferris wheel. We wandered the crowded fair and shopped in pavilions called Morocco, Iran, Iraq, Egypt, UAE, Kuwait, Oman, Yemen, Afghanistan, Saudi Arabia, Eastern Europe, China and Palestine. Curiously, one big tent was identified as "Africa." Rozz suggested that Noor choose where we'd eat. The food of many nations was to be had.

"I know what he's going to pick," I laughed.

Tony furled his brow. "So, Noor, what will it be? Mutton with rice? Or are you more in the mood for rice with mutton?"

Noor shot me a pleased look. "This is a special occasion. We will have mutton with rice *and* rice with mutton. Maybe something else, too."

At the Afghani restaurant, Noor selected the rice/mutton order, which came with large loaves of naan and the standard vegetables, and added finger-lickin'-good butter chicken. This being a Pashtun establishment he also picked up the tab. Tony tried to argue, but I explained how I'd lost that dispute every time. "Pashtun cannot let a non-Pashtun pay the tab in a Pashtun eatery." To him and Rozz, I gathered, this seemed a reasonable point of etiquette.

Noor went off to find the prayer hall for the *Isha*, the fifth and last prayer of the day. It was after midnight as we watched him stroll off into the still-jammed parking lot. Tony, Rozz and I crammed into Tony's Porsche for the cruise back to Dubai. I intended, no matter what, to head to Al Ain the next day, maybe take the intercity motorcoach. Noor had offered to come back to Dubai to get me but he had various jobs to see to and I insisted I'd find a way down, *insha'Allah*, on my own. I still had to find a bed, too, but there was time for God to work his will.

Saturday, *insha'Allah* did its thing. A friend and UGRU colleague of Brian's, still teaching at UAEU, happened to call Tony in the morning to see about meeting for lunch. Felicidade, whom I knew moderately well, was coming to Dubai for an outpatient procedure at the American Hospital. Tony duly mentioned that I was visiting and intended to travel later that day to Al Ain. The attractive Portuguese expat offered a lift and her guest room. It was early evening when we departed Dubai for the hour-long drive down E-66. Only four other colleagues who started with us, Felicidade remarked, remained at UAEU. The buildings where I had taught, 66 and 71, no longer existed. They had been demolished, taking with them Room 04, the Women's Toilet. Felicidade promised to give me a tour of the new, multi-zillion-dollar campus adding, "You won't recognize it."

From the Civic's passenger seat, I noted familiar landmarks—the Dubai Outlet Mall, the conning tower of Zayed University, signs to the still-undeveloped Dubailand and the Global Village.

"Remember a few years ago," Felicidade was saying, "when Finland had the top-ranked schools in the world? Well, the Emiratis went to Finland and hired as many teachers as they could. It lasted about six weeks. Emirati children, it turns out, are very different from Finnish children."

As we entered the Abu Dhabi emirate, I noted how the road widened from six lanes to eight. Palm trees now lined the median. "Didn't this used to be just two lanes each direction?" I asked.

"Not only does Sheikh Khalifa now have his name on the Burj in Dubai, but E-66 is wider on his side of the border than in Dubai. It shows who has the money."

At dusk, once settled in at Felicidade's, I called Noor, finding him at a mechanic's shop in Sanaiya. Something on his tipper truck had broken. Getting it fixed might keep him stuck there late into the night. *Insha'Allah*, he'd see me soon, but not till the next night. He had five tipper-truck runs scheduled for Sunday, *insha'Allah*, to deliver the extra-soft sand used to embed underground cables.

Next I called Fatima to confirm our plan for the evening. "We are all here, Uncle. My father has just returned from camping in the desert. Everyone will be happy to see you. Do you still know the way?"

After dark, I was repeating my reply to a Pashtun taxi driver, his company uniform as prim as his silver Camry: "Go to the Zoo roundabout, make a U-turn, then a right on the first street past the Women's Technical College, through the roundabout by the apple-green two-minaret mosque …"

The meandering ride through Al Ain's familiar streets gave me time to collect my thoughts. My eagerness for the reunion and my apprehensions were clouded by an uncertainty as to the gifts I had brought. Lying now on my lap in a canvas bag were presents for Faraj, Amna and certain others. The origin of these presents was a long series of random errors and misfortunes. Hilal, my guide and teacher at the camel farm and the family member I'd grown closest to after Fatima and her father, had died two years before. The circumstances, when I learned them, struck me as pointless and needless as those that had made Brian's heart attack fatal. Hilal had gone to Tawam-Johns Hopkins Hospital in Al Ain to have his hypertension seen to. In a chain of mistakes, whatever could go wrong did go wrong. I learned of Hilal's death soon after, but only came to understand the story a year later when Fatima and Amna accompanied Abdulla for a medical procedure—gastric bypass—at the real Johns Hopkins in Baltimore. Meeting them in Charm City I learned the family's faith in God's will remained unshaken, but its confidence in the UAE knockoff of a global healthcare brand was finished.

Hilal's sudden death had devastated the family. Fatima kept me updated. She asked whether I had photos of her late brother. She wanted to give them to Hilal's widow and son, Hilal bin Hilal, born after his father's death. I clipped a big selection to an email, but learned months later that Fatima's account had been hacked and the photos lost. And now here I sat with two iPhoto books—one devoted to Hilal—on my lap, two copies of each.

Coming through the metal gate, drawn back to welcome me, I noted that Faraj had followed through on the expansions of the two secondary villas, but had yet to break ground for the structures near the gate for his eldest daughters. Light spilled out of Door #1.

Fatima stood at the entrance in a vividly colorful sari and head-scarf. She put her finger to her lips as I bounded up the four steps, toting my heavy canvas bag. "Uncle, I did not tell my family you were coming tonight. If I did they would have made a big fuss all day, and I know how you don't like big fusses. Let's go in and surprise them, *insha'Allah.*"

Out through the doorway poured canned laughter. Stepping inside I spotted the sixty-inch flat-screen TV showing an over-the-top Egyptian comedy-melodrama. Faraj, in the same white leather recliner in which I had left him the night of Fatima's birthday party, gazed at the screen. Amna, talking to Layla, spotted me first. She threw her hands above her head. "Doctor, welcome, welcome!"

Faraj jerked his head around and shot to his feet. "Doctor!"

I crossed the cluttered room, we kissed on both cheeks, then touched noses.

"Brother, sit by me." He motioned to the sofa.

I sat and placed the canvas bag on the floor. The laughtrack from the TV filled the room. The family *majlis*, it struck me, was a disaster zone. Couches were pushed haphazardly into walls and construction materials littered the floor. "I am doing a project," Fatima apologized, "making one room into two. It's a big problem. I think the contractor is cheating me."

I raised an eyebrow. Fatima got the implication right away. "I'm using my own money."

Mariam hurried in with Sarah, not so little any more, at almost fifteen. Wearing a black *sheyla* and *abaya* and taller than her eldest sister, Sarah extended her hand, as she had at age eleven, when she exclaimed, "I love you." Faraj watched me shake his youngest's hand while keeping an eye on a fierce Egyptian lover's quarrel playing out on the flatscreen. I noted how tired he looked—even exhausted.

Mariam sat to my left, Sarah a few cushions away. "How is Max?" Mariam inquired. She had taken a strong shine to him during his visit. I told her about his new job in Washington. "*Al ham doo lielah!*" she exclaimed. Mariam enjoyed her own new job in UAEU's accounting department. A movie *aficionada*, she also had a new obsession—Japanese anime. A young man in a white *kandura* approached, and at first I didn't recognize him. Since I'd seen him last in Baltimore, Abdulla had shrunk by half.

"Doctor, I didn't know you were coming to Al Ain!"

"Apparently, Fatima wanted to keep it a secret," I said, getting to my feet and offering my hand. I sized him up. "You're half the man you used to be. That's quite an achievement."

"Yes, I feel good now." He paused. "But, Doctor, I hope you have not forgotten your promise that you'd teach me how to make cheeseburgers?"

If he provided the ingredients and the proper grill, I said, I'd teach him. But I felt obligated to add that he really didn't *need* cheeseburgers, that he'd had surgery to reduce his stomach, that I rarely ate a cheeseburger myself, and my abstinence had nothing to do with cheeseburgers not being kosher. We were comparing notes on Five Guys when Mohammed rumbled in. At the sight of me, he did a truly classic Hardy & Hardy double take. Of course, he was Hardy on his own now as Abdulla was a lot closer to Stan Laurel. Mohammed was twenty-four, a newly minted UAEU graduate in chemical engineering, and due to begin a job with a company owned by the crown prince that had something to do with retarding corrosion. Issa, the second-oldest surviving son after Sultan, and the father of little Mimi, now had four children, all in tow. After sustaining an injury in an attack by a prisoner at the Al Ain jail, he had been reassigned to test guns. "I shoot the gun and I say 'good' or 'no good.' Do you want to come shooting with me?" he asked.

As I agreed, and was about to ask what we would shoot, Fatima arrived with a cup of chai tea, set it for me on a small table, and sat to my right. She stage-whispered, "My father is very tired. We will eat dinner soon and then he will sleep. I couldn't tell him you were coming or he would not have gone camping. He spent three nights in the desert. He will spend more time with you later during your visit."

Faraj nodded. He'd heard and approved. Clearly, Fatima now ran the household. It was time, I felt, for the canvas bag. I reached in and pulled out four white books encased in plastic. "Fatima, I've made two picture books, and have two copies of each. The first is about Hilal. One copy is for his son. The other book is about your family and me."

I handed one Hilal book to Fatima. "Please give this to your mother." Fatima grasped it, removed the plastic case, and handed it to Amna. I handed the other copy, sans plastic, to Faraj. He removed the book from its slipcover and gazed at a closely cropped noble portrait of his first-born son. The title above read, "Hilal Al Falahi: A Tribute."

"Thank you, thank you," Faraj said, staring at the cover, a tear welling up in his eye. "Thank you, Doctor. Thank you, brother." He removed his glasses, wiping away tears, and rubbed his eyes. Amna kissed her forefinger and touched the picture of her son. *"Masha'Allah. Masha'Allah. Masha'Allah."* She pointed toward the ceiling and the heavens. *"Masha'Allah. Masha'Allah."*

Her daughters crowded around and the women carried the book to the dining table. Faraj opened the volume and slowly flipped the pages. *"Masha'Allah,"* Doctor," he intoned. *"Masha'Allah."*

Masha'Allah was a word I remembered hearing, in Baltimore. When a Muslim is born, Fatima had explained to me there, his or her death is already on the books. It had been Hilal's time. God's work is unexplainable. Only *He* has the answer. Now, Fatima further schooled her former teacher. "Uncle," she said, sitting down next to me once more as the books were passed around. "Do you know what *masha'Allah* means?"

"Literally?" I asked. I shook my head.

"*Masha'Allah* means, 'God has willed it.' What my mother and father are saying is that this book is the best gift, that there are no words good enough to express how they feel. Nobody could have given them anything better. Nothing. It is priceless."

I had learned the ins-and-outs of *insha'Allah,* but had failed to grasp the significance of what came next. What comes after God's will does its work? When God *wills* it… something *real* happens. Good. Bad. Indifferent. But real. Ineluctable. *Masha'Allah.* The operation of God's will then moves to the past tense. God wanted it to go this way, or end this way, and that's all there is to it. How could I have missed that?

Right after we'd eaten, Faraj peeled off for bed. Before Mohammed ran me back to my accommodation, after midnight, Fatima told me I was expected the next evening as well. I told her I'd like to bring Noor. "Of course," she said. "We are your family. I would like to meet Noor."

Felicidade made good on her promised tour of the new UAEU campus. A world I had known had been wiped from the face of the earth. Buildings 66 and 71 had vanished leaving an empty sand lot. The Women's Toilet swept away, too. Like Bizarro World in a Superman comic, the old Maqam girls' campus had become the boys' campus. Black was now white. The boys lived in the girls' old hostels. The girls had moved to the new part of the campus. The big news was that the perimeter was now free of barbed wire. Steel gates granted access via smart cards so everyone's comings and goings were tracked and recorded. There was enough covered parking for everyone, a world-class natatorium, spas, shopping and a fitness center. "Boys" could have vehicles and come and go at will, but "girls," if they lived in hostels, were still confined to campus. As before, the sexes did not mingle.

I visited on a school day but at six p.m. and the public areas were nearly deserted. The best that money could buy, the physically modern, architecturally distinct, shining-new education plant, with its massive Crescent Center, smartboards, and iPad-equipped students, remained devoid of student life.

Noor parked near where the rooms for Mariam and Fatima had not yet been built. Within Door #1 the family gathered in the messy *majlis*. Faraj, dressed in his sheikh's finest, rose from his sheikh-white recliner, stepped to Noor and greeted him warmly. My little brother had shown the depth and veracity of his true grace just as the rest of the family would. Mariam, Sarah, Sultan, Issa, Abdulla and Mohammed swarmed Noor with greetings. Faraj nodded toward me and I watched as he silently departed through Door #1.

"My father is leaving for a meeting tonight and for the next several days," Fatima said. "It was scheduled before he knew you were coming. He waited before leaving to greet Noor and see you." She quietly added her assurance that I would see him again during my visit. "You are here for a month."

My whole trip would run a month. But there was no need to tell Fatima this now. This visit was an end, and an event, in itself. Fatima turned to Noor. "My uncle says that you know about construction."

Noor glanced quickly in my direction. I nodded.

"Yaya, I know about such things."

"Good," Fatima said. "I have asked the man to come over tonight. I want you to talk to him. It's a disaster! Come with me and let me show you."

During the hubbub of dinner I managed to let Fatima know I'd be leaving Al Ain within a few days for a stop in Abu Dhabi where I had a work assignment. She assured me she'd line up time with her father. "But maybe it wasn't such a good idea that I made your visit a surprise."

We agreed that everything would, *insha'Allah*, work out. On the return drive to my host's, Noor offered his assessment of Fatima's project. "She is right. The Bahtan builder is cheating her. He is charging Emirati prices for poor materials and workmanship." He smiled. "I can help her."

This time she was not the Girl in Pink. Just before noon, I sat at Costa Coffee in the upscale addition to Al Ain Mall, nearly empty but heavily merchandized for Valentine's Day. A woman in a crimson blouse approached, sunglasses perched on top of her black *sheyla*. Samah gave me a big, warm, confidant smile. I thought, *The Woman in Red*, and corrected myself—the Wife, Mother & PhD candidate in Red. Coffee in hand, she joined me in the cushy chairs and set her cup on the low table. Samah confirmed that it was "just by chance" she'd contacted me via Linkedin, adding "You've been in my head for the last four years."

I chuckled. "You've been in mine, too. In fact, you are a central character in that little book you've searched for on the internet that isn't quite finished yet."

She gave me a look of curiosity.

"Remember how I said writing is rewriting and rewriting and rewriting, and that you have only one chance to tell the story the right way? Well, that's not actually always true in journalism. There are deadlines, press times. With a book, it is true. My 'little book' is not just my story, but parts of a lot of people's. It's your story, too. I don't want to screw that up."

Samah nodded. "I have to learn how to write as an academic and I don't like it at all."

I told her I was in the UAE because I was intent on a sort of closure, a completeness, to close some loops. "People ask me what's become of you and Noor. I had to come back and see for myself."

She was curious about me and over the next half hour I filled her in. Then it was her turn. She began on a bold note, her eyes locked onto mine. "You changed the way I look at people."

I'm sure I looked stunned, but no doubt pleased as well.

"I've told your story to everyone." Samah lifted her coffee, taking a thoughtful sip. "I've told my family and friends, and I plan to tell my children and grandchildren. Before I met you I saw all Jews as the same. All Jews were just Zionists. I would say, 'He's a Jew. They're all the same.' I'd give it no more thought. Now I give it thought. I look at everyone differently. I would not have done that if not for meeting you." She returned the cup to the table. "If I had known at the start you were Jewish? I would have dropped the class. But I didn't know, and now I see the world through different eyes. I see it better."

I was eager to hear more about what her life had become since we had last seen each other. Her two-year-old son, Saif, was her love and joy, along with her Emirati husband, now a banker, whom she had met at UAEU. They lived in university housing, one of the perks of the scholarship that was letting her work toward her doctorate. In two years, once she had been married five years to an Emirati, she would be permitted, under a new decree, to become a citizen and acquire a UAE passport. That would be the first real document of national identity she'd had her whole life. As a Palestinian, specifically the offspring of native Palestinians, she had had to rely on a makeshift Egyptian travel document, though Egypt was in no way her country. Citizenship would come with many privileges, including "more money, free land, a real passport," but she admitted to a certain ambivalence.

"Do you understand what I'm saying?" she said, tilting her head. "I mean, I am thankful and grateful to this country. It's given me so much. Things will be so much easier. I know my life is so much better here..." She paused and leaned forward. "But something is missing. My family was from the countryside in Palestine. My mother tells me stories about how the flowers in the orange groves smelled and I want to smell those flowers. Those *very* flowers. I want to walk that same land."

Naturally, as Samah voiced her longing to know the land of her parents and grandparents, I thought of the Jews. For two thousand years many had longed to return to Zion. I had never quite felt that longing, but I would visit Israel again within a few days transiting through Amman.

"I think I understand. You are a Palestinian Zionist."

Samah raised her eyebrow skeptically and laughed. "You might call it that. I don't. I talk to my son in Arabic, using my family's Palestinian dialect so he will always remember where he comes from and how we speak." She paused. "Remember when you said you believed there could be peace in Israel?"

I nodded, struck that she said "Israel." In previous conversations she had called it "Palestine."

"As a teacher," I said, "I wanted to instill hope about the future, not gloom. But I agree with you. I don't see peace coming in my lifetime. But I hope in yours or in Saif's."

"Obama has been a complete bust," she editorialized, shaking her head, "when it comes to peace in the Middle East. I don't believe there will ever be peace in Palestine. The only way there will ever be peace is if only *my* people are living there."

I was innately inclined to ask whether she believed that might happen with the Jews or could only happen—in her view—without them. But that was not our subject. Our subject was Palestine, not Israel, nor the chimerical two-state solution. The Jews, I knew, might be pushed out again. The Iranians are crazy enough to try anything. Sorry—some Iranians. I had to correct my kneejerk inclination to tar all Iranians with the same brush. Egypt and Syria had begun to writhe in sectarian and political chaos. All this had fierce implications for Israel, and—for that matter—for Palestine, too.

Before we parted Samah asked a simple question. "Do you mind if I call you David?"

Future salutation agreed, we arranged to meet two days later, on my last evening in Al Ain. The mall had a new indoor playground and Samah wanted me to meet her son. So, I realized, I had come not for closure, but for continuity. I left the mall understanding something else, too. That I was going to Israel the hard way. Not via the simple connection of flights—one cannot, of course, fly non-stop from UAE to Tel Aviv. I was not going to link up air connections, but make my pilgrimage overland.

The next evening Noor took me to Sanaiya. Dinner would be the traditional menu of mutton with rice and rice with mutton. Maybe soup, too. Just prior to the *Asr* prayer, the industrial zone was teeming. Walking the gritty streets I noticed Noor was jumpy, which he'd never seemed before here with me at his side. My senses also went on point; I noted that I was the only Westerner among hundreds of Pashtun swarming to pray. Noor quickly maneuvered us to an Afghani cafeteria.

Over the first course, soup, he explained his concern. "The drones make everyone crazy. Everybody knows somebody who has been killed by a drone. I was worried that some crazy person would be angry and jump out and attack you."

I acknowledged Noor's concern. Yet I also felt entirely safe being with him. His God might not look out for me as he did for Noor—Allah had no reason to. But I was protected, I knew, by the protection Noor enjoyed. If there was a Pashtun equivalent of *wasta*, I felt snug and dry under its umbrella. Still, after dinner we took care to tread lightly.

Samah and Saif were late and I was anxious. Noor was collecting me for a final dinner with the Falahis. Just as I was giving up, I spotted a bright yellow blouse and black *sheyla*. Their wearer was holding the hand of a curly-haired boy in a green jacket and white t-shirt. I grabbed my digital from the table and clicked off a few shots before my cover was blown. Samah pointed to me, Saif pranced right up and we exchanged high-fives.

For the next fifteen minutes we huddled around a small table with soft chairs and "played." Saif reminded me of my grandnephew, Eliezar, and I watched his eyes convey amusement as we performed non-verbal games expressing joy and happiness. The call of the *muezzin* sounded throughout the mall. Samah excused herself to go pray. She hoped I'd still be around when they returned. I watched the boy and his mother stroll away and sat pondering what had just transpired. Saif will get older, and someday, Samah has said, she'll tell him more about the man he met as "Uncle David." She'll tell these stories to his siblings. The seeds of peace? My mobile rang; Noor would be out front in five minutes.

During my visit I'd shot rifles with Issa, Mohammed and Abdulla at the Gun Club. Issa proved himself an Emirati Davy Crockett. In addition to scoring a few near-bulls-eyes on my target at fifty yards I managed to hit Mohammed's, to my left, too. The sight of the two of us sprawled out prone gave the UAE para-Olympic rifle team practicing nearby a good laugh. Sultan called me "my father." He brought his only child, Zayed, to meet me and urged me to go into business with him by being his American partner buying and selling vehicles. Issa and he were off to Baltimore in a week for a checkup at the real Johns Hopkins.

Fatima indeed ran the household. Her mother, sisters, brothers, nieces and nephews looked to her for decisions. Faraj had once told me Fatima was the most like him. She earned a good salary working in PR at the Transportation Ministry in Abu Dhabi where she reviewed press releases. She suggested that I should start a PR firm in Abu Dhabi and work with her. But she wanted a fuller life than just a job.

"How can a life be complete if I am not married and with a family?" she asked. "I'm twenty-six and want to have a husband and children. Uncle, do you have a husband for me?"

As the family—Faraj was not present—gathered around a large carpet on the pavers in front of the main villa for the dinner, I peeled off for a closer inspection of the expansion project. I wished Faraj could be showing me how his plan had come to fruition. I glanced over my shoulder and watched Abdulla and Mohammed grilling cheeseburgers, as I had taught them, on a hand-held double-sided grill used to cook kebobs over a wood fire burning in a low metal box.

Fatima had pulled Noor into the house to inspect the latest development of her remodeling project. Aunt Mira, a year younger than me, sat on the carpet next to Amna. She wore a metal faceplate, called a *burqa'* in the UAE, spoke no English and was, according to Fatima, one of the richest women in Al Ain. When I returned Mariam handed me a plate with a cheeseburger. Noor, Fatima, Amna and Aunt Mira were fully engaged in a robust conversation, in Arabic.

Noor brought me up to speed. "There had been a problem with Fatima's mother's sister. She was seven years old and had never spoken. A holy man was consulted and he told Fatima's grandfather that he should pluck the food from the fingers of a great sheikh, rush home immediately and feed it to his daughter. In two days, the holy man promised, *insha'Allah*, she will speak and be normal."

Fatima picked up the story. "Since my grandfather's home was in the Al Ain Oasis, behind Zayed's palace, and since every night Zayed fed all who came to visit, it wouldn't be a difficult task. The next evening, as Zayed picked up a piece of food, my mother's father snatched it from his hand..." she pantomimed grabbing food ... "rushed home and fed it to his daughter. As prophesied by the holy man, within two days my mother's sister was talking up a storm, never stopped talking, gave birth to eighteen healthy children—nine boys and nine girls—all at home without a doctor, and became one of the most-beloved women in Al Ain."

I'd never heard that story. "What has become of her?"

"At age fifty-three," Fatima said, "she was killed in a car accident. *Masha'Allah.*"

I raised my eyebrows. Fatima shrugged.

It was a night to tell stories and Aunt Mira began the next one about three famous men from Al Ain who had set out by camel to make the *Hajj*. Via Noor's and Fatima's translation I learned that the three men had, before embarking, made wagers regarding smoking and divorcing their wives if they didn't return within a year. Travails encountered on their journey made it impossible to get to Mecca for the *Hajj* on time when out of nowhere a stranger appeared to them in the desert.

"One of the pilgrims," Fatima said, "hopped on his back and was transported instantly to Mecca landing in the middle of the moving throng. When the stranger, a holy man—a *carrier*—returned the pilgrim to his companions a few days later the man described the *Hajj* in detail."

"So this *carrier* is a kind of prophet?" I asked, immediately knowing that was wrong.

"No!" Noor corrected. "Mohammed was the Last Prophet. A *carrier* is a holy man who performs miracles. There have been many and at night sometimes light shoots up into the stars from their graves."

"Noor is right," Fatima added. "Sometimes we see it from the grave of a holy man buried here in Al Ain, in an old cemetery owned by my mother's father's family. A *carrier* is a very special messenger from Allah. They appear all over the world."

I waited alone in the Corolla, the passenger door open, parked near the mosque next to the ADNOC on the Abu Dhabi Road. Noor had insisted that he drive me to the capital and it was time for the midday prayer. I grabbed a Diet Pepsi from the sack Noor had brought along, popped the top and took a swig. Next I picked out a foil-wrapped spicy chicken shwarma, and nibbled the end. I took a peak at the odometer while I was at it.

Ten minutes later, back on the highway, we followed the high-tension lines cutting across the swelling red dunes under the brilliant blue February sky. Noor was chatting on his mobile. When his conversation ended I asked, "Noor, your old Corolla has traveled more than seven-hundred-and-thirty-six-thousand kilometers. That's almost a half million miles. Is that accurate?"

"Yaya, that is true. It's had many engines, but the distance is accurate." He laughed. "On the phone was my friend. I told him that I was driving you to Abu Dhabi. Everybody who knows me knows our story." I nodded. "This friend knows about our spiritual friendship. So he says to me, 'Noor, do you think that maybe David is a *carrier*?' I tell him that I don't know. I say, 'Maybe he is.'"

Harboring no delusions of holiness, I let out a laugh. "Noor, if someone in this car is a *carrier* it certainly is not me."

Thirty minutes later he dropped me off at my Abu Dhabi hotel. That would be the last time, that trip, I was to see Noor. We said our goodbyes in the parking lot.

A few days later an intercity bus was how I got to Dubai and a final evening at Tony and Rozz's flat. Toward the end of the night, before we turned in, Tony summed up the reasons expats come to the Emirates, and why they leave. "You know, young David, there are three kinds of us—missionaries, mercenaries, and misfits. Only the misfits stay. If you come as a missionary one of two things happens. You leave bitter, your mission unfulfilled. Or you become a mercenary. I came as a little of each. Now I'm here for the money. I love to teach but they make it so hard. Haven't sold out. Never will. So I'll take their money as long as I can stand what I have to do to get it. Then I'll walk away."

The following morning, in pre-dawn light, the marine blue 2003 Dubai Porsche Show Car of the Year sped north toward Sharjah International Airport, a veteran Aussie driver at the wheel. Rozz sat crammed in the small back seat. Tony got us doing a good two hundred kmph.

"I think a final run in the porker is in order," Tony announced. "Don't you? A fitting end to your time in the UAE, wouldn't you say, Young David?"

I'd booked an early morning Air Arabia flight across KSA, three-and-a-half hours across two time zones, over massive oil fields and the Empty Quarter, to Amman. A taxi would take me from Queen Alia International Airport to the Jordan River, and the crossing near the Dead Sea. Once I was across the Israeli border, I'd hop a Palestinian *sharoot—insha'allah*—up to East Jerusalem and the Damascus Gate.

Crossing Allenby Bridge, a piece of history, I thought of Samah. As I completed my journey, my own idiosyncratic version of *aliyah*—literally "going up," as one can only approach Jerusalem, from whatever direction, by ascending—I thought of my friends and family in the UAE, of my friends and family in Clevistan. And of my nephew, Ethan, awaiting me in Jerusalem where he was studying.

On my last night in the Holy City, the Fast of Esther, touching the ancient stones of the Kotel, the Western Wall, I said the *Shehecheyanu* and tucked the requisite personal note to God into a high crevice. I asked Him to watch out for my family, friends, the Jews, Israel and then boldly asked Him what he had in store for me. Of course, I never expected any form of answer.

Stepping back I watched my nephew join other men to *daven* in the twilight. I stood at a distance, recalling Tony's litany: "missionaries, mercenaries, and misfits."

No, there was a fourth kind of expat who ventured to these parts.

The family provider. The miracle worker. The holy man. I thought of one in particular. He hailed from an ancient mountainous land, and carried a *Clevistani* on his back to places he could never have reached alone. Tony was not wrong, just overlooking something. Noor's friend was, too.

I was hardly a *carrier*, just another Western arsehole. A missionary mercenary misfit who'd seen he didn't fit and was too little missionary and not enough mercenary to stick it out.

The *carrier*? Noor Islam, the Light of Islam, from North Waziristan.

God's will—*insha'Allah, beshert*, Kismet, whatever you want to call it—works in mysterious ways. In the summer of 2013, a long-time friend was named the president and chief executive officer of the world's largest Jewish campus organization. We hadn't spoken in several years and I'd sent him a brief congratulatory note; a month later I was hired on as Hillel International's first-ever Chief Administrative Officer. For the first time in my career, I was a "professional Jew." Was God playing a cruel cosmic joke on me? Most likely. Had *He* directed me to this job and this place at this time?

Tony and Rozz are retired and live in a village outside of Bezier in southern France where my new wife and I have visited. Fatima remains my primary contact among the Falahi family and is starting her own business. During the Summer 2014 Hamas War in Gaza, Samah contacted me alarmed that I worked for a pro-Israel organization, told me that many of her family members had been killed by the IDF, and severed our friendship. She told me never to contact her again.

Mohamed is remarried, to a Yemini woman who earned a PhD in Egypt, and is the chair of his Oklahoma state university's engineering department. His children moved with him to the Sooner state. His daughter, Sabah, is excelling in college and son, Akiel, is in high school. His family in Sana'a is under threat of the al-Houthi, who have taken over the capital city. I have made inquires about Yemen's last rabbi and his family and have heard no credible report. Did they march into the sea?

Noor and I communicate frequently via the wonders of social media and free international phone calls. I think I'm Facebook friends with nearly every Dawar in the UAE. Noor and I currently own a piece of land together in Peshawar where he intends to build a home for his family because they cannot return to "crazy North Waziristan." Currently they are renting and saving money to build a house. He tells me during every conversation that his family prays for me and that everyone in his tribe knows our story. Some Dawar think, he still tells me, that "you are a *carrier.*"

During our last conversation, during Ramadan, I was lamenting about something or other to do with my job and saying that "all Jews are crazy, not just me." As usual, Noor put me in my place. "David, my friend, God will take care of you. Everyone is too crazy because the world is too crazy. So I tell my family that I look forward to the day that you and I can walk together in Paradise forever. This is a short life and that life in paradise is for eternity."

I think often about Noor's wish to "walk together in Paradise forever." I wonder where that stroll through eternity would take us. And in who's "Paradise" we would walk? Muslim? Christian? Jewish? Do they overlap? Surely others would join us. I have some people in mind. Jews, Muslims, Christians. All cousins, as Faraj said.

What a brilliant adventure that would be.

ACKNOWLEDGEMENTS

I'd like to thank the United Arab Emirates University for giving me the opportunity to teach and to "see for myself." What impressed me was its ambition to become a foundational national university. I'd like to thank my students, many of whom you met in these pages by name, for permitting me to get to know them and educating me about their world. Among those at UAEU I'd also like to thank are Dean Don Baker and Dr. Beverly Merrick for hiring me, Dr. Carol Barnett for her camaraderie and guidance, Felicidade Van Acker for her friendship and hospitality, and Dr. Mohamed Binjbr for sharing his world and transporting me to Yemen.

My sincerest and deepest gratitude goes to my wife, Laurel Hamilton Eden, a great "reader," keen editor and thoughtful sounding board. My deep appreciation also goes to Jess R. Taylor, who helped me shape this narrative and understand that it is all about the people and telling a story that matters. And also to my colleague and friend, Joanna Connors, who helped me bring this story to light, and to Al Margolis for the maps of the UAE and region. Then there's Jack Rosen, who gave me a bed when I needed one, and Bob Stevens, who told me to be a "Canadian."

This story would never have happened without my dear friends Dr. Tony Jewels and Dr. Rozz Albon. Tony truly is that true foxhole buddy and Rozz holds her own in that carve out. Laurel and I have visited them a few times at their new home on a few acres outside a small village near Bezier in the south of France.

My most sincere love and affection flows to my Emirati family, the Falahis, especially Faraj and Fatima, who filled my life with warmth and companionship, and embraced me unconditionally as they welcomed me into their home. There generosity is a great testament to their whole-hearted embrace of their faith and heritage.

And, finally, my deepest admiration and affection goes to Noor. Thank you for making me strive to be a better human being and being my constant reminder of what that person should be. We have become family, which is another story.